I Don't Want to
GO HOME

I Don't Want to
GO HOME

★ THE ORAL HISTORY OF ★

The Stone Pony

Foreword by Bruce Springsteen

Nick Corasaniti

HARPER

An Imprint of HarperCollinsPublishers

HarperCollins books may be purchased for educational, business, or sales promotional use. For information, please email the Special Markets Department at SPsales@harpercollins.com.

Portions of this book have previously appeared in the *New York Times*.

FIRST EDITION

Designed by Nancy Singer
Photographs pages i, ii courtesy of Nancy Singer
Paper background art on pages v and vi © Yevhenii/stock.adobe.com

Library of Congress Cataloging-in-Publication Data

Names: Corasaniti, Nick, author.
Title: I don't want to go home: the oral history of the Stone Pony / Nick Corasaniti.
Description: New York: HarperCollins, 2024. | Includes bibliographical references.
Identifiers: LCCN 2023054962 | ISBN 9780062950789 (hardback) |
    ISBN 9780062950796 (trade paperback) | ISBN 9780062950802 (ebook)
Subjects: LCSH: The Stone Pony (Asbury Park, N.J.) | Music-halls—New Jersey—
    Asbury Park—History | Rock musicians—Interviews. | Rock concerts—New
    Jersey—Asbury Park—History. | Rock music—New Jersey—Asbury Park—
    History and criticism.
Classification: LCC ML3534.3 C67 2024 | DDC 781.6609749—dc23/eng/20231212
LC record available at https://lccn.loc.gov/2023054962

24 25 26 27 28 LBC 5 4 3 2 1

Contents

Cast of Characters

Michele Amabile: *Asbury Park Press/Radio DJ*, HTG

Tony "Boccigalupe" Amato: Musician, Cahoots

Jack Antonoff: Musician, Bleachers

Mike Appel: Former manager, Bruce Springsteen

Nicole Atkins: Musician

Jim Babjak: Musician, the Smithereens

Mark Bahary: Bartender, Stone Pony

Brian Baker: Musician, Bad Religion/Minor Threat

Bobby Bandiera: Musician, Cats on a Smooth Surface/Asbury Jukes

Chris Barron: Musician, Spin Doctors

Dan Beck: Head of Promotions, Epic Records

Al "Doc" Berger: Musician, Asbury Jukes

Susan Blond: Chief publicist, Epic Records

Rachel Bolan: Musician, Skid Row

Gary U.S. Bonds: Musician

Lisa Brownlee: Cofounder, Punk Rock Museum

Bob Burger: Musician

Glen Burtnik: Musician

John Cafferty: Musician, John Cafferty and Beaver Brown

Ernest "Boom" Carter: Musician, E Street Band, Lord Gunner

Eileen Chapman: Asbury councilwoman/manager of Mrs. Jay's/manager of Stone Pony

Kenny Chesney: Musician

Chris Christie: Governor, New Jersey

Jake Clemons: Musician, E Street Band

Danny Clinch: Photographer/founder, Sea.Hear.Now

Richard J. Codey: Governor, New Jersey

Marshall Crenshaw: Musician

Russell Crowe: Musician/actor

Michael "Buck" Crowell: Artist manager and promoter

David Cruz: Reporter, NJTV

Dave Davies: Musician, Kinks

Eric Deggans: Reporter, *Asbury Park Press*

Judy DeNucci: Bartender, Stone Pony

Dennis Diken: Musician, Smithereens

David DiPietro: Musician,
T.T. Quick

Tim Donnelly: Founder,
Sea.Hear.Now

Miles Doughty: Musician,
Slightly Stoopid

Mike Doyle: Musician, Lanemeyer

John Easdale: Musician,
Dramarama

John Eddie: Musician

Brian Fallon: Musician,
the Gaslight Anthem

Danny Federici: Musician,
E Street Band

Vinnie Fiorello: Musician,
Less Than Jake

Stanley Fischer: Union organizer

Larry Fishman: Chief operating
officer, Asbury Partners

Donavon Frankenreiter:
Musician

Stacie George: Promoter,
Live Nation

Stan Goldstein: Journalist

Joe Grushecky: Musician, Joe
Grushecky and the Houserockers

Patrick Hallahan: Musician,
My Morning Jacket

Bruce Haring: Reporter,
Courier News

Billy Hector: Musician,
Hot Romance

Erick W. Henderiks: Bouncer,
Stone Pony

Nick Hexum: Musician, 311

Kate Hiltz: Empress Dowager,
Bouncing Souls

Doc Holiday: Musician/producer

Benny Horowitz: Musician,
the Gaslight Anthem

Dan Jacobson: *triCityNews* publisher

Paul Janeway: Musician,
St. Paul and the Broken Bones

Jack Johnson: Musician

Joe Jonas: Musician,
Jonas Brothers

Kevin Jonas: Musician,
Jonas Brothers

Nick Jonas: Musician,
Jonas Brothers

Bobby Jones: Head of security,
Stone Pony

Ben Jorgensen: Musician,
Armor for Sleep

Tomas Kalnoky: Musician,
Catch 22/Streetlight Manifesto

Jorma Kaukonen: Musician,
Jefferson Airplane/Hot Tuna

Lenny Kaye: Musician, Patti
Smith Group

Jeff Kazee: Musician, Asbury Jukes

Bryan Kienlen: Musician,
the Bouncing Souls

Darius Koski: Musician,
Swingin' Utters

Lance Larson: Musician,
Lord Gunner

Chris Layton: Musician,
Stevie Ray Vaughan and
Double Trouble

Harvey Leeds: Manager,
Stone Pony

Stan Levinstone: Promoter,
Stone Pony

Huey Lewis: Musician,
Huey Lewis and the News

Pete Llewellyn: Bartender,
Stone Pony

Nils Lofgren: Musician,
E Street Band

Vini Lopez: Musician,
E Street Band

G. Love: Musician

Southside Johnny Lyon:
Musician, Southside Johnny and
the Asbury Jukes

Clint Maedgen: Musician,
Preservation Hall Jazz Band

Jesse Malin: Musician,
D Generation

Peter Mantas: Former manager,
Bon Jovi/Atlantic City
Expressway

Dave Marsh: Music journalist

Tom Marshall: Musician,
Amfibian/Phish

J Mascis: Musician, Dinosaur Jr.

Mike McCready: Musician,
Pearl Jam

Jim McGreevey: Governor,
New Jersey

Bob McLynn: Musician, Step
Kings/Manager, Crush Music

Andrew McMahon: Musician,
Something Corporate/Jacks
Mannequin/Wilderness

Monte Melnick: Manager,
Ramones

David Meyers: Musician,
Blackberry Booze Band

Jean Mikle: Reporter, *Asbury Park
Press*

Ryan Miller: Musician,
Guster

Joyce Moore: Manager,
Sam Moore

Sam Moore: Musician,
Sam and Dave

Tom Morello: Musician

Gary Mottola: President,
Madison Marquette

Lee Mrowicki: DJ, Stone Pony

Philip D. Murphy: Governor,
New Jersey

Willie Nile: Musician

Tony Pallagrosi: Musician,
Asbury Jukes

Graham Parker: Musician,
Graham Parker and the Rumour

Reverend David J. Parreott:
Minister, Asbury Park

Mark Pender: Musician, Asbury
Jukes/Hubcaps

Tom Petta: Musician, Bigwig

Butch Pielka: Cofounder,
Stone Pony

Matt Pinfield: Radio DJ

Dave Pirner: Musician,
Soul Asylum

John Popper: Musician,
Blues Traveler

Carrie Potter: Granddaughter of
Upstage Club owner

Margaret Potter: Owner,
Upstage Club

Tracey Story Prince: Bartender,
Stone Pony

Joe Prinzo: Consigliere,
Asbury Jukes

Lexi Quaas: Former nightclub/
concert promoter

James Ramen: Musician,
Fury of Five

C.J. Ramone: Musician, Ramones

Robert Randolph: Musician,
Robert Randolph and the
Family Band

Geoff Rickly: Musician, Thursday

Jack Roig: Cofounder, Stone Pony

Richie "La Bamba" Rosenberg:
Musician, Asbury Jukes/Hubcaps

Billy Rush: Musician,
Asbury Jukes

Rich Russo: Free Form
Radio DJ

Dave Sabo: Musician,
Skid Row

David Sancious: Musician,
E Street Band

Domenic Santana: Former owner,
Stone Pony

Bob Santelli: Journalist/
executive director for the
Bruce Springsteen Archives

Heath Saraceno: Musician,
Midtown

Howard Saunders: Institute for
Labor Education and Research

Al Schnier: Musician, moe.

Steve Schraeger: Musician,
Cold Blast and Steel

Wesley Schultz: Musician,
Lumineers

Ed Sciaky: Radio DJ

Patti Scialfa: Musician,
E Street Band

Tony Shanahan: Musician,
Patti Smith Group

Nancy Shields: Reporter,
Asbury Park Press

Patti Smith: Musician

Ronnie Spector: Musician

Kenny "Stringbean" Sorensen:
Musician

Bruce Springsteen: Musician,
E Street Band

Pete Steinkopf: Musician,
the Bouncing Souls

Bill Stevenson: Musician,
Descendents

Don Stine: Former chair,
Asbury Park Historical Society

Dube Sullivan: Bartender,
Stone Pony

J. T. Sullivan: Bartender,
Stone Pony

Tim Sweetwood: Promoter,
C3/founder, Sea.Hear.Now

Garry Tallent: Musician,
E Street Band

Christopher Thorn: Musician,
Blind Melon

Henry Vaccaro: Developer

Stevie Van Zandt: Musician,
E Street Band, actor

Kenny Vasoli: Musician,
Starting Line

Max Weinberg: Musician,
E Street Band

Adam Weiner: Musician,
Low Cut Connie

Carl "Tinker" West: Manager,
Steel Mill/Bruce Springsteen

Christine Todd Whitman:
Governor, New Jersey

Zakk Wylde: Musician,
Ozzy Osbourne/Black Label
Society

Dave Wyndorf: Musician,
Shrapnel/Monster Magnet

Foreword

Locals, first and foremost; the Stone Pony was a local bar, a neighborhood joint. I started out at a place up the street called the Student Prince. When the Prince cooled down, I wandered up to the Pony, because Steve and Southside Johnny were the house band. It quickly became my main hang. There were a lot of good musicians, cute waitresses and bartenders, along with some decent bands coming through, but it wasn't a venue for many national acts at first. It was just your club. That said, Asbury was a lively place socially at the time. The club had a group of spirited regulars who kept the place vital and afloat. Outside, the town was crumbling, the amusement rides were on their last legs, the boardwalk dead, the city largely vacant and gangland dangerous. But the club was safe due to a heavy team of bouncers who insisted on the peace. Women don't go to dangerous clubs, and where there aren't any women, there sure aren't gonna be any men. The boys at the door could occasionally be rough. They did not suffer dope shenanigans. Danny Federici went flying out belly-to-the-sidewalk for some drug hijinks in the Pony's men's room one summer night. My buddy, a bouncer called Payback, was the blond hulking, humorous, glass-chewing black belt who weekly policed the joint. Together we drove Steve's red Cadillac on the boardwalk from Bradley Beach to Asbury after a night on the town club tripping. There were a lot of good local bands who were never going to go any further but who served an important and honorable purpose on a sweaty Saturday night when the beach crew wanted to dance and down drinks like Sex on the Beach. I drank Jack Daniel's, Ol' Blue Eyes' favorite, and it served me well. The club was a great place to get high and jam a few songs during the last set. I'd sit at the bar in a slow burn all night, waiting to blow the roof off the place; where I would sweat so much in forty minutes, I'd leave the place stone sober. Southside Johnny on Wednesdays, Saturdays, and Sundays was probably the best house band in the nation at that time. With a full horn section, they regularly wrecked the place. Steve was an incredible bandleader-arranger, and Southside had the voice and real grit. The place was filled with local eccentrics. The owners, Jack and Butch, big and capable bouncers themselves, kept a tight lid on everything, and everybody was happy. It was a good time to be young and amongst a community of people who felt about music the way you did. I spent a lot of weekday and weekend nights there for quite a few years right through the height of my popularity and never had a problem. Folks were glad to see me, and I was glad to see them. Staying local all through the crazy high times was the smartest thing I ever did. The Stone Pony and its patrons allowed me to continue to be one of them, and for that I'm forever thankful. At seventy-four, I don't get down to the Pony as much as I used to, but I'm still glad it's there. Long may she run.

—*Bruce Springsteen*

Author's Note

This book is based on hundreds of original interviews conducted by the author. Some comments have been edited for brevity and clarity. In rare cases, quotes were excerpted from other sources, including speeches, recordings, and newspapers, especially for important voices who are no longer with us. A list of these sources and the pages they correspond to appears on page 299.

Introduction

I'd like to start with a clarification for those whose familiarity with the Jersey Shore begins and ends with a certain abomination of a reality television show: the Jersey Shore is a diverse stretch of 141 miles of coastline that is far from monolithic. There's alcohol-free family resort towns like Ocean City; mansion-lined, Hamptons-esque hamlets like Spring Lake; and kitschy, carnival-vibe boardwalks in Seaside Heights and Point Pleasant. There's pockets of surf and fishing communities in almost every town.

Asbury Park, however, was always different.

A brief history lesson: In the early 1900s, Asbury Park was an entertainment resort town seeking to compete with Atlantic City, building theaters and convention halls to help fill its many hotels. In the middle of the century, it was becoming a destination for touring acts looking for a gig between Philadelphia and New York City. Led Zeppelin and the Rolling Stones, for example, arrived in town in the 1960s.

Yet like many towns at the time, Asbury Park was segregated. The oceanfront, or east side of the train tracks, remained a largely white population. On the west side was a largely Black community with a thriving music scene, as jazz and blues clubs littered Springwood Avenue.

In the 1960s, as the civil rights movement rippled across the country and Black communities fought back against racist Jim Crow laws and segregation, the west side of Asbury Park began to grow frustrated with dwindling economic opportunities in town and a shrinking housing market.

Those tensions would erupt into riots in July 1970, when protesters destroyed nearly all of Springwood Avenue.

Though no one was killed, the damage and unrest sparked a flight from Asbury Park, the beginning of a slow, precipitous decline that would bottom out in the 1990s.

That era was my introduction to Asbury Park and the Stone Pony: inching through the crumbling west side of town, as the six-CD changer shuffled through Blink-182, Bad Religion, and Bigwig, in single-lane traffic for the 1998 Vans Warped Tour, held in the Stone Pony lot. Cars were backed up five miles along a mostly single-lane road to the Garden State Parkway.

It was a two-plus-hour crawl, in swampy Jersey Shore summer heat, for my dad and me in an aging Ford station wagon, as we crossed into a ghost town.

Dubbed "Beirut by the Shore," the once-proud beach resort town of Asbury Park looked more like bombed-out Dresden in World War II, the shattered remnants of the city ripped apart by decades of corruption, segregation, tough luck, and the unsparing whims of economic change.

Even with the Warped Tour stages providing a temporary skyline to the beachfront and a surge in summertime population, the scars of the struggling town were everywhere.

Bars were shuttered and closed. Homes deserted. A rotting, abandoned condo project twelve stories high cast a shadow over the concert area, a warning visible from blocks away of this city by the sea that fortune seemingly forgot. It was not the kind of ruins that presented options to the opportunistic and bold; it was just dead.

But I couldn't stay away.

It was quickly becoming central to the booming New Jersey punk scene. Bands that started with shows in basements, legion halls, and firehouses were getting signed to major labels and headlining tours. That recognition drew other national punk bands to Asbury Park. And with them came me, to the Pony and other venues in town. My friends and I, hooked on the scene and the permanent hearing damage that came with it, tried to go to everything.

Then I discovered the world of Bruce Springsteen.

He had always been there, omnipresent in my life as a lifelong New Jerseyan born to two lifelong New Jerseyans, with a father who filled every car ride and silent moment in the house with classic rock or

Q104.3 on the radio. But it took my own journey into music as a fledgling guitarist to move deeper than "Born to Run" and "Thunder Road," and discover the canon of the greatest American rock star in history.

That someone as galactic as Springsteen was from the same state as me, and kept coming back to the same dingy venue I trekked to, made me obsessive. No matter the band, no matter the genre, there was always that 1 percent chance (or perceived chance) that "Bruce might show up." It made every gig at the Pony just a bit more intoxicating, spellbound by the potential of a surprise appearance. It was those same four words that, for some time, kept the Pony alive when the town around it wasn't.

Indeed, some fifty years from its opening in 1974, the Pony is still here, sitting on prime beach real estate in open defiance of the expected life span of a rock club. Famed venues like CBGB and Max's Kansas City are long gone. The original Cavern Club, where the Beatles started, was knocked down. But the Pony remains, no longer a neighborhood bar with a legendary stage but now a destination venue with major industry support.

As the town has experienced a resurgence in the past fifteen years, sparked by a vibrant LGBTQ community, persistent developers, and a rich musical history, the Pony proved the lone constant. Its white-speckled concrete walls are now surrounded by multimillion-dollar condos, trendy new hotels, and destination restaurants. That rotting, failed condominium structure is now a gleaming, seventeen-story glass tower, with penthouse condos fetching prices north of $6 million.

Even now, as a major music venue, there's a sense of community at the Pony. I check in with my Summer Stage bartender Frank at every show, always stationed near my "secret spot" in the lot where I'm guaranteed some standing room. Being able to say "I know Bobby Jones" is like knowing Butch and Jack. The camera (and harmonicas) of Danny Clinch provide that signature spontaneity. Southside Johnny and the Asbury Jukes still sell out the Pony every winter, and put on a big party every summer, including one in 2019 where Bruce did indeed show up. (My dad and I still talk of that show, especially the "Sherry Darling" jam, with reverence.)

Though I never got to experience the Pony of old, I feel that spirit regularly at show after show, perhaps no more so than on the Saturday night of the Sea.Hear.Now festivals. The first day culminates in an epic super jam known as the Ocean Avenue Stomp at the Stone Pony that lasts deep into the night. Each song break is laden with that same addictive anticipation: Who might show up? I've seen Brandon Flowers jam with Jake Clemons, Mike McCready with Christopher Thorn of Blind Melon, St. Paul and the Broken Bones play house band for Wesley Schultz from the Lumineers and Nicole Atkins, and all of My Morning Jacket take over the stage. Lenny Kaye, of the Patti Smith Group, wandered over one night just to get a beer and ended up onstage with the Tangiers Blues Band blasting "Gloria." And these were all unbilled.

When I first came back to New Jersey and its shores after years on the political campaign trail for my day job, I began to see Asbury Park differently—not only as living history of American music but as an unwitting microcosm of the changes in blue-collar towns I had seen across the country. Indeed the story of Asbury Park—the rise and fall of a local economy, the daily struggle for civil rights, a proud town's resilience and revival—was happening in mining villages and steel mill towns, midsized cities and industrial exurbs across the country. The scale, and the success, may have varied from town to town, but the foundations were the same.

Asbury's, however, had a soundtrack.

So the best way to tell the story of Asbury Park, it became clear, was through the words of the people who got blisters on their fingers and sweat stains on their clothes building that very hymn. I spent years tracking down the bartenders, photographers, musicians, bouncers, politicians, revelers, staffers, and boastful locals. Like everyone else, my days again became filled with the hope of an unbilled performance or impromptu jams, eagerly scanning the Pony concert calendar every week.

Because there is, after all, always that chance. Bruce might show up.

I Don't Want to Go Home

1

Flames

The foundations of a once-prosperous beach resort begin to fray. Though the jazz, blues, and R&B clubs scattered across Springwood Avenue, on the west side of town, continue to thrive, the economic ills caused by decades of segregation combust in the summer of 1970.

Bruce Springsteen: I was in Wanamassa at the surfboard factory, and there was a huge water tank nearby. Vini Lopez and I climbed this water tank and sat near the top. And you could see Asbury burning off in the distance.

Garry Tallent: Before the riots, there were a lot of clubs. We played five nights a week. Year-round. All summer, all winter. We were there for years.

Doc Holiday: Asbury was the deal. It was a place to go and it had clubs. I mean, the nightclubs were such that you could actually get thrown out of one bar, roll over on the street, and be at the entrance of another one. And they all had live entertainment. The Pillow Talk, Mrs. Jay's, Steve Brody's, they were all over the place. So if you were going to be a musician, that's where you went to work. And we were going to Asbury Park to play music for two reasons: to get paid and get laid, period.

Southside Johnny: This small area of Asbury Park has always been clubs and bars where musicians could make a few dollars.

Stevie Van Zandt: We had tried to do some things with different bands. We had a different band every six months in those days.

Vini Lopez: I lived over by Springwood Avenue, where Neptune High School is now, and we'd ride our bikes down there, and all the clubs would have bands in them, sit there and listen to the bands outside. Every corner had a different band playing at one point.

David Sancious: At that time, I lived on what's called the west side of the tracks, the other side of the tracks. I didn't live here in this area. There was a real division between the clubs on the east side and the clubs on the west side. On the west side was predominantly African American, much larger population. There wasn't a sort of free flow of musicians back and forth. In other words, I can't think of a lot of Black musicians who were playing these clubs on the east side, with the exception of Clarence Clemons. Apart from Clarence Clemons, myself, and Ernest Carter, the second drummer in the E Street Band, we were the only sort of Black musicians that you see on the east side occasionally. And on the west side of the tracks, Garry Tallent was the only white musician who could play clubs on the west side of the tracks.

Ernest Carter: My father used to take me to the Orchid Lounge when I was eight or nine. I was young and I was just beginning to play. I stayed mostly in Springwood Avenue, going up and down the streets playing in those clubs since I was eleven years old. The music scene there was magical, so much music going on. It was our own little world on Springwood Avenue on that side of the tracks, man. It was just beautiful.

Lance Larson: I used to go down there, to the Orchid Lounge, to see a lot of bands, Black artists played in that place. It was right across the street from Fisch's; it was a department store.

Tony Pallagrosi: The sounds of Asbury Park were a mixture of things. But there were a lot of sounds in Asbury Park. On the west side of town, it was jazz. There were jazz clubs. And funk bands. But the majority of clubs east in Asbury Park were Top 40 clubs. I don't recall tensions between white and Black performers here in Asbury. I would go to the Orchid, for instance, to see jazz. And I never felt uncomfortable there.

I felt like that's how it's supposed to be. We're all supposed to draw off each other's energies.

Ernest Carter: Asbury had everything you could just imagine, and want, from the blues or rock and jazz, to the gospel, to everything. And it was kind of "keep to your side," but they called me Fidget. I couldn't stay in one place too long, so I would cross over and go there, and hear things, see things. Just to go to Convention Hall mainly because Convention Hall had a lot of solo acts there and a lot of nights for the Black people to go down and have a good time. Then I would go see all these other bands too that didn't have anything to do with the culture on my side. I was just open-minded because this is what my father taught me. I would go there to see Mountain, Jefferson Airplane, Steppenwolf, Chicago. If I couldn't get in, a couple of buddies of mine, we had a way to get in on top of the roof and stay on the rafters up there and watch the show.

Reverend David J. Parreott: Springwood Avenue was like the living room for a lot of people. That's where they played, where they had fellowship, what recreation it had, shooting pool and eateries that were here on Springwood Avenue at the time. Plus they shopped there. And during those years, a lot of people on the west side in that particular time in the early fifties and before, they didn't venture much across the tracks and go to the beachfront. I was born right here in Asbury Park in 1934. My family had been here for over one hundred years at that particular time, much more than that right now.

Bruce Springsteen: It was coming, because there was no representation at that local level for the African American population in town. And it was just something that was in the air and it was something that needed to happen.

Reverend David J. Parreott: Generally, any kind of civil disturbance of this kind of activities stems from lack of jobs. In Asbury Park, it was because many of the jobs that the young people had on the beachfront every summer would have been taken all by young relatives of the business owners down there.

Southside Johnny: If you ever had gone down Springwood Avenue, you'd see how people live. I mean, I would have rioted too. I mean, it was horrible there and nobody ever did anything about it. Because we had gone through the Martin Luther King riots and the Watts stuff and all of that. The way people were treated across the railroad tracks made it a real powder keg . . . And the city fathers knew, the city council knew that it was right on the edge, but they didn't do anything about it.

Reverend David J. Parreott: The other thing that lends itself to these kinds of things was the crowded housing that we had, particularly on the west side of Asbury Park, especially the southwest side of Asbury Park. And there was a lack of coordinated recreation in the city, like basketball, no basketball courts. We never had one. Tennis courts or playgrounds and other planned activities for the youth. During that particular time period that this initiated, I was the juvenile officer for the city. The young people came and spoke with me and talked about this lack of activities, jobs, et cetera, and what are we going to do, there's no place to go, and I can't get a job downtown anymore.

Bruce Springsteen: These were the times. So it didn't really catch you by surprise. I would say it was happening on any given day. It was in Newark or Asbury, or in Freehold. It happened in my little town of Freehold. And so it was part of the cultural picture at the moment.

Stevie Van Zandt: These times were very volatile. I mean, there's riots, seemed like all the time, every year or two. There's a lot of frustration, and it was just the beginning of the birth of consciousness. That whole decade really was the birth of consciousness in so many ways, including racial consciousness. And up until then, people were tolerating a lot of the racial injustice. It was just a normal part of society. And then at some point, it just was like, "Enough is enough."

Reverend David J. Parreott: It started right after a concert on the beachfront and the kids walking in and cars intermingled with the gathering that was turning out, letting out at the Westside Community Center. The group coming home from the beachfront and those coming out onto Springwood Avenue, they started name-calling and started bottle throwing, which really was something of copycat from other cities and states that had several disturbances in those areas.

Ernest Carter: These people came to our high school and started making all this noise about the rights of the Black people. . . . But what blew my mind was they were blowing up their own things.

Judy DeNucci: My father, he was a newspaper photographer for the *Asbury Park Press* and the *Long Branch Daily Record*, and he also was freelance for the *Daily News*, so he was right in the middle of it. There were nights he didn't even come home, he was there all night long, taking pictures of everything. . . . We drove through all the blockades, streets, and everything and it was the saddest to see what happened and how it changed the whole facade of Asbury, the business district, and Springwood Avenue.

Patti Scialfa: I went to Asbury Park High School, which was a predominantly Black school at the time. It was sad to me. It wasn't frightening. It's just heartbreaking when no one's listening to your voice and they're not seeing you, and your needs are invisible. And that leads to problems. I'm not saying it's right or wrong, I'm just saying I have great sympathy for that. That's the only way you feel you can be heard. And it was sad because mostly, a lot of the damage was in the neighborhood of Springwood Avenue across the tracks.

Reverend David J. Parreott: When the riots did break out, I was at home, and they gave me a call and told me, "Hey Dave, your kids are acting up out here." I came out and rounded them up and took some home and sent some home. That was the first night. The next night they were throwing bottles and things. That particular night broke a few windows down Springwood Avenue. The next day and night, and several days, of course, things escalated. They were making these Molotov cocktails and setting fires, et cetera. Quite a few kids were taken into custody and a lot of adults. Some of the things were escalated by law enforcement, even though I was part of law enforcement, but some of them kind of roughly treated these youngsters. But once they started the fires or right after that, and state police came in and they drove up and down Springwood Avenue in high speed with vehicles with no license plates, so you couldn't recognize, as you didn't get the badge numbers.

Ernest Carter: These guys came in, they were some fake Black Panthers. They had the right clothes on, but I knew Black Panthers. It had nothing to do with those guys. They were just agitators, frustrated Black people about what's going on, which I don't blame them, because shit was bad, man, but on that side of town, we were surviving and everything was moving on up. But man, when it came and started on Springwood Avenue, I was like, "No, man, please don't do it there. Go across the tracks or something, make something over there," but no, they just fucked up everything that I grew up around. Everybody got messed up, even their own homes. All the clubs I loved and played in got all destroyed. My street was gone.

Bruce Springsteen: The entire west side burnt to the ground. An entire cultural way of life and entire huge cultural chunk of Asbury Park, where it was incredible music and just an amazing neighborhood, burnt to the ground.

Vini Lopez: When those riots were going on, Tinker [West] had the surfboard factory up in Ocean Township, and it was up on the hill, and we went there. Because from up there you could see out to the ocean, and you could see the place burning down. So, we just stayed up there, and it was a crowd of people up there with us.

Southside Johnny: On the day of the riots, I was working at the post office. I was at a substation down on the boardwalk, a little kiosk, where you sold stamps or postcards and packages would come in. My friend Phil Moses drives in and said, "You got to come back, because they're having riots in Asbury Park." Our boss, Les Bush, great man, had said, "Go get John." And I had to pedal this old bike from the thirties, which weighed a ton, with all my cash and money orders and stuff, were in this heavy wooden box. And I'm going past everything, and I mean, they burned down Big Bill's and Fisch's Clothing Store and it was a terrible time.

Stevie Van Zandt: We were just hunkered down and avoiding the whole thing. We weren't really out on the street witnessing the thing because it was a real dangerous time. I remember people on the roofs with rifles, defending their turf and all that.

Jack Roig: Coming down on the train one night when we were leaving Allenhurst, they said, "Everybody on the floor," and the train blew right through Asbury, Bradley, and then stopped in Belmar.

Reverend David J. Parreott: It wasn't something that was good for the west side because we eliminated jobs on Springwood Avenue, many jobs. Eliminated the housing. You had housing on top of the storefronts that were below, and that was not a good thing. . . . Springwood Avenue, for the west side, was like the playground. It was like the beachfront. It was the way people promenaded up and down in fellowship and carried on with each other on the avenue. All of that was taken away as a result of this civil disturbance.

Billy Hector: When I went to bed, it sounded like there was a football game going on. I used to live about a mile away from the stadium. You could hear them shouting and screaming. Ocean Grove put armed guards on the fucking bridges in and out of the place.

Vini Lopez: The guys that worked at the Upstage, they all got their guns and went up on the roof to protect the Upstage. But I don't think it ever really got that far. But it was bad over on Springwood Avenue.

Carl "Tinker" West: The bouncer there [at the Upstage], at that time he was a motorcycle enthusiast, and he went down and sat behind the door during the riots. And one of those rioting people opened the door and he said, "Do you want to live or die?" And they closed the door and went away. He had a shotgun.

Tony Amato: We were musicians, so we didn't give a shit about all this racial baloney. I was playing with the bass player, Norman Perkins, Black guy from the west side. That screwed us up for a while. We couldn't go out and play as much or rehearse because the parents were tense. It was the older people. It wasn't the kids.

Bruce Springsteen: I believe it also put the kibosh on the boardwalk for quite a while. And it was one of the few towns where there were rides also on the boardwalk.

Vini Lopez: It kind of just fell apart. Asbury became, in my opinion, like a ghost town at some point. People didn't want to go there because of the riots. They were afraid to go there. But we lived there, so we didn't stop by any means.

Patti Scialfa: At the time, the papers were just always feeding you one-dimensional ideas about the Black Panthers, anybody who was out there making a change that was a little frightening for people. They never looked at anything good that the Black Panthers did, like making places that the kids could go to before school, having hot breakfast and all this. They were just vilifying every person of color in the media.

Tony Pallagrosi: The riots really put a damper on how the suburbs viewed Asbury Park. I mean, just the fact that there were Black people in Asbury Park. That was a thing even before the riots. As the years went on, people became fearful. And the only people who didn't were people who liked music.

Southside Johnny: I remember that it was a lot more paranoid to go out at night. But that didn't last long. We were all long-haired hippie guys, or probably past that. I think there was a certain affinity to that. They knew that we were no threat. I mean the Black people didn't look at us as the people who had neglected them.

Ernest Carter: I lived a beautiful life growing up in Asbury. Springwood Avenue before the riots, it was everything, but after the riots, I don't understand why it went down like that, but it did. It broke my heart and I had no reason to stay there really musically.

Bob Santelli: It completely changed. Overnight. I mean, the vibe was spooky. It was like something really bad happened in the town, because it did, you know? You could feel it. I mean, many kids would come up and go to record stores in Asbury on the other side of the tracks, buy your clothes up here, especially if you were in bands and whatnot. It was kind of a cool place. Steinbach's was up here. It was a big place for school clothes for when you were in high school and whatnot. All of that on my end stopped.

David Sancious: The whole tone of the town was changed after the riots. Commerce was different. There were a lot of shops and stores that were closed. Everything was very, very different after the riots. It was a sort of big diminishment. But a few places hung on.

2

The Upstage Club

An all-ages, third-floor club above Cookman Avenue with amplifiers built directly into the stage hosts jams that would not end until the sun breached the sea to the east. Opening in 1968, two years before the riots, it offered a young Bruce Springsteen, Stevie Van Zandt, Southside Johnny, and many future E Street Band and Asbury Jukes members an introduction to the stage.

Vini Lopez: Before all that happened . . . the Upstage was in full swing.

Southside Johnny: The Upstage Club. I'm sure you've heard a lot of the stories about that. I'll give you a quick rundown. It was opened by a guy named Tom Potter. His wife, Margaret, played in bands. She was one of the first rock-and-roll chicks I ever met. She was older than us. They both were. But anyways, he starts this club, up above a Thom McAn shoe store, a three-story brick building on Cookman Avenue. The second floor was this folk kind of small stage, near a little cooking place, where they could make coffee and sandwiches and things like that. And the third floor was this big long room, with a stage at one end of it and it had built-in speakers, a PA, a drum kit, had amplifiers and a double keyboard. So you just had to come and bring your guitar or mic kit and harmonicas and play. It just was a magnet for musicians. I mean it was open from, I think it was eight or nine until five in the morning, at one point, and no alcohol was served. So the kids could go.

Al "Doc" Berger: They had amps built into the stage. You just plugged into the stage.

Stevie Van Zandt: Bruce told me about it. He says, "Man, there's this new thing, Upstage. You got to check it out, down in Asbury Park." Now Asbury Park, that was a little bit exotic for us. I mean, I had been there to see the Rolling Stones at Convention Hall and the Byrds. That was a regular. That was our venue for the big acts coming through from in between Philadelphia and New York. They would always usually play Asbury Park. And I had been in a couple of band battles down there, but it was good forty-five minutes away. It was a trip. Bruce told me, "Go down there and ask for Margaret," who was the wife of the co-owner. And that was it, man. It became a second home. Or no, it became home, first home.

Bruce Springsteen: When I wrote that record [*Greetings from Asbury Park*] I was living on my own above the Upstage, in Asbury Park. So it all just came naturally.

Margaret Potter: Bruce came up very politely and said, "Excuse me, but would you mind very much if I borrowed your guitar? The gentleman downstairs said it would probably be okay." I said sure and stuck around awhile while he plugged in, to make sure he understood the system. He played some blues thing, and I said, "Oh, Lord," and went back down to the second floor. Vini Lopez, the first drummer in the E Street Band, was sitting down there, and Miami Steve, and Southside Johnny, all playing Monopoly, which is what you did while you waited to get up, and I told them they had better get upstairs. They were involved in the game, and asked why. I said, "Hey, guys, there's some kid up there who can really play." They said, "Where are you going?" I said, "Where do you think? Upstairs."

Stevie Van Zandt: We all moved to Asbury Park because of that club. We were literally living off of that club, only making like fifteen dollars a night.

Bruce Springsteen: In the beginning, there was "Mad Dog" Vini Lopez, standing in front of me, fresh out of jail, his head shaved, in the Mermaid Room of the Upstage Club in Asbury Park.

Vini Lopez: I happened to be lucky, me and Big Bobby, to be the house drummers at the Upstage and got to play with a lot of different musicians and learn what we do. And that's what it was all about, was the learning experience in those days. The young kids could go in there at the Upstage from eight to midnight, and they were dance kids, and it was still a jam session in there. And then, either Big Bobby or me would be the house drummer for the early session or the late session, which was from one to five in the morning. But you never really knew until the night of who was going to be there, and Tom Potter would assign you on the stage when he wanted you there. It was quite a scene.

Stevie Van Zandt: Jamming had become a thing. The whole blues revolution going on with all the stuff coming out of England, the Yardbirds with the rave-ups that they were doing, basically, which was just jams. Songs started to go from two and a half minutes to be extended, because guitar playing started to become fashionable. The lead guitar, basically. Eric Clapton and Jeff Beck and the Yardbirds guys basically were responsible for just making guitar the king. Suddenly, playing guitar was as important as the songs. So jamming suddenly happened. It was all blues jamming, basically. The Upstage concept was built on that.

Garry Tallent: The Upstage became a kind of guitar-slinger Dodge City. Every guitar player in at least a twenty-mile radius heard about this place and showed up and tried to outdo each other.

Bruce Springsteen: We first saw Garry Tallent along with Southside Johnny when they dragged two chairs onto an empty dance floor as I plugged my guitar into the Upstage wall of sound. I was the new kid in a new town, and these were the guys who owned the place. They sat back and looked at me like, "Come on, come on, punk. Bring it. Let's see what you got." And I reached back and I burnt their house down.

Patti Scialfa: I knew of Bruce back then because he was known as the fastest guitar player in town.

Danny Federici: When Vini Lopez and I first saw Bruce play at the Upstage we basically said, "We've gotta have this guy in our band." So we decided to start a band. So he quit Earth to put a band together with me and Vini. And we found a bass player, Vinnie Roslin. And that band was called Child. And that's how the whole switcheroo thing—getting him out of Freehold—began.

Southside Johnny: We got the job to jam there, either Big Bobby, or Vini Lopez was the house drummer. Garry Tallent was the house bass player. Steven, or Johnny "Hotkeys," or I forget the other guy's, Ricky DeSarno was the house guitar player and if they needed a singer, I was the singer. So we were there all the time and it was just a great education. I mean people would come and say, "Let's do this. Let's do that." We'd try to do it. You had to be very flexible, you had to think on your feet, and it was really our college.

Vini Lopez: John Lyon would play the bass. Or he'd sing a little bit here and there and play his harmonica, but he never was Southside until the Pony.

Southside Johnny: We were getting paid to stay there from nine till five and jam with whoever wanted to jam. Of course, we would have been there anyway. But you get a lot of, if you had a gig and you got off at one thirty, two, you'd go from your gig to the Asbury Diner and get something to eat and then you'd go to the Upstage for the rest of your night.

Patti Scialfa: The one that everybody wanted to go to was the one that started at one a.m. in the morning. That was supposedly the real deal.

Tony Pallagrosi: If you went to the Upstage, what was played there was bluesy rock and roll and a lot of R&B tunes. And some blues, and you wouldn't hear that in other towns. You heard that in Asbury. And it was because there was ethnic diversity in Asbury. And because at a point, you had a place where you can play that music and get paid.

Patti Scialfa: I did have a band back then. It was called Ecstasy. I was young enough where I couldn't drive, and I remember being dropped off there by a friend. I told my mother I was sleeping over somebody's house, dropped off by a friend at about one o'clock, met the band that was in there, and went upstairs and sang "White Rabbit" and "Somebody to Love." I was a big Grace Slick fan. I remember that as just being out-of-my-skin exciting. "Okay. I'm in a real venue right now." But then I didn't know how to get home. Actually, I tried to hitchhike, and then I got a little frightened. It was on Cookman Avenue. It was like three in the morning, four in the morning, and then somebody called their father and had them pick us up. I think that's what happened. I tried to hitchhike. I was a big hitchhiker in those days, but then just feeling, "This isn't the smartest thing to do at three in the morning, being fifteen or sixteen."

Tony Amato: Some of us would sneak out of the house, 'cause I was a little young for the Upstage, but since my father, basically, was the accountant for Margaret and Tom Potter, I used to be able to get in there because they knew who I was.

Patti Scialfa: Margaret and Tom Potter. I remember Margaret came up to me and she was very lovely. I mean, basically, I think I was fifteen, sixteen at the time, and she came up to me and she complimented me. It was odd. Something like, "Wow, you've got something. I don't know what it is, but you do have something," I remember. I took that as the largest compliment in the world because I was a kid.

Ernest Carter: I would go up there by myself, but I wouldn't play. And these other cats would come in, Bruce and everyone, but the only one I would remember is Garry Tallent. I just was up there just listening and hanging out, figuring out what the hell was going on up there. Tom Potter would warn me: "Your dad's coming down." I'd say, "Where?" I shot out the back door when my father was coming in because I wasn't supposed to be there at that age.

David Sancious: I'd go and listen to what they were doing and I would dance and it was very psychedelic back then. The walls were all painted psychedelic as a vibe.

Southside Johnny: We played anything we wanted. At one point, he had this screen, the stage would be here at the far end of the room and he had this movie screen that would come down and cover the band and everybody would be sitting out there and looking at the screen and they played W. C. Fields's silent things and shorts and we'd be playing along with it, watching W. C. Fields from behind. It was kind of bizarre. It was the sixties. There was some acid and all of that and it was just, we reveled in the silly old aspects of all of it. It was just perfect for the time and it also gave us a chance to jam, try different music. Because people didn't really care, as long as you really were good and you really played your heart out. So it was good. I met a million musicians there and it lasted I think three years, something like that. I was doing some of the acid, so I don't remember all of it.

Vini Lopez: I remember one time, I think it was Garry, me, Ricky D. And we got up and the place is packed. What are we going to do? What are we going to do? Let's just make noise. So we ended up there and just started making noise, and we did it for twenty minutes.

Garry Tallent: The miniskirts contest, though, that was . . . Tom Potter, he got to judge the miniskirt contest.

Vini Lopez: Around here it was all these cliques. If you were in Freehold, you were Freehold clique, if you were in Middletown, you were in Middletown group. Asbury Park, we had our own clique too. There was a clique of musicians everywhere. The Upstage brought the cliques together. And Potter would mix and match.

Garry Tallent: It's funny how cliquey it was.

Vini Lopez: And the Upstage took care of all that, smoothed it out.

David Sancious: Bruce has been famous locally for all of his life, really. He had several bands that were popular locally before the configuration that became the E Street Band. Quite a few. So I met him when I was fifteen. I dropped out of school when I was fifteen, in the middle of my junior year. And one night, as I'm going into the Upstage, I walked up the stairs and Bruce was standing next to Garry. Garry and I had met a couple weeks before on a recording session, just a private recording session for an amateur musician. Didn't have a record contract or anything. We had met and sort of clicked right away. And I'm walking up the stairs, Garry recognizes me, and he introduces me to Bruce. The two of them were standing at the top of the stairs trying to organize who was or wasn't going to be involved in this next jam session coming up. So I went up, shook Bruce's hand. He said, "Hey, we're organizing this jam session. Do you want to sit in? You want to be part?" I said, "Yeah, absolutely."

Bruce Springsteen: Davey was very, very unusual: He was a young, Black man who—in 1968, Asbury Park, which was not a peaceful place—

crossed the tracks in search of musical adventure, and he blessed us with his talent and his love. He danced like Sly Stone and he played like Booker T, and he poured out blues and soul and jazz and gospel and rock and roll and he had things in his keyboard that we just never heard before.

David Sancious: As we're walking towards whoever the ride was, Bruce said to me, "Hey, listen, I'm, I'm about to break up this band I have called Steel Mill." They were huge down here. And I had seen Bruce in Steel Mill before that. I was like, "Wow." It was a very different band. And Bruce back then was the sort of local gunslinger on the guitar. He was playing the best electric guitar around. Nobody was playing better, taking solos and playing really, really good guitar. So that one night that we actually physically met and played together. He said, "I'm going to start something else new. I'm going to end this thing." And, "Would you be interested in being in it?" And me fresh out of high school with no job or no anything, all I had was my desire to do exactly what he was doing. So he invited me in.

Mike Appel: The local clubs in Asbury Park were terrific. And it was a great oasis for musicians who needed nurturing, like Bruce Springsteen to become a Bruce Springsteen and to give them even a place to hang their hat for a while. And to be in front of a crowd, a live crowd. And to play people their wares. "Here's my wares, here's what I've got. What do you think?" So that's very, very important. That's a great role, a nurturing role that a club like that plays in an artist's life and in a manager's life.

Stevie Van Zandt: You're analyzing songs, you're pulling apart those two-and-a-half-minute hits, your favorite songs, and analyzing what instruments are doing what and all that. So that was extremely important. But now we've gone on to musician craft. This was a new stage of development within the evolution of the rock thing. So we started to learn how to play longer guitar solos, which I eventually very quickly realized, I just didn't really dig that whole thing. In my heart, I really wasn't a musician per se. Me in my heart, I wanted to play guitar good enough to play a cool solo in the middle of a two-and-a-half-minute song.

Tony Pallagrosi: The Upstage, even though it was only around a couple of years, the right people met there. The right alliances, musical alliances, were formed of like-minded, musical people, like-minded people with talent. It's the "we liked the same music, we liked the same clothes."

Patti Scialfa: It's like you cross some kind of threshold into the real world of music. It felt that way. It was so looked up to. When you're young, you look at anyone who's doing something, whether it's acting or it's music, it's another planet. And you're always wondering, "How do I get there? How do I get to that spot? It just seems impossible." So, being at the Upstage felt like, "Okay, this is your first little step of getting closer to what you feel people speak your language is."

Eileen Chapman: I had a good friend Jimmy Miller who was a guitarist, who had turned us on to the Upstage up here on Cookman Avenue. We'd all be going to bed eleven and he'd be heading to the Upstage. Finally we're like, okay, we have to do this. He kept saying you have to come see this guitar player. It was, of course, Springsteen.

Lance Larson: I used to go to Asbury every weekend; every night I could I'd go to Asbury. Go to the bars and go to hear all the bands, and I went to the Upstage a lot. I never played because I was too young. But I saw Bruce and a lot of the guys play there.

Bobby Bandiera: I was playing D'Jais with my friends Holme, and a couple of the bartenders and the actual owner of the Upstage would tend bar at D'Jais. And at the end of the night, he would plead with me, because the Upstage wasn't doing well. It just wasn't getting enough clientele to stay alive. "Can you announce it on the mic? People from here, come up over to the Upstage?"

Bruce Springsteen: Tom Potter had split up with his wife, Margaret, from Margaret and the Distractions. He was crushed. And he closed the Upstage down and went to Florida, and I never saw him again. Hard as it's to believe. I figured I'd run into him somewhere along the way, but nope.

Carrie Potter: My dad told me that Tom struggled for over a year keeping the Upstage open and was losing money. Finally with only $10,000, after selling what he could, a renovated bus and an MG car, he told Margaret he wanted to close up and cut losses and move to Florida, where his sisters and relatives lived.

Southside Johnny: The Upstage Club was, to us, it was just magic. It was a golden time and we knew it. We knew we were getting away with murder. The police weren't bothering us too much. We didn't have money worries because we were younger. We got food stamps. Al got food stamps. And Steve would go next door to the Greeks and turn them in for money and go to the racetrack. That's true.

Stevie Van Zandt: It would be a stretch to say the Upstage saved Asbury Park, but it saved us. It certainly saved us. We had nothing else we could possibly do. It was absolutely a miracle for us.

Bruce Springsteen: I just think it was one of those things. It had its moment and its moment was over.

3

Tiny Horse

As Asbury grappled with post-riot realities, the "circuit" formed by Kingsley and Ocean Avenues was still littered with beach bars, stained by the salt air and summer sweat. In February 1974, amid those crowded environs, two former Jersey Shore bouncers hoped for a future.

Jack Roig: I never wanted to open a rock club. And I definitely didn't want anything in Asbury Park.

Bruce Springsteen: Once the Upstage closed, we had the Student Prince for a while. But you were still in hostile territory in those days. There weren't many places you could go and play what you wanted to play. Most of them were Top 40 bars.

Stevie Van Zandt: The riots had pretty much cleared what was left of the town out. It was left to us mystics and rogues and renegades and outcasts who moved in.

Jack Roig: I grew up in an Irish neighborhood. Upper Manhattan. There's a gin mill on every corner and probably a couple in between. Always wanted to have a bar. I was kicking around down here, and one Sunday afternoon in September, October of '73, I call up this real estate guy. Never heard of him before. I said, "What do you have for sale?" He said, "How much money do you have?" I said, "Just show me what you have." When I say I had no money, I had no money. And I should have.

I was a computer programmer systems consultant at that time. So, I went up. I was talking to him and I said, "Look, I don't want anything in Asbury Park. I definitely don't want anything in Asbury Park." It was not too long after the riots and he said, "Well, I've got a place up in Deal to show you, but do you mind if we stop in this other place? I don't even have keys for it yet. I just got the listing an hour ago. I don't have keys for it yet." We strolled up to the Magic Touch. It was the Pony. The front doors, still the same front doors. They were painted black. Each door had a circle in it. I looked in the door, and I said, "Okay, I'll buy it." Never went in the place. Talk about stupid.

Bruce Springsteen: At some point the place next to Mrs. Jay's turned into the Stone Pony.

Jack Roig: You want the true story of the name? I was married at the time, and . . . Well, she's dead, so it doesn't matter . . . And I was out with some girl, and I woke up the next morning. She had this thing on with little horses on it, this little T-shirt. Don't ask me where the "Stone" in Stone Pony came from, but that was it. That was it, man.

Jack Roig: I was working in the city every day. It was commuting to the city. I was looking for somebody to run it because I couldn't be there every day. My first choice was a salesman for one of the local distributors, and he didn't want to do it. Then I asked Butch. He said, "Yeah." He wanted to do it.

Steve Schraeger: Butch was the guy that helped physically build that place. He knocked down walls. He built the back bar with guys that worked there with him. Butch did all kinds of carpentry, and of course he had a guy, friend of mine, who was a mason. This guy's an electrician. And they worked to make the place bigger.

Jack Roig: The first day of the Pony. The closing was in East Brunswick. I had about eleven loans out just to pay off the down payment. That's what I mean, not too smart sometimes. It was snowing. I think about eight inches of snow fell on Asbury Park that night. Thank God the band canceled, because one person showed up that I knew from the train. That was it. One dollar, rang one dollar. I wanted to give him a beer for nothing. He said, "I want to pay the first dollar." That was the first night. But basically, from there until Labor Day, we did okay. We were in the black until about, I'd say, two weeks after Labor Day. Then the bottom fell out. I mean, when I say the bottom fell out . . . It stayed open because I always believed if you close, people will never come back. But we were down. I mean, I was out. It was just, "Why would they come there?" You know? It was nothing special. Had no name, had no nothing.

Al "Doc" Berger: In the beginning, the Pony was a dump.

Jack Roig: We were like in foreclosure, basically. And the first mortgage guy, Joe Stein from Stein Cadillac, wouldn't give you an inch. Not an inch.

Erick W. Henderiks: In the beginning of the Stone Pony, they didn't really have a during-the-week crowd. As a matter of fact, at one point, Jack put up Ping-Pong tables on the dance floor. He was trying anything to try to get business in there.

Jack Roig: I don't know if anybody ever talks about the nights we had hypnotists. You needed something to do on a Wednesday night, so you served something different. So you book a hypnotist, and they could bring in two hundred people and do things.

Glen Burtnik: Somebody that I knew had tickets, I guess, to go see a band called Flame at the Pony, it was the name of the band. They put out one album. This was 1974, so right when they opened. It was weird. What is the dance floor now they set up chairs and tried to make it a theater in a way, just these stupid chairs. We sat there and watched this band that I'd never heard of.

Erick W. Henderiks: One time, it was like a cabaret. He had all these tables on the dance floor and he had waitresses. Then finally with the music, when the music started to happen, then things started to take off. The Pony became known as a music-friendly place. Initially, what they did was a lot of cover bands like everybody else.

Butch Pielka: The first year we were pretty strapped for money. Jack worked another job and held things together. Then half the roof blew off in a windstorm and we found out our insurance company had gone bankrupt. I don't think we ever got a penny for that roof.

Jack Roig: December 1, 1974. It was a nor'easter. Blew the part of the roof over the stage right off.

Stevie Van Zandt: They were just able to basically barely keep it open, kinda halfway fix the roof. I think it was, I remember it being the last half of summer, so they were trying to take advantage of, at that point, even though the residents had all fled town, some of the amusements were still open on the boardwalk. The Ferris wheel and stuff was like, still there.

Butch Pielka: It seemed like everything was going bad up to that point. This is a very rough business to get started in. You spend all sorts of money for liquor and bands, then you pray like hell somebody walks in the door.

Jack Roig: In the beginning nobody came from Asbury.

Stevie Van Zandt: People would come down on the weekends from Jersey City, from up North Jersey, they were still coming down to Asbury even though its glory days were long over. So the Pony was just trying to stay open, take advantage of the end of that summer, grab the money they could grab, and then they were gonna close the club.

Lance Larson: We were in the disco era, you know? They just wanted disco bands and stuff.

Tony Pallagrosi: It was a deep disco scene. There was a station in Newark, and I think it was WRVR, which was a very deep Black-oriented disco station. And you hear bands that didn't really make Top 40 radio all that much, like Function. And you'd hear deep cuts off the Heatwave album, not necessarily the hits and things, bands of that ilk. You'd hear Parliament on that that you just weren't hearing elsewhere. And some of those bands or bands that played in that vein would play at the Pony. They were primarily, from what I recall, Black bands. And they were playing deep disco. You didn't see that elsewhere. It was kind of like what was happening musically on the weekends, even though it was completely different than what the Stone Pony would become.

Dube Sullivan: We had to put up with the disco crowd. The girls would always dress up, and they'd always want to dance. All the hard-ass rock and rollers, they didn't dance. You know who they wound up dancing with? It'll be all the Black guys always dancing with the ladies because they knew how to dance.

Butch Pielka: We had a real solid year of disco, and then it sort of died off.

J. T. Sullivan: We used to get guys in here with four hundred dollars' worth of clothes on their back and they wouldn't drink. Disco people don't drink at all; they're heavily into ice water, though.

Tony Pallagrosi: Springsteen talks about Spanish Johnnys, and you had Spanish Johnnys dancing to that music at the Stone Pony. Which really, if you think about what happened at the Stone Pony later, we became this bastion of white rock and was, I don't think the Black community in general felt all that comfortable for many years at the Stone Pony.

Butch Pielka: Rock-and-roll crowds are better and easier to deal with. They also drink more. The disco crowd was more plastic and phony. They came in all dressed up, but they had a dollar in their pocket.

Jack Roig: We did some disco stuff. And I just couldn't stomach it. I walked in there one night off the train and looked around and I said, "Pay 'em, close the bar down, we're done. I'm not going to do this anymore. Just close it down right now and throw 'em out."

David Meyers: I had this band, Blackberry Booze Band, and we needed a new place to play. And my sister-in-law, married to my brother, tells me about this club that just opened, and her brother is a co-owner of it. His name was Butch. Butch and Jack. I went to meet Butch and he knew me and we talked. I told him I had the band. I said, we do not play commercial music.

Stevie Van Zandt: Up till then, the rules were, the bar band rules were, if you play the bar, you had to play what they call the "Top 40." Which was the hits on the radio. There was no exceptions to that rule.

David Meyers: At that time when I went into that club, there was nobody there. And they had Top 40 music, like groups like Waterfront, stuff like that. And Waterfront was a good band. But we don't play that kind of music. We play our music, which is R&B and the blues. So I said, "Give us your two off nights. Thursday night, Sunday night. And we'll draw in some people and I think it'll work well here. I can feel the club had a good vibe to it." So he says, "Okay, how much you want?" So we booked the club, I booked it for $135, the four of us. And our PA. So that's when we started playing there.

Jack Roig: Butch had a cousin that was playing with the Blackberry Booze Band. We paid them $135 for the night. No one really came. And we did a second night. Not much again. And I said, "Hey, I'm so far in the hole now. Do it again."

Butch Pielka: They started out bad and we lost a lot of money every Tuesday for the first couple months.

Dave Meyers: After the first week, Jack goes, "I don't know if I'm going to have them back." Butch says, "This is going to work. Just give it some time." It was a crowd, but not a killer crowd, but a crowd. So he goes, "Okay, we'll let you play."

4

Jukes Origins

It seemed every beach bar had a band, and every band played the same Top 40 songs. Pop. Disco. Radio hits. That did not appeal to some of the locals, like Stevie Van Zandt and Southside Johnny Lyon.

Southside Johnny: I had joined a blues band with some forgettable name, playing harmonica, but the main guy who played guitar, he wouldn't let me sing. I wanted to sing. And another friend of mine was playing harmonica with the Blackberry Booze Band and they made him sing, and he didn't want to sing, he just wanted to play harp. So we switched bands without really asking. And the Blackberry Booze were such hippies that they went, "Oh, okay, man. Whatever, man. It's cool."

Dave Meyers: Paul Green, who was our harp player, said he was leaving the band. He goes, "I'm going to leave, but I got a replacement. His name is John Lyon, and he's a good harp player." So John Lyon comes over into the ranch, to meet Paul Dickler and I. We run through some songs, and John sang a few and played the harp. He wasn't like Paul Green, who was a very excellent harp player, but he was good and he fit the bill. So we put him in the band. And that's when I got the gig at the Stone Pony.

Southside Johnny: The Blackberry Booze Band was really a hippie band and they would take extended solos and after a while I just went, "I don't really like this." So I said, "I'm going to reform the band."

Dave Meyers: We're playing at the Pony, so John says, "I have a friend who was playing, I think in a group," maybe the Dovells. And he says he needs a band right now to play, and he's not playing with anybody. I said, "Who is he?" He goes, "Well, that's Steve. His name is Steve, Steve Van Zandt." I know Steven, because I heard him play guitar, and I heard him sing. He's a very good guitar player.

Stevie Van Zandt: I had come off of the oldies circuit, where I was playing with the Dovells and Dion. There was this thing called the oldies circuit at the time, which I'm not sure, some parts of it may still exist, but basically, when the British Invasion came in '64, the Beatles and Stones and Yardbirds and everybody basically put all the heroes out of work. Those guys were in their thirties, maybe forties and they were in the prime of their lives and they suddenly got put out to pasture into this thing called an oldies circuit. Which if you weren't on the circuit, you wouldn't even know it existed. We played Vegas, we did the oldies shows, the Garden with Richard Nader, but mostly it was hotels.

Southside Johnny: Steven Van Zandt was working jackhammer on the turnpike and he needed a place to stay. So my wife and I had this house on Collins Avenue and he stayed with us. I said, "Steven, you're killing yourself." He had been playing with the Dovells and leading the band in the oldies thing. I mean it's great, a great paying gig working on the turnpike, but it destroys your hands and he was such a great guitar player. He would come and he would be covered with asphalt and his hands would be like this. So eventually, we conned him into joining us.

Stevie Van Zandt: It's a confusing time for me, in my memory. Whenever there was time off, whenever I got home on the oldies circuit, which lasted almost exactly like a year, I would go down and see them jamming. And I probably jammed with them now and then, although I pretty much had my fill of jamming for life after doing it for eight hours a night at Upstage. To this day, I'm not interested in jamming ever again.

Dave Meyers: So in comes Steve Van Zandt, and we're playing the blues. On a Sunday night, most of the club were guitar players.

Stevie Van Zandt: I negotiated with Butch and Jack, who were, you know, at that point, not the nicest guys in the world. They were typical club owners. They were like those tough-guy type of bouncers more than owners, but I said, "Listen. We'll come in on your worst night," which I think was Sunday night or Monday night, and "we'll charge you nothing. We'll just take the door. You guys take the bar, but we get to play anything we want."

Dave Meyers: One night John and Steven went to Butch, or to Jack, and renegotiated the financial gain, financial price. It was not $135 anymore, it was more, but he did that. I told him he shouldn't do that, that he was really overstepping. And then one night at the Pony, John said, "Dave, I want to talk with you." I said, "Okay, John." He says to me, "Dave, I'm going to have to let you go." So I said, "What does that mean?" He goes, "I'm just going to let you go. We're going to another bass player." By then, I was really fed up with this whole scene. I mean, it was more of a shock, and something I couldn't figure out. Maybe my focus should have been on myself. But that particular night, I said, "John, if I'm hearing you correctly, you're saying you're going to fire me." He goes, "Yeah." I said, "John, but if my memory searched me correctly, I'm the one who hired you. And not only that," I says, "I'm the one who got the gig at the Stone Pony, and brought the band in. So John, I fire you." He looked befuddled. He didn't know what to do, but I wasn't serious. I said, "John, I'm not serious." I said, "When would you like me to leave?" He goes, "Whenever you'd like to." I said, "Well, I'll be gone in two weeks." And I left.

Southside Johnny: I got fed up with the lack of direction in the band and I fired the guys that started the band. Kept the drummer. I brought in some new people, Kevin Kavanaugh on keys, for instance.

Al "Doc" Berger: I had been on the road with the Dovells and with Steve, with Miami, and we played for about a year on the road. We played Vegas. We were doing sets, our sets, and then the Dovells would come out and do one or two shows, or whatever it was. And Steve said, "I got this song." It was "I Don't Want Go Home."

Stevie Van Zandt: I had met Ben E. King and the Drifters, and I decided to educate myself about songwriting, because I had been songwriting for years and didn't like anything I'd written. And I just decided I need to educate myself here. And I need to go to school. And I decided, "Well, where's it all begin?" And I decided, "Well, it begins with Leiber and Stoller." And so I intentionally sat down and said, "Okay, I'm going to write a Leiber and Stoller song for Ben E. King and the Drifters." And that's "I Don't Want to Go Home." And that was the first song I had ever written that I really liked. And I didn't give it to Ben E. King. I ended up giving it to Southside for his first album.

Al "Doc" Berger: We were playing "I Don't Want to Go Home" in the Dovells sets in Vegas, then all over the country. Then I kind of lost track of him for a little while until I got a call and he says, "Look, I'm in Asbury Park. I got a band, Blackberry Booze Band, and you want to come play bass?" So I said, "Hell yeah."

Billy Rush: I was playing in other bands, but my main linkup was a good friend of mine, Michael Scialfa. We used to play in his house in Deal. We used to set our amps up and blast them out at the ocean. Put those twin reverbs on 10 and just crank them up. He had heard from Kevin Kavanaugh, the keyboard player, that the guitar player in the Jukes at the time, whose name is Paul Dickler, really great guitar player, slide player too, had decided to leave. So I went to audition and that was like a dream come true because I was actually going to be a lawyer. I went to law school and my illustrious law career lasted about two weeks.

Al "Doc" Berger: Steve came up to me one day and he said, "We're changing the name." And he said, "It's kind of a long name. Hope you're going to like it." And it was Southside Johnny and the Asbury Jukes. So I said, "It's a long name, but all right, let's go with it."

Stevie Van Zandt: We had gone to see Sam & Dave, which just completely, permanently, forever blew our minds. I mean, it was just one of them moments. So me and Johnny decided to be the white Sam & Dave, and do this hybrid thing of rock and roll, guitar with horns, because we are digging soul music.

Southside Johnny: Steven and I went to see Sam & Dave and we realized that we really wanted horns. I mean we all loved that Otis

Redding and all that stuff. So we went out, trying to find horn players, and they were all jazz heads. So it took a while. We made a demo of "I Don't Want to Go Home" with four kids from Asbury Park High School band. Because we couldn't find anybody.

Tony Pallagrosi: Ed Manion and I ended up in this really crappy club band called Papa Banana and the Bunch. That never really went anywhere. I don't think we ever played anywhere. It was just horrendous. So one night I freaked out and quit. I turned literally there and during rehearsal, and I turned to Ed and I said, "What are you going to do?" And he goes, "Well, I guess I'm gonna quit." So we both quit. And then we kind of walked upstairs out onto the street and kind of looked at each other, and it was like, now what the fuck are we going to do? And we just said, Well, let's go to the Stone Pony. See what's going on there. So literally, we went to the Stone Pony that night. A band called the Shakes was playing. Vini Lopez was the drummer in the Shakes. And Vini knew Ed, and walked up to Ed literally that night and said, "Ed, you're looking for a gig? Because a friend of mine is looking for a trumpet player and a baritone sax player." And Ed happened to be playing baritone sax at the time. And I was a trumpet player. And that turned out to be Southside Johnny. Wow. So a week or two later, we auditioned and we were in the band.

Stevie Van Zandt: We didn't know we were doing it, but we completely revolutionized what a bar band was by having the horns and that combination of rock and soul. It was really a new idea. Now, that's become the standard sort of configuration for a bar band. Not only that, but we took a bar band from basically an insult, that if somebody was called a bar band, it meant somebody that really couldn't make it in the real world, couldn't make it in the music business. We kinda gave it some credibility and after the Jukes' record came out, you could see, you saw "bar bands" in the reviews. You saw it in the way people described them, like Graham Parker and the Rumour or Huey Lewis and the News. Even Elvis Costello, all those guys were suddenly part of this new garage-related bar band genre which the Jukes started without knowing we were starting it.

Garry Tallent: It was so uncool, it was cool again. There were all kinds of horn bands around Jersey before, and they were all terrible. All of a sudden, with the Jukes, a horn band can be good. I guess more like Chicago. We didn't dig the real slick stuff.

Billy Rush: The horn band, it came to be because that's what Johnny and Steve loved, that kind of music. So they wanted to have a band like that, where they could replicate the songs that they wanted to sing. Like those old Stax songs and whatever, Otis Redding, New Orleans stuff. So that's why the band came to be. And I think the fact that we were a horn band did make us unique in the area, and probably all New Jersey in a way.

Tony Pallagrosi: It was music that was popular at the Stone Pony, but nowhere else in any of the other clubs. And that's what the Jukes were. I mean, we couldn't necessarily go to the Royal Manor or go to the Osprey and draw people at that point, but we'd have hundreds of people coming to see us three nights a week in Asbury Park. So it was a home for music that had no home elsewhere.

Tony Pallagrosi: The kids who came to Asbury were different. You had a bar next door, Mrs. Jay's. There would be, you know, fifty to a hundred choppers lined up down the street. The Pagans were there. You had gay nightclubs. That didn't happen in Sea Bright. That didn't happen in Point Pleasant Beach. That didn't happen in Seaside. So it was always an alternative. Shit happened here that didn't happen in other Jersey Shore towns.

Eileen Chapman: It was already a scene, and then watching these guys, the Blackberry Booze Band into the Jukes, sort of developed that fan base and drawing up crowds to play three, four nights a week. You couldn't deny that there was something going on there. And it was more and more people were coming. Everybody was dancing.

Stevie Van Zandt: At that point we were a dance band, but we were rock and roll. People were not dancing to rock and roll back in those days. People forget that. It was almost like a revitalization of that concept of being a dance band at that point because as of like, I don't know, as of '67, '68, '69, people had stopped dancing to rock and roll and started listening to it. The whole vibe changed during those years. So we kinda were like a throwback to what the Rolling Stones were doing when they started, what the Beatles were doing when they started, the Who, and the Yardbirds. They were all dance bands and their job was to make people dance. And so was ours, so we were able to combine this new idea of playing, not original music yet, but album tracks and odd combinations of songs that were, that was a new idea for bar band music.

Bruce Springsteen: People danced. They didn't watch. No matter who was up there most of the time, they just still danced. And so it was a big dance club.

Judy DeNucci: Once I started going, I was hooked. I was there every night, even before I started working there, because I love to dance.

Stevie Van Zandt: For whatever reason in the bars, that culture kept that thing alive. Well, I mean, it was a mixture of rock and roll in the bars and disco starting to take over. But between the two of them, dancing was still the thing. And the bar owners wanted people dancing so they got thirsty and drank more booze. I mean, that was the business model. And this turned out to be extremely important. Because it was a weird little phase of the evolution that could have very easily not happened. And that made us play a certain way, more aggressively, to make people dance. Because if you didn't make people dance, you were out of there. So we would carry that extra aggression and force right into the concert world a few years later, when the E Street Band really started going. So it was a very, very helpful part of our evolution to actually be in that bar band scene, and having to make people dance long after it had stopped being fashionable.

Southside Johnny: We wanted to do more than just jam. We wanted to do songs. Steven actually liked reggae back then and we did some reggae songs.

Stevie Van Zandt: Some of that early reggae stuff was very poppy, very poppy, very danceable. "Struggling Man," "Harder They Come" from Jimmy Cliff. A lot of the stuff on *The Harder They Come* album, actually, is still one of the greatest reggae records ever made. We rocked them a little bit. We gave a little bit more rock to it, but it fit in because we weren't doing the slower things.

Tony Pallagrosi: We were playing some reggae. Nobody played reggae then. We're playing obscure Sam & Dave songs. We're playing obscure R&B songs. Not to R&B fans. These are white kids. Suburban kids, Jersey Shore clam-digger kids.

Stevie Van Zandt: I was just trying to write contemporary soul music– type songs. I mean contemporary versions of those sixties type of soul music songs.

Southside Johnny: A lot of rhythm and blues, a lot of soul, a lot of blues, a lot of rock and roll. We just liked all of that music. So we wanted to play all that. Unfortunately for the Stone Pony, they didn't know any of the songs that we were playing. They had a band called Colony, a very good cover band, and they did Top 40 and the place would be mobbed on the weekends. But they wouldn't give us the weekend. So we got Tuesdays, Thursdays, and Sundays, the worst nights of all. We started to attract an audience.

Al "Doc" Berger: When we first started out there, yeah, twenty people in the room. And luckily for us, ten girls that would be dancing with each other.

Stevie Van Zandt: First week it was fifty people, then next week a hundred and fifty, and then three hundred. And then they fixed the roof and before you know it, we had the first successful residency really ever. And went to three nights a week and they expanded the club and went to like a thousand people a night.

Garry Tallent: If you're bringing them people, you could play whatever you want.

Stevie Van Zandt: Making people dance, man, it was a part of our thing now. We were playing whatever we wanted to play. We weren't playing the Top 40 anymore on the radio. That was the revolution that we staged. That was the coup d'état that we won, but we still had to make people dance.

5

A Jukes Scene

The best bar band in Jersey. In 1975, that did not mean much. But word was starting to spread about this new rock band that played three nights a week at the Stone Pony. Their frequent guest and collaborator, Bruce Springsteen, was just dubbed "rock and roll's future," and his face graced the cover of *Time* and *Newsweek*. And here he was, appearing at the Stone Pony. His bandmates, including Clarence Clemons, Danny Federici, and Max Weinberg, quickly made it a home too.

Stevie Van Zandt: Bruce had belonged to the music business by then, which had a whole different set of rules that he was supposed to follow in terms of the venues he could play and all of that, and because his first two records didn't do very much, he couldn't tour that much.

David Sancious: The booking agency, I think we were with William Morris agency at the time, and they booked us a better quality, let's say better, a notch up of club from the Jersey Shore, with a larger room, more people. But they also booked us in theaters and colleges.

Mike Appel: But the band would not just do what I would call William Morris dates. They had their own little connections to clubs and they could make some money. And nobody gave a shit. "Fellas, knock yourselves out. Take the money, take the door, take it off." And William Morris doesn't give a shit either. These are all big boys. They don't need your two hundred dollars. All right, trust me.

Stevie Van Zandt: So Bruce just ended up hanging out with us. He just would come down, just to play. Just to hang out. He was there, pretty much from the beginning almost, or close to it. He'd go on the road for a few weeks, but then that's all he could do. So he'd be home. What are you gonna do? You can't record a record every month, so you gotta find something to do.

Bruce Springsteen: I was living in the same general area, and that was probably where I was living in the 1970s. In Long Branch or Atlantic Highlands or somewhere, so I was still very much a part of just the local scene and I hadn't moved away or anything. So the success was just something that was there to navigate. I still pretty much lived the way that I, you know, same circle of friends, and same hangouts. And the Pony made it comfortable for me to be there.

Max Weinberg: When I joined the E Street Band, I had a car. When Roy and I joined at the same time in August of '74, this was an opportunity for me to move to Long Branch, which I did. And I had a car and Bruce didn't have a car, and he lived in this little cottage on West End Court, which actually, it was so small, it was a half a number. And it's still there, the cottage. Seven and a half West End Court. And I lived a couple blocks away in a garden apartment. So I had the car, so I was kind of the designated driver. The only new car I could afford was a yellow AMC Gremlin. And we drove down to the Stone Pony.

Bruce Springsteen: I went up there to see Steve and Southside Johnny because they actually started at the Pony. They had a regular residence at the Pony, so we used to all go and hang out there and play.

Southside Johnny: I loved it when Bruce came up, because I could take a break and he'd have to do a bunch of singing. But there was real tangible excitement when he showed up. The downside of it was that people would be coming to see him, and he didn't come every night. So people go, isn't Bruce going to be here? I said, no. He's got a life. He goes on the road and he's gone for months. When he comes home, he may want to sit home on a Saturday night. So you get some of that. But our audience was still our audience. Of course, they loved Bruce and all. So when they came to see us, they were happy to see us. And if Bruce came, or Steven, or whomever, that would be an extra thrill.

Max Weinberg: In those days, the Pony, it was a third of the size of what it is now. In fact, it ended just to the right of where the stage is now. And then behind that wall there was the kitchen, and you couldn't even really call it a dressing room, but it was open from eight to something like five a.m., which was really unusual for a number of reasons. Bands had to play that long. And the Blackberry Booze Band was a band you could sit in with. So Bruce sat in, I played. I was the new sort of kid in town, and the only person I knew down there was Bruce, and I had the car.

Southside Johnny: And Bruce had given us "The Fever." He came into the Pony one day while we were rehearsing and said, "You should do this song." And I went, "What? That's a fucking amazing song, why don't you do it?" And he just says, "Doesn't fit on the album."

Bruce Springsteen: I had the song "Fever," which I had ambivalent feelings about, as far as myself singing it. And so I said, "Well, Southside's got a great voice. He'll sing this very well. Southside, here's a song." That's how it went. And he liked it and he started singing it and then it was a big hit for him.

Billy Hector: "The Fever," of course, they still play today. Funny how Bruce just gave that away.

Max Weinberg: Bands and musicians like Bruce and others were able to develop their own distinct musical personality. And the Pony encouraged that too. As long as you brought in a crowd that drank, you could pretty much do whatever you wanted. And that was one of the first things I noticed when I started going to the Stone Pony. And then once we kind of, I wouldn't say get established, but '75, '76, we were virtually all there every night. There was no place else to go. And we were night owls and young guys. So I had the Jaguar XKE, which if I was lucky, wouldn't break down on the way home someplace. This was before it became a national scene.

Jack Roig: The same week that Bruce was on the cover of *Time* and *Newsweek*, there were about three hundred people lined up outside waiting for us to open. I walked out front and I looked down the line, and

I stopped in my tracks. "What the hell is that?" And there is Bruce, digging through his pockets. He never carried any money, but he's at the end of the line and is looking through his pockets to pay the cover charge, which was like three dollars. So I went and dragged him past the line and into the side door.

Butch Pielka: When I first started here, I was talking to somebody and they said to me, "Bruce is here tonight." I said, "Who's Bruce?" I had never heard of the guy.

Dube Sullivan: Some of those nights in early '75, it was maybe a hundred and fifty people in there in the winter at night.

Stevie Van Zandt: He was hanging out with us and he added a lot to the scene because he was great and because he was in the music business a little bit, that gave a little added credibility, I think, to what we were doing anyway. It was a nice combination of just creating a scene for the dance band and then Bruce would jam and other people would jam too.

Bruce Springsteen: I brought no guitar. I would come to the Stone Pony. I would sit at the bar, I would have some drinks, and then I would get onstage and we would just play until the cows came home.

Max Weinberg: We were going there pretty much almost every night, at least that's my recollection of it. Of course I was his ride, which was great because we got to know each other and just sort of thrown into each other. It was going to the Stone Pony every night, and then going, whatever time we'd leave, going to the Inkwell, which was in Long Branch. It seemed like it was open twenty-four hours a day because I remember eating there and seeing the sun come up.

Bruce Springsteen: Southside was there every . . . I forget what it was, but two or three times a week. They were obviously one of the greatest bar bands working on the planet in that particular moment. And Stevie was there. He was in the band. So they had great songs and great arrangements. And the band sounded incredible for a small house band in the seventies, to have a residency. They were very sophisticated and it's getting quite exciting, because of the horn section and Steve knew how to arrange and he knew how to choose good material. And so it was great times, some of the most fun times in my life.

Stevie Van Zandt: The Stone Pony was everything. That was home base, and we all lived within blocks of it.

Bruce Springsteen: We did go to some other places. We were at the Green Parrot in Neptune, and they had original bands, and there were a few other places we went. We went to quite a few other bars during that period of time. But there wasn't any place quite like the Pony. The Pony was our home away from home, and that was just the way it stayed.

Jack Roig: They were good for us and we were good for them. So if you were going to be there, it made sense to let them set up base for practice. But, nobody realizes how much it costs to have somebody like that practice. Because the electricity and the air-conditioning you're running. It's crazy. Back then in the seventies, I remember my electric bill was over three thousand dollars a month.

Erick W. Henderiks: The Bruce thing, I think that was always good for the locals because everybody knew Bruce. He'd been in a lot of bands, he'd been around for a long time. Everybody knew somebody that knew Bruce.

Dube Sullivan: Back then, we were open to three o'clock. The last set would start at one forty-five a.m. Bruce would jump up there and the last forty-five minutes, it would just be him with Southside and playing the old blues stuff, and all this stuff that they grew up playing, Chuck Berry, all that stuff.

Billy Hector: I would see the Jukes play and Bruce came up. That's the first time I saw him. He came up near the end of the night and started singing "Oh Carol" [by Chuck Berry]. He actually threw his hat on the ground, was pulling his hair out, really into it. It's his last tune he was going to sing. It was amazing. It was only twenty-five people in the place. But they all ran up front to see this thing happen . . . I says, "Okay, that's what you got to do." You can't . . . There's no phoning it in. This guy's going for it, just pulling his hair out. Screaming "Oh Carol." I mean, "Oh Carol," for Christ's sake. I love the song, but it was the delivery. He definitely had some magic happening there.

Billy Rush: When Bruce came up, it was like the place would go into complete bedlam.

Stevie Van Zandt: There was no formality. No formality. I mean, I'd known him seven, eight years by then. He was a local guy. We had been playing locally a long time, so it wasn't like he was bringing celebrity to the party. He was already a local celebrity, in the sense that we all were. It just strengthened everything by the fact that he had gotten signed.

Erick W. Henderiks: One day, Bruce came into the Pony, and he had two versions of the album cover. He was in black, and Clarence was in white, and then he was in white, and Clarence was in black. He had two covers. One where he was black and one where he was white. He was asking the guys in the bar, his buddies, "What cover do you think is cooler?" We were all picking the cover. He did that. He was like that, just a regular guy. "What do you think looks cooler?" Certain people he trusted. He's smart enough to tap into other people's ideas.

Bruce Springsteen: The Pony was laid out very strange. The stage didn't project into the club longways. It was kind of on the side of the club. And so there was a relatively small amount of people that could fit in there and really experience the band. You were close to everybody, and the ceiling was low, and it was a classic sort of rock club. You were close to the audience, very close to the audience. And there were other clubs in the area that we played where the stage was higher or set in a more logical place, but I suppose they didn't end up having the same down-home atmosphere as the Pony had.

Jack Roig: We had to keep making the stage bigger. I mean, the Jukes were getting bigger. They had, what, they had eleven guys on the stage at one point. You had to fit everybody.

Bob Santelli: Once Bruce connects to the Stone Pony, once that happens, then all bets are off. Then it just explodes, right? And he starts to hang out there, and word spreads among the locals, and then it spreads elsewhere. And before you know it, there are lines to get in.

Governor Chris Christie: Hearing stories from older guys in high school, we were in junior high, about them going to the Stone Pony to go and watch bands play and having fake IDs to get in and all the rest of that stuff. I was sixteen when I first went. Had a fake ID. And I went with a friend, like most of us went the first time, on a rumor Bruce was going to be there that night. So we hopped in our car. It was a friend who was a year older than me, had his license. We jumped in his car. We drove down to Asbury Park, and Bruce didn't show up.

Dube Sullivan: I think they were only charging three dollars a head back then to get in on a Tuesday, Thursday, and Sunday nights. Literally, when that first came on, there used to be two bouncers at the door, one guy checking ID, and one guy taking cash, because there was no cash register, just cash in hand. The guys that we'd be working, we'd just hand off the pile of money to the next guy that was taking cash. Then Butch and Jack would come by and pick up all the twenties and tens, and we'd be left with the change to keep cash. I can remember personally running through the night after stocking the bars and whatnot and coming back and checking in my back pocket, and there was another ten or fifteen twenties. "Hey, Jack here." "Hey, Butch here." "Here's the twenties here." They got wise to that pretty soon and they put a register up.

Al "Doc" Berger: With the people there, with the lines around the block, that kind of thing, that told us we were doing something good. In the beginning, we had this manager, I think his name was Tony. He was too small for us. So later, we got somebody else and he was a jewelry guy. So he made these little lockets and that was the Jukes rocket pins. And Steve came up with the jackets and all the different ideas that he came up with promoting. So at that point, when we started doing merchandise and stuff like that, I thought, "Oh, this might be real."

Stevie Van Zandt: Relative to the overhead you had, relative to the bills you had to pay, with the crowds we drew, I'd never been that rich. I never, never will be again. Three dollars a head. We had three thousand people a week. Nine thousand dollars back in 1976 dollars. Course, we blew it all at the racetrack, but that's beside the point.

Billy Rush: That was the scene. Are you kidding? Hey, we're young-blooded kids. That was the scene and sure, you were known then and so it was a great place for meeting people, girls especially.

Southside Johnny: There were girls that would talk to you. The girls in the neighborhood wouldn't even look at you twice. Once you got offstage, they'd go, "Hi." They'd go, "You're really great."

Stevie Van Zandt: It was wildly good. It was wildly crowded, and it was a scene, man. It was the hottest thing. Everybody from North Jersey would come down on the weekend, and it just was like a real classic residency like everybody else had done in the early sixties. Beatles at the Cavern, the Stones at the Richmond Crawdaddy Club. The Who, everybody, all of those bands had residencies, even the Byrds, I think at Ciro's. It just becomes a real social scene, and in those days, not a lot of drugs, but there was a lot of sex and drinking. And it was this great, I mean, the world before AIDS was just paradise. There was a lot of sex in the bathroom in between sets, or in the office.

Billy Rush: The bartenders would just give us drinks. And the mostly female bartenders, if I remember correctly, they would just give us drinks. Probably Butch and Jack didn't know . . . who knows what they were told to do or not told to do.

Al "Doc" Berger: One night I'm playing and we're cooking, we're doing good. And a girl jumps on a stage and she gets me in a headlock. And I'm telling you, it hurts but I'm playing, I'm keeping playing. Of course they're grabbing her arms off and she was holding on tight. But got to keep playing.

Billy Rush: I got walking pneumonia once. I had set up a garbage can on the side of the stage. So I was sick as a dog and playing one of those really spectacular high-energy shows where I should have been in a hospital bed probably. But I'm standing there and throwing up on the side just in the dark. No one could really see the garbage can.

Jack Roig: They were making a lot of money. We made this big sign, big neon electric sign. We put it up on the board like who was gonna be playing, Southside Johnny and the Asbury Jukes, home of Southside Johnny and the Asbury Jukes.

Al "Doc" Berger: The Pony was our second home. Practice, rehearsals. Somebody else playing, we're there. We're playing, we're practicing. And Jack and Butch, they were great. They were great to us. Of course, we built their second room, or whatever you want to call that, their addition, and they admitted and said that. And as a matter of fact, in the second room, they had a little wall, like a wood wall or something that had pictures of all of us glued on to the wall. They had a sign out front on the marquee, HOME OF THE ASBURY JUKES. And I'm telling you, I loved that.

Jack Roig: Stevie did not like it one bit. Of course, we didn't ask him if that was okay. We thought it was a great thing to do for us and them.

Stevie Van Zandt: We were fighting now and then. We had to threaten to leave the Pony at one point to go across the street. That's when we got the most radical change in bar culture in history. At the time, we were going from five sets to three, which was just unheard-of. But we had to threaten to leave to do it. So every once in a while, there'd be something. I mean, I basically joined Bruce because I was tired. . . . It was always something. There was always some kind of fight about something, it seemed like. I was managing the band at the time. So it's just a little bit aggravating pretty regularly. I don't remember about what exactly, but there was regular confrontations with the owners. We're friends, but then, I don't know, something weird would happen, and I don't know.

Billy Rush: The Pony had this guy, Erick, the guy must have been six feet eight, I think. And built huge. Just a monster. Sweet guy though. Really good guy. And my position on the stage at the Pony was on the stage right by the door that's going out. There was a side door there and I would stand there on the stage and I'd see Erick, I mean, he'd pick up guys by the seat of their pants and by the scruff of their neck and literally kick the door open and throw them out. People that were misbehaving. I don't know what they were doing, but we were just playing along, grooving along. And I turned my head to see Erick's throwing someone out the door. So that was pretty funny. He's the one who kept the peace there. I mean, no one messed with this guy. He was a monster.

Erick W. Henderiks: I went in there one night and it was busy. The Pony back then was like the Wild West. It could be weird depending on who's around, like a lot of motorcycle guys, a lot of, I don't know, different people. I went in there by myself. I'm at the bar and I'm having a beer. These two big guys bump into me, so I said, "Hey, man. Take it easy." I spilled my beer. The guy looks at me, he smiles, he turns around, and then he tries to coldcock me with a mug. I dispatched him quickly and his friend. Then the bouncers ran over and they were going to throw us all out for fighting. Because the thing is, if you're in a fight, you're going out. They were going to throw me out, but then Jack, who I didn't know at the time, walked over and goes, "No, not him. Those two guys." They threw those guys out and Jack came over to the bar and says, "Can I buy you a beer or something?" I'm drinking a beer and then he walks away.

About ten minutes later, he comes back to the bar and he says, "Can I talk to you for a second?" I'm thinking. "Oh, shit. Now what? Am I in trouble for something?" He goes, "Here, come with me." As we're walking through the maze in the back, I'm opening the doors, but I'm opening them all the way up because I'm thinking somebody's going to do something back here because I'm already a little rattled, like "What's going on here? These two monsters just tried to get me." Now this guy is a monster. He's about six feet ten at the time. (He shrunk a little bit like all of us.) He comes in and he said, "Listen, I like the way you handle yourself. Do you want a job here?" I said, "I would love a job here."

Al "Doc" Berger: The Pony, if you ask any of the Jukes I think, one word if we had to say, we all would say, it was hot. I mean literally hot. You can hear Johnny on, I got all kinds of discs and tapes go "Oh it's so hot in here." And he goes on with his speech, but we're all sweating our asses. And me, I'm in the three-piece suit and I didn't take off my jacket and my vest, and I played that way mostly in the Pony the whole time. I don't know why. I don't why. I didn't take anything off. Steve and everybody, they stripped down a little bit. But I kept it on, I don't know. I'm a bass player, what can I say?

Billy Rush: We would do five sets a night and end at three in the morning. It was really the nightlife type of thing. And it kept getting more and more crowded within those months, and then we got a record deal.

Dennis Diken: Summer of '76, We took a drive down to see the Jukes one night because there was such a hoopla about them. We were very excited about that, that a Jersey band was making some noise, and we liked the record that we heard on the radio. We thought this would really be cool to see them live. We just got shut out. It was sold out. We knew that there was something brewing there, and we wanted in. Yes, we were going to CBGBs, we were going to Max's, we were getting real hungry for live music.

Billy Rush: We would do our set at the Pony and end it at three in the morning and then get in the cars and drive up to the studio in New York where we would get . . . I think that Steve had worked out some kind of deal where we were getting time overnight. Bands did that a lot. And Jimmy Iovine was the engineer and we were all exhausted. When one guy was doing his session, the other guys were half asleep all over the place, including Iovine. I remember Iovine sleeping under the board sometimes. Because I think he did sessions in the day and then we'd do them . . . he'd set up the board for that particular musician and then maybe cop some z's under the board.

Bruce Springsteen: When a band plays a place for three or four weeks, people depend on it. I think maybe they were actually away a week and a half. They made a record. They had champagne here when they came back.

Southside Johnny: When Steven came to write the songs for the album, he wrote this song, this kind of New Orleans thing. He talked to Steve Popovich [the vice president at Epic Records]. It was kind of a Lee Dorsey song. So he said, "Why don't we get Lee Dorsey?" Steven said, "Can you?" And he did. Lee came up. So Lee stays at the Travelodge, because we don't have any money. He comes up. He's got this beautiful three-piece suit on, matching. We put him in the Travelodge and we get him a bottle of Chivas Regal, which is what he wanted. We said, "Lee, we're going to do it tomorrow at ten in the morning and whatever." So, "All right." "Here's the tape. Learn the song." He said, "I'm real excited." So I figured, "I'm going to call Lee and see if he's okay." So I call him at the Travelodge around nine at night. So we're mixing and doing it.

No answer. Okay, ten o'clock. No answer. I'm going, "Fuck. I brought Lee Dorsey up to New York City for him to get mugged and killed." So I'm frantic. So the next thing, Lee comes walking in decked out, knew the song cold. I said, "Where were you?" "I was out with B. B. King drinking."

6

May Day

The record was cut. It was time for a coming-out party. The Jukes were going national and were about to bring the Stone Pony and the entire scene with them.

Al "Doc" Berger: Steve told us in the beginning, "You know, you get signed, that don't mean shit really." You get signed and you sell five records, you're in the same place you were the day before.

Dan Beck: Steve Popovich [Epic Records executive] knew Southside's music wasn't rock in the sense of what was on rock radio at that time. In those days, if you ask somebody, "What's the marketing plan for such-and-such an act?" It's like, "Put it on the radio, idiot." There's nothing else. "Put it on the radio." So I think Steve knew that Southside didn't necessarily exactly fit any format. So he wanted to come up with a way to get radio involved. So he basically had the idea of, "Hey, Bruce and the Stone Pony, let's launch this in this huge way."

Southside Johnny: Once Steve Van Zandt met Steve Popovich, they became the two Steves. They were as thick as thieves, scheming, planning, dreaming. They were just amazing to watch together. They would come up with the most outlandish things. This was one of them, said, "We're going to do a live radio show." I think there was going to initially be like five radio hookups, MMR, MMS, NEW, and whatever.

Dan Beck: They thought, let's get all these stations on board, because there's no station in Asbury Park. But can we get NEW and WMMR in Philly?

Stevie Van Zandt: That show was the genius of Steve Popovich, who really dug the fact that we had created a local scene, just like the old days. People used to do that in the old days. Get residency and start a scene and that was how rock and roll really flourished in the early days. Steve Popovich loved the fact that we had brought that back and made the radical decision to do something that was only done in New York and LA and do a live national broadcast out of New Jersey. No one had ever done that.

Southside Johnny: We had nine, I think it was nine or eleven, FM radio hookups in all these different states, Cleveland, and wherever. Towns, cities, wherever you want.

Jack Roig: I was still working computers. I was still in the field and remote stuff was a myth. So I said, "I don't know how you're going to do it. But, sure, that's great."

Lee Mrowicki: At the time I was working at WJLK. At the radio station, one day the general manager comes into the office, my studio, he says, "Do you think we can do a live concert?" And I says, "I used to do them all the time in college, so I don't see why not. We can put together the equipment and everything." We used to do football games on remotes. And I said, "We've got the remote equipment. It's not in stereo though. That's the one thing." And WNEW-FM wanted in writing that Bruce would play. And of course Bruce doesn't do that kind of stuff. So they refused to air the concert. So Steve Popovich at Epic Records, at the time, the guy that was vice president that signed the Jukes originally, knew the local station. He lived in Freehold, commuted to New York every day. They had the guys for Epic give us a call, and they go, "Can you handle the production and put it on the air for us?"

Dan Beck: Popovich came to me, and he said, "I think we should film it." He said, "But I can't pay for that out of the A&R budget." He said, "You could pay for it out of the publicity budget." So I was in, and we got Susan Blond, who emceed it all. She was a personality. She was very close friends with Andy Warhol, and she was one of those Warhol people. She had had some kind of crazy indie cable show in Manhattan that was semifamous back then. So it's like, "Yeah, we should have Susan do this."

Susan Blond: There were a lot of people at the company that really loved the Jukes. And so as soon as I met them, I loved them and I wanted to help them do whatever I could for them. I became the head of publicity rather young there. The liner notes were done by Bruce. It was the right person to have done them. The music appealed to us all. We loved the Southside Johnny boys.

Billy Rush: She was a publicist for CBS at the time, Susan Blond. She was everywhere. She was the one with the mic going around sort of interviewing people, I think. I'm trying to remember. And she's just one of those New York, bighearted, big openmouthed girl.

Susan Blond: I'm wearing like a Sonia Rykiel. That's a certain designer, that blue sweater I'm wearing, even though I had the slicker on the outside part, the sweater is, it's so me to be wearing like this kind of designer sweater to the Stone Pony. It was so out of place but I didn't know I was gonna be on camera that night. That just kind of came together as we were doing it.

Butch Pielka: They really went first-class with everything. They pulled up with a $250,000 sound truck.

Stevie Van Zandt: We knew that we were making history by being the first broadcast out of Asbury Park. I mean, that was obvious, and we were also revealing our identity to the world at that point. That whole Jersey thing. The nicknames. I mean, we brought in Kid Leo from Cleveland. Dave Marsh was the Duke. [Jon] Landau was the King. La Bamba was La Bamba, Southside was Southside. I was always Miami Steve. And yeah, that was a new thing. That whole culture, that Jersey culture was kind of a new thing.

Southside Johnny: It was a chance for a club in Asbury Park, New Jersey, the Joke State, and one of the joke towns of Joke State, to get some recognition all around the country because there was this night of live music.

Tony Pallagrosi: There were media trucks in the street. And there were people in the street. It was electric. And it was scary. I mean, I still had fucking sand between my toes.

Stevie Van Zandt: Jimmy Iovine, my friend, and at the time our engineer, he says, "Why don't you write a song for the occasion?" And I was like, "Jimmy, we're going to promote the first album. That doesn't make any sense at all." But I thought about it and I did it. And it was "This Time It's for Real," and it completely would change my songwriting, because it was the first song that was autobiographical. It was the first song actually about what was going on, rather than just trying to write classic love songs or whatever soul music was doing. And it really was only that one song on that second Jukes album. The rest of the second Jukes album went right back to doing as close to classic soul music as I could write. But that one song, man, would be the future of my songwriting, and very, very, very important in my evolution.

Al "Doc" Berger: Steven came into rehearsal the day of the show and was so excited, he said, "I got a new opener. I got a new opener. We got to play it. It's a new opener." It was "This Time It's for Real." And the first bass line I came up with for that show wasn't even what we would use on the record.

Southside Johnny: We were ready. We were ready. We had rehearsed, actually rehearsed, and we had material down. We were ready to be heard. One of the thrills about that night is that we finally got to show what we could do to people who never had seen us before. We had been playing to an audience that had seen us. And they knew, and they liked us. But this was a chance to kick ass on a somewhat national stage, and I was champing at the bit to do it. I couldn't wait to get onstage and just whale away.

Dan Beck: I've been to thousands of club shows over the years for new acts, veteran acts, whatever, and my feet are still sticky from all the floors. I don't think I can recall a show that was more packed than that. Throw out the fire laws. That place probably had three times the people in it that were allowed in there. It was probably so damn dangerous.

Jack Roig: Control was a big thing that night. You knew it from the start. It was going to be different. It had the feel.

Bob Santelli: You could not move. And it was extremely hot. And I remember just being totally jammed. And the excitement level was off the charts. It really was off the charts, because basically, here was the house band being celebrated. This is our band, our house band now being recognized nationally on this broadcast.

Erick W. Henderiks: I worked that night. I carried more beer that night than ever. I must have lost six or seven pounds that night. I was carrying kegs on my shoulder. You couldn't even get through the crowd with a dolly. I just said, "I can't manage this crowd. It's so busy." I started carrying kegs on my shoulder. Which Jack didn't like that very much because he was always afraid that one falls and, well, he really didn't like that very much.

Jack Roig: These fucking gorillas. I kept saying, "Use a hand truck." I don't want to say you can't cure stupid, but you can't cure muscles.

Billy Rush: Everybody came down from the record company from New York, so the crowd complexion was changed. It was kind of a record party. And then the regular folks, I don't know if many of them actually made it in there that night. I remember it being bedlam, but again, I don't remember how many of the regulars I would say made it in there because it was full of record people, radio people, news journalists, that kind of thing.

Harvey Leeds: They were a great live band. And that was just like, you know, the hype and the mystery of this is where Springsteen's from, so it had the Bruce mystique all over it.

Eileen Chapman: Having Ronnie Spector there, and Kid Leo there, and Ed Sciaky, and all these famous names, I guess, maybe realized that this had sort of leaked outside of Asbury Park. It's not just our local band anymore. These guys are going somewhere, and they're doing something a little more special than I had anticipated.

Southside Johnny: It was mobbed. It was ridiculous and of course we had all the equipment and things like that, yeah. We had Lee and Ronnie.

Ronnie Spector: I just thought it was something exciting to do. I know when I first started out in the business I wanted somebody to help me out. So I think I should help somebody else out, because I know it can be rough.

Lee Mrowicki: The town had declared Memorial Day to be like New Year's Eve and they let the bar stay open till five in the morning. That was just because of what it was for the whole entire town.

Dube Sullivan: The night opened up with the Shakes. They were the house band that was playing right about the same time as the Jukes. I remember Bobby Campanell, who's the lead singer of the Shakes. As soon as they got to the recording thing, he's up onstage. He goes, "Hey, great to be here. It's nice to be radioactive."

Vini Lopez: We had to be more on our Ps and Qs because it was a live recording, and they recorded us too. And we did mostly all original material too. But the main thing is in the years prior to that, you'd always go in and go, "Okay, we're going to blow the roof off this place here." I don't care who's opening. I don't care who's going to end the show. Well, there, we didn't want to take the spotlight away from anybody. We wanted to just hit and get out and let Southside have the spotlight because it was their show.

Southside Johnny: I just put my head down and did what I did. Sang, tried to be funny. Interacted with Ronnie, interacted with Lee [Dorsey], Bruce. It was just one of those nights where it was a real free-for-all.

Bob Santelli: Of course, everyone figured Bruce would show up. And when he shows up, of course, the place just goes absolutely crazy.

Bruce Springsteen: It was "Hey, Southside's going to be on the radio." "Let's all go down." It was as loose as that in those days. We didn't really say much about it. Everybody got up, like we do on any other Wednesday or weekend night, and sang the songs.

Al "Doc" Berger: Clarence was there and he sang on "The Fever," that bass vocal part that he sang. Everybody played that night.

Bruce Springsteen: I forget what we sang that night, but I'm sure it was the same stuff we were doing the rest of the time. Oh, "Having a Party." That song had been done several thousand times before that.

Al "Doc" Berger: So, after we finished a set and I'm not sure which set it was, we jump off the stage and we try to make our way to the front door. And we're sweating, three-piece suit, but it was cold outside, it was great. I'm looking at my watch, almost time to come in. All right, got to go back. I open the door and the nightclub heat hit me in the face. That became "I Remember Last Night." That's exactly what happened. That's exactly how the song got written. And it was about the Pony and it was about that moment.

Lee Mrowicki: They did their show, it was about an hour show, on the radio, and then the two owners afterwards made 'em play another set, since it was their normal night. They played the second set, and I have both sets, which is really kind of interesting, because some of the songs on the second set were better than the first set.

Dan Beck: They played for forever. It wasn't a half-hour set. I'm thinking that show probably went on four hours.

Bruce Springsteen: It was just a great, great night.

Lee Mrowicki: The place was open until five o'clock in the morning, so after the Jukes did their second set, I guess they took about a half-hour, forty-five-minute break, went and did another forty-five minutes.

Southside Johnny: I don't remember what happened after we played. I'm sure there's plenty of stories. I'm sure I was half in the bag.

Dan Beck: I think the event that we did was really about taking the record industry down there. I think that's probably what's pivotal about that event. I don't think any of us really knew what the hell we were doing. I think we were acting on Steve Popovich's instincts, and that was we needed to find a way to fast-start Southside Johnny, because the music wasn't as automatic. It was more of romance music.

Bob Santelli: That show was really something that was a monumental, historic event on the Jersey Shore, because it, for all intents and purposes, identified this place as a place where something very serious was happening in rock history. And that's when the analogies . . . I'm not so sure they were accurate, but the analogies with Liverpool. Like, okay, there's that whole . . . The Beatles hit, like Bruce, and then all these other bands followed. And that was the thought that, okay, here comes Southside Johnny and the Asbury Jukes. And then of course, right after, the place would be teeming with A&R people. And they would call me all the time: What bands are you covering? Who's hot? And there were a few bands, of course, there were the Shakes, and Cahoots, and Bill Chinnock, and a number of others, because there were some really great players. But everyone then started to change their sound to sound like either the Jukes or Bruce Springsteen and the E Street Band.

Dan Beck: We expected it to be really good. But we were amazed. It's like, "Oh my God. Look at this." We knew it was still going to be hard, breaking Southside, because of radio formats. As it proved, it was hard. He was never really given the commercial opportunities that he and the music deserved. But that night was just spectacular.

. . . .

Ed Sciaky: It was really incredible, and hotter than anybody could have dreamed. Southside proved himself, and he had to, and the band was hot. The energy level was so high, you could feel it on the street, you could feel it in the hot dog stand next door.

Dave Marsh: I'm more excited about Johnny than anything in a long, long time. Because they play music that, to me, goes right to the heart of what rock and roll is all about, which is to say soul music. There is one musical form that is the rock bottom out of which all other forms grow. And the music that Southside Johnny and those boys play is that form.

. . . .

Jack Roig: That show, getting that big, it seemed like it made it more monetary. Of course everybody was getting paid more, not that they didn't deserve it, but then you had to charge more.

Erick W. Henderiks: That show definitely showcased not only the Jukes but the Pony. I think more people were aware of the Pony, it became more internationally known. I have relatives in Europe that asked me about the Stone Pony, what it's like to work there. We're talking the Netherlands, where they're huge Bruce Springsteen fans there.

Dube Sullivan: Tuesday, Thursday, and Sunday nights were never the same after that. It got crazy. We had celebrities coming into the Pony. I can remember guys like Boz Scaggs hanging out, Jim Messina, actors like Michael J. Pollard, and sports stars. There was the Taylor brothers, Bruce Taylor and—I think his name was Brian Taylor. They were pro football players for San Francisco.

Harvey Leeds: We thought we could be world domination. But you know. It was hard . . . But the Jukes, there was nothing like it.

7

A Booming Jukes Scene

The Jukes. The Shakes. The Shots. Cold Blast and Steel. Cahoots.
Lord Gunner. It was boom times at the Pony. Marquee local bands
playing multiple sets every night. Music fans and Bruce fanatics
running high bar tabs. A growing cast of regulars, a mix of Jukes,
E Streeters, musicians, bartenders, and locals, all who don't leave
until sunrise. The Jukes' Memorial Day show had put the Pony
scene on the airwaves, and everyone wanted a piece of SOAP, aka
the "Sound of Asbury Park."

Bob Santelli: There was this immediate post-'76 thing. When that
happened, there was just this incessant need for bands that carried
the so-called Asbury Park sound. And Vini was right at the front of
that. Lance Larson. And then all of a sudden, there's this explosion of
original bands in and around the Jersey Shore. And many of them are
really, really good.

Stevie Van Zandt: That combination of rock and soul became the
definitive format, the definitive genre. A lot of the bar band thing was
Top 40 music up until the Jukes. And we changed that into classic soul
music, and rock as well. Not exclusively soul music, but that combination, and suddenly that became the definition of a bar band.

Lance Larson: We ended up as Lord Gunner; we did a lot of original
stuff. But we did half and half, you know, half covers. Still had to keep

the people happy. We started there in '75 I think. Seventy-five was the year Lord Gunner finally got together.

Vini Lopez: I was in the Cold Blast and Steel when it was myself, Steve Schraeger on drums. We had two drummers. We had John Luraschi on bass and Ricky D playing guitar. And we played stuff, all kinds of stuff. But we convinced Jack and Butch to let us play at the Pony. They gave us a Sunday afternoon one time. And we did pretty good on a Sunday. So, he says, "Eh, let's try it again."

Tony Amato: During that time, most of 1976 to the middle of '79, these were the four bands that had the sounds of Asbury Park. Bruce Springsteen E Street Band, because he used to come in with his whole band to play there, just to keep fresh. The Jukes, Mad Dog and the Shakes, and Cahoots. Eventually in '79 you had the Shots. The Shakes used to open up for the Jukes. Then all of a sudden one night the Shakes can't play. Steven turns around, looks at me. "How's your boys? Your boys ready?" I said, "Yeah, I'll be back in about an hour." So I went back out to the house where we rehearsed and said, "Hello, fellas, forget doing the laundry. Get the shit. Let's go." We went down the Pony. We played, and we opened up for the Jukes. So after that, it was Tuesday night was Cahoots and the Jukes. Thursday night, it was Mad Dog and the Shakes and the Jukes. Friday night was Cahoots and the Jukes. Saturday night, it was Shakes and the Jukes.

Max Weinberg: The Jukes were the house band. They played two or three nights a week. And the other nights, these bands like Cahoots, Cold Blast and Steel, the Shakes, and the Shots. I used to sit in with all of those bands.

Patti Scialfa: My older brother, he's eighteen months older than me, played in a band called Cahoots. That was George Theiss, when he left Bruce's band the Castiles. He left the Castiles and formed Cahoots, and my brother was in that band. They were a big band down there, and everybody would go see them. So that's why I started going down there, but I didn't really know anybody. I would just hang out once in a while, bring my mom or a friend.

Bruce Springsteen: They were pretty open to the original bands, original local bands that came in and played, and then there were cover bands too, that we played with all the time. And it became like a Wednesday, Saturday, Sunday thing, Friday, Saturday, Sunday. And depending on who was playing, there were a pretty decent amount of other local bands that played also, and I'd sit in with them too, very often from time to time. It picked up that sort of locals thing. It was a place where the local community musicians went.

Max Weinberg: I don't know of any other place that really had that kind of thing in rock. I mean, that was in the jazz clubs in New York, that was particularly uptown, way uptown New York. That was not uncommon. But no, I don't really know any other [rock] place that was [like that]. I guess that was an outgrowth of just people's mindset coming from the Upstage, which was sort of sitting in jamming, whoever showed up that night.

Steve Schraeger: We were comrades, everybody back in the day. Us, the Jukes, the Shakes, you know, we were all buddies. We had each other's back. It was a good time to grow into the music scene. I learned a lot just watching the Jukes rehearsing, watching Steve Van Zandt lead. It was where you hung out, even if you weren't playing.

Patti Scialfa: I lived in New York City. I would come down on the weekends from New York. My parents had gotten divorced. I have a younger brother who's thirteen years younger than me. I would come down and spend the weekend at home just to try and fill up the house and be supportive, be there for my younger brother. And then at nights, I started going to the Pony. I don't know how that happened, but I started going down there. I guess I knew some of those guys. I became friends with Bobby Bandiera's band, Cats on a Smooth Surface, and he would just say, "Hey, come and we'll do any songs you want to sing." So I would just jump up and sing when I first started coming down on the weekends.

Ernest Carter: I could go in there and jam with people that would see me just hanging. I played with Lance Larson. I played with John Luraschi, bass player, a couple of other people. Cahoots, those bands. I would go in and spin with them. I would jam all the time. Then I had my friends Gary Smith and Harry Boyton and Tommy LaBella.

Bruce Springsteen: The people that came were really drawn from that area. And as such were eccentric in their own way. I think if you were living and breathing in Asbury Park at the time, you were a bit of an eccentric. So there were a lot of local musicians, a lot of funny people into their own thing. It was just a place that had its own personality. It was when localism was still very local.

Jack Roig: We'd be setting up the band in the daytime, and there were always people outside taking pictures. If I was around, I'd bring them around and let them come in and take pictures. It was good publicity. It was great.

Governor Chris Christie: Every time I went on a rumor, he never was there. So it was just you wound up going, and you still had a good time. There was good music there. As you know, it's a cool atmosphere. So it wasn't a totally wasted trip. The people who were there, the way people reacted to the music at the bar, even the way the bartenders reacted to the music, you could tell these were people who loved music and thought it was cool and thought where they were was a cool place to be.

Eileen Chapman: The whole house band thing was one of the reasons why we all continued to go with the Pony. You knew every Thursday night you're going to get Lord Gunner, it's going to be amazing. Music's going to be great. You're going to know . . . your friends are going to be there. The Diamonds on Monday night, Cahoots, Cold Blast and Steel. I loved all the whole house band mentality there at the Pony. And it gave each of these bands the opportunity to play there long enough to create more and more fans for their music.

Lee Mrowicki: You have a focal point, singer, whether he had a gruff voice or not, and horns, and that kind of sound became, quote-unquote, "the sound of Asbury Park," although really, Asbury Park had other bands that were just as popular, if not more so, and they were different bands. They were hard rock bands, things like that. Everybody said, "Well, that's the sound of Asbury Park," but the sound of Asbury Park didn't sell a whole lot of records.

Stevie Van Zandt: Popovich was very much into turning it into a scene, which we did. And usually, with a scene goes a sound, a certain thing. And we did have that thing, between me, Southside, and Bruce. I mean, we very much were influenced by the same things, and that rock-meets-soul thing. So that was true. It wasn't completely fabricated, but there were some other things as well. I mean, just a few miles away, Bon Jovi was doing something very different. But as far as the hardcore scene, the Asbury Park sound, I think was that rock-meets-soul thing that all three of us had grown up with.

Bruce Springsteen: All the bands sounded different. There were rock bands, pop bands, reggae bands. The only sound was the sound of Southside. And then there were a couple other bands. I think Jonny Bon Jovi's first band, the Atlantic Expressway, was very influenced by Southside. And he had a horn section. And then there might have been one other group. So the fact that people were simply using horns alone was a big part of what people I think relate to now as the sound that came out of Asbury Park. But no, there wasn't a scene where everybody had a similar sound or anything, except for a very few groups. I think just because of Southside's residency there at the Pony for such a long time, and then because he had some success. And a little bit of our own R&B influence in the E Street Band at the same time, mixed it into what people began to think was the sound that came out of Asbury Park. But I don't hear any sound of Asbury Park myself, outside of Southside, maybe.

Southside Johnny: There's no sound of Asbury Park. The fact is that there was a hotbed of musicians. Everybody had their own likes. Everybody sounded differently. And there was so many great bands. There wasn't a single sound. No. It was just a scene.

Lance Larson: Everybody would compare us to the Jukes. Except we were rock-'n'-roll with horns. We played a lot of stuff, a lot of other people's stuff with horns. We were completely different from the Jukes, but everybody started out like the Jukes. We used to dress up and strut around.

Garry Tallent: It was all bullshit. There was no sound of Asbury Park.

Tony Amato: The Jukes did not sound like the Shakes. The Shakes did not sound like the E Street Band. E Street Band didn't sound like Cahoots. Yeah, we were all playing the same type of R&B music, but nobody sounded the same. Maybe the only thing that we all had in common is everybody had a sax player and a B3 [Hammond organ]. Maybe that's what they were, but there was no sound. That's bullshit.

Jack Roig: They were all around all the time, and they all knew each other. All the musicians knew each other, so it was like a spiderweb. The musicians knew Bruce and all the people knew the musicians. They all knew each other.

Patti Scialfa: You'd come up and sing four or five songs. It was unique to the Pony. It was a very comfortable place to do that. I'm sure there were other little clubs around town, sometimes I would go in and just sing with somebody and just have fun. But mostly it was the Pony. You just end up knowing a lot of people there because I grew up, like what, fifteen minutes from the Pony. And the original bands that were big there, like Cahoots and Bobby's band, they were extremely welcoming. Musicians would come, "Yeah, come on up! Come out and play." Or do this, do that. That, I think, set a tone for it just being open and friendly, and people could go and play music. Musicians are usually nice to each other, so it was always a camaraderie, a deep camaraderie. That's why I love music.

Max Weinberg: Jack and Butch were kind of visionaries and letting that scene develop. And I remember thinking at the time, particularly coming from North Jersey, where pretty much all the bars and clubs were organized-crime owned in North Jersey, and this was like a breath of fresh air. You could pretty much do what you wanted in terms of the music you played. There was a place up near Fort Lee called the Point After, up on that, the Palisades, and it was absolutely a mob joint. You tried to play a blues song in there and the patrons looked like they were cast right out of *Goodfellas*. And it was a leap for them, for the owners of these places to put live rock bands in there. And you better play whatever hits of the day you could. And not too loud.

Steve Schraeger: Sometimes, Van Zandt would sit in with us. Bruce would sit in with us. Southside. They were there. They felt like coming up and singing a song. It was great. That's when the place would go nuts, any of the three of them, the place would erupt.

Richie "La Bamba" Rosenberg: Around Thanksgiving time of '76, when the Jukes were working on songs for *This Time It's for Real*, they were looking to add a trombone as a permanent fixture into the horn section. And I got the call from one of my Philly friends who was play-ing with the Jukes at the time, Rick Gazda, to come to Asbury Park. So I went to the Pony for the so-called audition, and the band was set up on the dance floor of the Pony. Johnny obviously there, Steven obviously there, and Bruce was there too, because Bruce was writing material for the Jukes at that time. But they weren't set up on the stage. I guess they were having whatever the stage was going to be used for whatever band was there that night. So everything was just set up on the floor, and that's when it started.

Tony Pallagrosi: We would all go to the Pony because that was kind of our home. You could walk in 1976 and see me and a chick, La Bamba and a chick, Bruce and his girlfriend, Joy, at the time, slow dancing on the floor of the Stone Pony. And people came there because they heard about the Jukes hanging out there and the E Street Band hanging . . . Max could be there. Roy never really hung out, but Garry could be there. And Clarence, certainly Clarence. And people would come from all over the country just to see if we were all hanging around.

Richie "La Bamba" Rosenberg: I was a fixture at the Pony. Since that day, since joining the band, I was like a fixture. I moved in with Ed Manion. We had an apartment, a house in Belmar, and then months later we moved into a garden apartment across the street from the Pony. We'd meet everybody and get up and jam whenever you wanted to.

Bruce Springsteen: Places like the Pony are just filled with characters. That's just the way it is. Asbury Park was filled with characters in 1973. That's where *Greetings from Asbury Park* came from. It's like the local areas, people, nicknames, and this, it's all common stuff. So Asbury was just filled with all kinds of characters, who did all kinds of jobs. And my social life, even during the eighties, I chose not to go to New York or not to go to LA or someplace else. I stayed where I grew up, and I went to the places I went as I grew up. And that's what made me feel safe and it made me feel centered, and it gave me a lot of joy. So it was filled with characters that I really liked and loved.

Billy Hector: This guy Marty, his name was Buzzsaw. He worked with chain saws. He was working with David Meyers. He would just come in, bring his congas and put them on stage at the Pony, and just start playing until he eyed a girl. Then he'd just leave. He would do it with the Jukes, he would do it with Hot Romance.

Southside Johnny: There were so many characters that came in. Erick the Great Big Viking, who would dance with karate moves and he was there when we first started out there. We had to do "It's Your Thing" by the Isley Brothers, two or three times a night, during every set.

Erick W. Henderiks: I was able to take the ceiling tiles out of the ceiling when I was young. I could jump up in the air. They played James Brown music and I would dance. I was a good dancer too. I could do all the shit that James Brown did. I could sidestep and split. I could do all that shit. Then Southside and the Jukes would once in a while play a James Brown song, and then I would just go nuts in the corner. That was my thing.

Vini Lopez: Erick. Yeah. I've seen him twirl those guys. They didn't touch the ground once they started being bad; they left the Pony by way of air from the dance floor to the door. Boom. Outside. But Erick was very, very nice. He took care of us all. And later on, they made sure they walked people to their cars because it was dangerous out there.

Erick W. Henderiks: It looked like a twirl, but it wasn't a twirl. It was more of like a—I don't know what it was. Mystical judo. I just probably put people out in a nice way. The word *judo* means "gentle way."

Bruce Springsteen: Erick, I believe, was a black belt in judo for real, and did a lot of studying and had some real skills in that area. He was also very funny. We stole Steve's Cadillac one night and drove it on the boardwalk from Belmar to Asbury. When we got to Asbury, we went in some club somewhere.

Erick W. Henderiks: A guy named Rick was a road manager for Bruce at the time. Him and Bruce said, "Let's take a ride." We're riding and then all of a sudden, we see a ramp. I lived in Asbury Park and I wasn't sure about that ramp, but I realized that that was the ramp that the police used to drive on the boardwalk to patrol the beach. I don't know if it was me or somebody who said, "Let's drive on the boardwalk." I can't even remember if Steven was with us. I don't think he went with us. No, because he'd be pissed off if we took his Cadillac. Stevie would've went nuts. It was a hell of a ride. We were on the boardwalk driving. We did see the police, and then Rick, he turned the headlights off and we were driving in the dark on the boardwalk. I'm in the backseat with Bruce and a guy named John Henry, who's a legend. We were in the backseat screaming. I think I was laughing so loud and Bruce said, "Yo, man, you're spitting on me." We drove back and forth on the boardwalk with the headlights off. That was our excitement.

Stevie Van Zandt: I don't remember that.

Lee Mrowicki: Steve had this red Cadillac convertible, and the license plate said MIAMI. You may hear this lady's name, Obie Dziedzic. Obie was his personal assistant at the time, worked for the Jukes, et cetera. Eventually she worked for Bruce. But she used to have to replace those license plates every two months because people would steal them.

Steve Schraeger: Stevie was crazy back in those days, man. He had a white Cadillac. Put MIAMI plates on the back. He always wore those big hats. Go to the racetrack. He was a piece of work.

Stevie Van Zandt: One night, I was coming home from the Pony and a guy crossed over in the lane. It was a four-lane road, and I was in the fast lane and he was in the fast lane. And he came over into my lane, and so I pulled over to the right lane, and so did he. Head-on collision. I smashed my head. And a couple operations, but they didn't really work out so well. So the hair never really grew in exactly right. So it was like, "What are you going to do?" And I was already wearing bandanas every now and then. So Bruce said, "Yeah, make it your thing." And I did.

Southside Johnny: There was a bartender, a little squat guy with a really muscular build, JT. He would come out and somebody would get belligerent and get drunk, some guy, and JT would just, "Be cool, man. Be cool." They'd go, "Fuck you." No, no, no, no. Take it easy. Fuck you, come on, they want to fight. So JT would come out from the bar, put a little paper napkin on the bar, take his teeth out, put his teeth on the paper napkin, and say, "Okay, let's go." And the guy would back off. He was like, "Okay, we're going to fight? I'm really going to fight." It's not like we're going to push each other, I'm going to hit you. It's hilarious to watch.

Dube Sullivan: He got his two front teeth knocked out playing tackle football, no pads, pickup game. He had the little plate in there, and when something was about to jump out, if it was a guy just challenged him, an out-and-out challenge, it's like, "Okay, outside." One by one, this guy would walk out, and they'd have their guy looking out for him, but the guy would be standing there, and then JT would just pull his front teeth out. The guy would go like, "This guy really means business."

Erick W. Henderiks: When JT took his teeth out, it was on. That was his signature move. He pulled the teeth out and then everyone said, "Okay, this is going to be for real now."

Dube Sullivan: It was a pretty intimidating thing to see that, all shapes and sizes. My brother [JT] was five feet eight, 230 pounds. Pit bull fireplug. He wasn't a pretty man, so he didn't mind going in. He could take a couple of taps, but as soon as he got in there and did his work, not too many guys walked away from it.

Pete Llewellyn: JT, Jersey Toughness. He couldn't stand bikers. I think he beat the hell out of half of them. He would take his teeth out so he didn't lose them.

Dube Sullivan: My brother had a little passion about confronting the bikers there. There was a president of the Pagans, this guy named Teddy Kendricks. His nickname was Nails. He was about Jack's size, six feet eight. He and my brother went toe-to-toe several times.

Pete Llewellyn: He was a one-punch knockout artist. If he missed, he was in trouble. He didn't miss. He was a little, short, potbellied, beer-drinking alcoholic. I liked him.

Tracey Story Prince: JT taught me how to bartend. "Service with an attitude and fuck you with a smile. That's all you need to know. Just keep on smiling. When they say, 'fuck you very much,' just keep on going." He was a very funny guy. He liked his Hennessy. He was short but big and looked like he wanted to kill everybody. He had a scowl on his face even when he was ecstatic, so he was very intimidating too.

Erick W. Henderiks: He must've been about five feet three. If he was a dog, he'd be a Staffordshire terrier. Tenacious as hell, wouldn't give up, and then more of a pain in the ass like, "This guy's not going to stop coming at me. I'm just going to turn around and run away," because he won't stop. He'll win the war by attrition. You'll give up because you're tired of fighting the guy because he just doesn't give up, so why even start? There's no reasoning with him, so you got to run away.

Bruce Springsteen: Erick began eating the glasses. Drinking the beer, and then eating the glasses. And that was his style of entertainment.

Erick W. Henderiks: We were stupid kids., To see who was a tough guy by biting a piece of glass out, and that was J. T. Sullivan. And eventually John Henry. One day, he did it, and he cut his mouth open real bad. That put an end to that stupid trend. Everybody was cool. Men wanted to be men then and women were glad they had men. That was part of their mystique. "I'm so tough, I can bite glass." With certain guys, like, I think Bruce would say in that song, "the boys were trying to look so hard." That's my only reference I can remember like that. All the guys back then, they tried to be a rock-and-roll macho kind of guy. They thought it was cool.

Vini Lopez: He'd chew those frosted glass. He'd chew one up. And we go, "Heeeey what? I ain't trying that."

Lance Larson: I used to break glasses on my head during a show. It started one night we were having drinks, and I just tapped a glass on my head and it broke. So I did it a few more times and the people at the Pony would cheer. So then people started handing me glasses, and I ended up breaking them on my head.

Vini Lopez: One of the bartenders, when we do "Kansas City," he would bring a tray of the frosted seven-ounce glasses, like thirty of them. And Lance had this Afro. And he'd smash a glass on his head to the "Kansas City" track. And he'd break every one of the glasses on his head. Now he had the Afro, so nothing would happen. And at the end though, he'd go like this to get the glass out of his hair and cut his hands and cut his head every time he did it. He never learned anything. I gave him a big comb one time.

Billy Hector: Lord Gunner would have me up to jam. I learned the songs on the stage, whatever the fuck they were, they were great. It was such great energy. His energy is the same as Bruce's when he is on the stage. Lance just takes it over. He'd be stalking the stage, looking at you like he's going to kick your ass and bang the glass on his fucking head. Then he starts bleeding. He's still singing, fucking doing his thing.

Lance Larson: I remember Rickie D. [DeSarno] saying, "Oh man, that's great, man. People love it." And I said, "Yes, it's not your head." I said, "This is killing me." So, certain glasses are easier to break. But people got to the point that they were giving me mugs, a beer mug, and I'd start bashing them into my head and thought, "Shit, I've gotta stop, I can't break that."

Ernest Carter: We were wild, man. We were doing everything you're not supposed to do but you're supposed to do at that job. Doing some lines of cocaine, drinking, all that good stuff. Then eventually say, "Damn, fuck that." We had a good time. Lance was cool. I would make sure he'd stay up on the money because he forgets he owes people every once in a while. But man, we had good people in the band.

Kenny "Stringbean" Sorensen: It was Labor Day weekend. I had been going to check out the band, and it was Monday of Labor Day. Usually sometimes bikers would deal bad vibes, but this time it was all coming from the stage. The bikers couldn't be bothered. But the guys onstage were all cranky. And it was Lance Larson and he started yelling at the soundman. And then I see him throw down the mic, and come over and punch the soundman. And then everyone onstage just started hitting each other. Like Vini Lopez. "Mad Dog" Vini stood up and punched Steve Schraeger. And he goes, "What the hell did you do that for?" And that was the end of the show. That was how I got to know these guys.

Tracey Story Prince: The regulars would hang out. The back bar was the place to be, of course. I used to bartend the back bar. That was when I started going, Judy and I would cocktail waitress. I really wouldn't do much because I'd hang out at the back bar, my waitress station with everybody. They were really good with that.

Patti Scialfa: I started singing there, not every weekend, but a lot. I saw all my old friends from school there, and then it became more of a social connection and a musical night. It was just fun.

Max Weinberg: It was almost like *Cheers*. I didn't know it at the time, but when I look back at the TV show *Cheers*, going to the Stone Pony, you'd see the same characters all the time. And it was a little like *Cheers*, where everybody knows your name, except it was focused around music.

Dube Sullivan: Originally, there wasn't a back room. There was the side bar where it is today, and then right around between the restrooms was the little bar called the Cave. Yes, the Cave. It was this white stucco-enclosed little bar with like four stools. That's where my brother JT and a waitress would come up and get the drinks, and that's where all the headliners would hang out. Steven would be there. He wore the fedora, and the polyester suits and stuff. At that time, I think it was only 275 occupancy. They tore that out, and that's when they made the back bar back there. I think they got to 400, four and a quarter, but we had well over 1,000 people a night when the Jukes were hopping and stuff.

Tracey Story Prince: Every musician in the town would be there. They had a thing called the "URINE" [pronounced "you're in"] card. It was, you get in free. The people that were regulars got their URINE card.

Dube Sullivan: You flashed a URINE card, you didn't pay, and you got right into the door. Skip the line, and you only got them from Jack. I don't even think Butch gave them in. Only Jack gave them out. If you had that, you were either cream of the crop, or you were very early. He was taking care of the guys that supported him on those first winter, summer nights that nobody was around.

Judy DeNucci: There was a little fireplace back there. In the winter, a lot of people came because it was a cozier spot if they weren't dancing in front of the band. Especially the nights that were a little bit slower. The back bar didn't really get that busy until later on when it became the place to hang out. Of course, when Bruce would come in, he'd always come to the back and hang out and when any of the national acts, Elvis

Costello or Gary Bonds, they would always hang back there. That's why people would always end up hanging out. In fact, I used to tell Bruce, "Would you please go up to the front."

Mark Bahary: I started bartending in '78, '79. That was when it was really cruising. The back bar is where Bruce would hang out. He'd be at a table on his own. He was drinking Heineken beers.

Southside Johnny: We knew all the bartenders. We knew 'em. Almost all of the fans knew us, we knew them. We'd go out and eat together. I always thought that one of my duties as a musician was to break down the barrier between the singer and the band and the audience, instead of that aloof thing. It just kind of . . . I'm having a great time, I'm getting to sing for my living. I look out and people are dancing and smiling. Couldn't be a better job for me and I just didn't want anybody to think that I was getting bigheaded about it. I was having as much fun as they were and I wanted them to know that. And that I wasn't stand-back or anything. And that way you get them to buy you drinks too. Chicks and alcohol.

Bruce Springsteen: As far as people drinking and all that, all that was going on. And there was that sort of thing. And everybody was young. We were in our thirties and younger, so there was an awful lot of rowdiness and people getting thrown out of the bar and things like that. But that felt just kind of normal.

Vini Lopez: And in those days it was open till three, everybody was drinking. It was crazy. You could get a container to go out.

Garry Tallent: You could get whatever you want.

Max Weinberg: The drinks were cheap and the pours were big, and that's a very good combination. The pours of the drinks were very generous. Without a doubt. I mean, they'd feed you, Jack and Butch.

Tony Amato: We were drinking for nothing. Because the bartenders, they were all local. They weren't going to charge us. So we were drinking for nothing. It's the way we was. The way we grew up. Each night playing, it's a jam session. Or it's like, "Oh, Jesus Christ. George Theiss is drunk. He's passed out. Oh, it's his birthday. What do we do?" Steven says, "Give me the fucking guitar." And Steve will come up and he'd play. He finished the night with us.

Dube Sullivan: It was sex, drugs, and rock and roll. Seriously, I mean, nobody got cut off of drinking. You really had to be a real ass to get cut off and thrown out. If you're a regular, we used to walk out of there cross-eyed. God, it was scary, how crazy it was. They used to do five sets a night. It was forty minutes on, twenty minutes off. Everybody used to go run outside and puff, or do whatever, and then come back in. That went on for like four or five sets a night. It's just nonstop going, going, going.

Steve Schraeger: There were some nights where we might have been a little too drunk.

Tracey Story Prince: Steve Schraeger would celebrate his birthday for three months. Anyone who walked in, he'd tell him his birthday and they had to buy him a drink.

Tony Amato: We would be staying there until five in the morning. Drinking Chartreuse.

Bruce Springsteen: Chartreuse. Terrible stuff.

Tony Amato: Butch and Pete, one of the bartenders, grabbed me one night, threw me up on the bar, got the funnel, Chartreuse. Within five minutes, I was never so drunk in my whole goddamn life. I went right into the bathroom, threw up, and thank God I only lived two blocks away.

Bruce Springsteen: Clarence, by the way, was the king of the green Chartreuse. He could down a bottle of it. Clarence was the king of green shot juice. He gave some to me one night and I blew up in the bar and my cheeks became the size of a frigging chipmunk's and I immediately made my way to the front door and the gutter.

Judy DeNucci: Oh yes, Clarence, loved Ivan the Terribles, which was green Chartreuse with vodka. Or sometimes if he ever got behind the bar, he'd make his own pitcher punch. He'd say "This is my pitcher tonight," and he'd put like twenty different things in a pitcher.

Jack Roig: For Clarence, that was a small price to pay.

Gary U.S. Bonds: I don't know how Clarence would do that. That's terrible stuff. Terrible. I didn't drink that stuff. Clarence drinks some weird stuff. Virginia boy. I used to drink corn liquor and chocolate soda. Yes. It sounds bad. It was delicious.

Southside Johnny: It was a honky-tonk town then, and that was a real honky-tonk, a real knock-down, beer drinkers, fistfights, rock-'n'-roll bar. And, of course, there were people in the city that didn't like it. But it was one of the few viable businesses after the riots. So it was vital that there be some downtown life on Friday night.

8

Pony People

Every bar has its regulars. This bar had some extraordinary regulars.

Bruce Springsteen: Jack and Butch were just classic bar owners. They were unintentionally, absolutely hilarious most of the time. But they were also very serious bar owners in that they believed that keeping the place safe was important, whatever that took. And they were two huge guys, first of all, and would narrowly bounce themselves. And they were just classic bar owners. Once they realized they'd stumbled on the golden goose, we owned the place. It was great. They said, "Hey, whatever this is, it's working out for us. Let's just keep it going."

Tracey Story Prince: Jack had a favorite line: "If you're not effing the help, you got to go." That was his big closing line, but that never worked with him. Because the people were effing the help.

Dube Sullivan: Big Jack was famous for chasing people. He'd be walking through the bar, "All right. You don't have to go home but you can't stay here." That would be his thing. He'd say that three or four times, and then finally, when it was getting three o'clock when he could technically be in trouble, he can be like, "Get the F out of here." He'd just be loud and scary. The guy is six feet eight. The musicians and the groupies that try to hang out, they would bust out, just literally run out the door.

Erick W. Henderiks: I got people out of the Pony. See, back then, everybody was entitled. "I know Bruce. I know Jack. I know Erick."

They wouldn't leave. I don't know. We tried to get them out by quarter to three back then; they wouldn't leave. I went out in the back, and I hooked up a garden hose to the industrial sink back there. I went in the back bar, and I just shot everybody with a hose. Shot everyone with a hose and they're screaming, "You fucking jerkoff," but they all left. Jack didn't like that too much. I said, "But it's better than a bullet, Jack."

Southside Johnny: You'd think Butch would've been the rough guy. Crazy because Jack was always a little saner, it seemed like. But when Jack got going, all bets were off.

Lance Larson: Jack and Butch, we were very tight. I used to go to Butch's house and use the swimming pool; we all used to hang out with them. Jack used to cuss a lot, but he had a rule for us onstage. He said, "Just don't say 'fuck.'" I said, "Okay." And then I got a point where we'd be onstage and I'd say, "Fuck this, fuck that." And he said, "I'm going to fine you every time you say that," and it got to be a joke. Because he would say, "Don't say 'fuck' tonight." And I'd say, "Okay." And the first thing I would say when I went out there was, "Fuck this, fuck that." And I said to Jack, "Don't say that to me before I go up there, because that's the one thing on my mind." So when I picked up money for that show, they charged me for every fuck, fuck, fuck. I'd get twenty dollars.

Max Weinberg: They were great. Those two guys were, I mean, if it hadn't been for them, that whole sort of seventies into the early eighties Asbury Park scene would not have developed, the two of them. Butch and Jack were maybe not a full generation, but a good eight or nine years older than the rest of us. So they were a little bit like, they were protective if you know what I mean.

Tracey Story Prince: I was actually thrown out of the Pony before I was hired there. I was dating a drummer. He used to play there every Wednesday, but I was underage. Back then, it was normal because eighteen, seventeen, y'all looked the same age. The band who called me Yoko Ono decided to tell the owners that I was underage. It was a band called Max. We were from Ocean Township. The town over from Asbury. They did real well there. When I went back when I was eighteen, Jack says, "I can't get rid of you, can I?"

Pete Llewellyn: Butch was one of my absolute best friends. He had a very cool personality. He was diabetic, badly, and he was very moody. He'd either sit there with you in the best mood in the world, have drinks with you, or he would walk by you without saying a word.

Vini Lopez: Jack has thrown me out of the Pony, and then he has also thrown me into the Pony. I got in trouble and I didn't play at the Pony anymore for a while. The lead singer in the band, Bob Campanell, had this double-neck guitar, it was a beautiful thing. One night I hear, "Aw, man, somebody just stole Bobby's guitar." One of our friends goes running out, stops this car that's leaving the driveway, opens the door, the guy gets out. Boom, guy knocks this guy out. [But there was] no guitar in his trunk. I went, "Ah, shit." I walked into the bathroom and I kicked the door shut. One of the ceiling tiles fell out. Well, Jack saw it. He grabbed me by my neck. I became the bouncing ball in the backstage area. Put my head through the wall. Right through, boom.

Erick W. Henderiks: Vini's a very noble character. If he thinks you're doing him wrong or if you're telling him a lie, or you're—he'll stand up to it but he's got a bad temper. He's one of those guys that may be better off saying what he needs to say and walk away rather than saying what he needs to say and throwing hands.

Vini Lopez: And I'm laying on the floor like this. Now, it's Jack, an Asbury cop, and Butch, and they're standing over me like this. I always had this briefcase with me, so Jack leaned down to get me, and I grabbed my briefcase and I went *wham!* and I hit him right square in his ear, and he went, "Whaa." I could see the stars. I got up and ran as fast as I could out of there, ran all the way home, because I lived in Asbury. I ran all the way to my house. I was black and blue, I was bleeding, from Jack.

Jack Roig: No, it was the other way around. I'm sitting there counting out his money, and he had this metal case he used to carry, right? Next thing I know, he hits me in the head with it. For no reason. That's why they call him Mad Dog, right? And I get up. I said, "Whoa, what the hell?" I know I can't hit him. I didn't put his head through wall. Did he say that? I did not. I picked him up, and I threw him through the wall.

I did not put his head through the wall, because I didn't want to hurt him. That's why you call him Mad Dog. I love the man.

Vini Lopez: Months go by. I wasn't going near that place. To hell with that, I don't need to get beat up by nobody, but I was walking by one night, and the side door opens up, the stage door, and there's Jack. Grabs me by the throat and throws me in. First time I've ever been thrown in a place. He goes, "Get over there and get a beer. What the hell's wrong with you?" And he started yelling. I said, "Jack, don't worry. I'm going to get a beer. Don't worry." From there on, we went back and played there again. They put a safe in front of the hole, because the hole was in that office for a long time. Then they made it where you can get food.

Bruce Springsteen: Danny Federici was coming in the front door, my recollection, and he made a mistake of laying out one of the "Do you know who I am?" quotes on the bouncer. And either the bouncer didn't know who he was or he did know who he was. Either way, the result was the same. Danny immediately met the concrete out in front of the front door. The facts are, most of the band members, as far as I know, did not object. Danny had a way about him that at the wrong moment and at the wrong time, he could be quite obnoxious. He was not above pulling out that "Do you know who I am?" And yet it didn't work down there. And I might have said something to the guys after that. "Please don't throw Danny out. Talk to me." Whatever, but it was just one of those things.

Jack Roig: I walked into the men's room, and Danny's in there doing lines. I said, "Danny, come on. Either go outside or tell me if you need privacy, I'll send you to the back room." He goes outside, he puts out a pile of shit on a table on the dance floor. Jesus. I walked over, I and two guys. I said, "Take him out." Two guys pick them up under the arms, walked into the stage door. I was there. I saw the whole thing, walked him out, put him on his side. He started rolling around saying he got beat up and everything. The next thing I know, about an hour later, Clarence was coming down. Clarence shows up. Federici used to go out there and tell us Clarence was going to come down and kill everybody. So Clarence came down. And I met him out in the street. And he believed everything Danny told him. I said, "Whoa, whoa." He said, "I'm going to come in there, I'm going to kill them." Now I'm much bigger than Clarence. Back then, I'm 290, 300 in the gym all the time. No fat. I said, "No, no, this is what happened. I saw it." We talked about it, we talked about it, and that was it. All you can say is, hey, shit happens. It wasn't our fault. It wasn't my fault.

Eileen Chapman: The Pony didn't even open till eight or nine at night. You figure it was open till two or three. But sometimes we'd be there till the sun came up the next day. We'd all hang out afterward and have some drinks and Jack would sometimes take out his gun and shoot out some of the lights. Yeah, a revolver. The neon lights. Depending on Jack's mood. Or get the hose in the back and hose everybody down. Jack was a fun and funny guy. And Butch was the real serious guy.

Tracey Story Prince: Pretty burly. Butch looked like a tank. Back when they were younger, they were very intimidating, extremely intimidating. One time, I don't know if I should say this, Jack wanted to get everybody out, and nobody would listen, so he shot two bullets into the ceiling and said, "Now we get the fuck out."

Jack Roig: Nobody would leave. Everybody knew somebody who knew somebody who knew somebody. The whole back room. There must have been a hundred people still there. Nobody would leave. Nobody listened to the floor man and the doorman knew they weren't supposed to start throwing people out because he's young. And I guess I was not too stable. And I got my shotgun and I walked outside. And I never liked that Bud Light sign across the bar, so I blew it away. They left. A couple of floor men quit.

Vini Lopez: Me and Lance and Lance's brother hot-tarred the Pony roof. The whole roof and Mrs. Jay's too. We did the hot tar job on it. Lance got really hurt, but that's a whole 'nother story. But now, a couple of weeks after, the tar was done, and it was good and stuff, Jack, or somebody, shot the gun up through the roof. Now, it rained a couple of days later and the rains come in. So, they blamed us. "You don't know how to do it." "But he shot holes through the ceiling. Come on."

Jack Roig: Those holes could have come from any place. There was a shooting gallery at night. Everyone set up. Have fun.

Erick W. Henderiks: The Pony guys were pretty professional. They really didn't start much, but if there was a crisis and there was a lot of shit going down, we were ready. We pretty much tried to keep it as nice as possible.

Bruce Springsteen: There was quite a bit of stability and there was some fighting, but not much. The bouncers were reasonably tolerant. And so it wasn't wild like that, like some other clubs in the area were, where you were guaranteed to get into a scrap if you walk through the front door. Stone Pony was actually . . . Butch and Jack were very, very intent on keeping it safe. They knew if they couldn't keep it safe, they weren't going to have a crowd, they weren't going to get the girls there. And then they're going to get the guys there. And so they had a small group of bouncers, who were initially somewhat ruthless on laying out the lessons of how you should behave at the club, at the time. But it did make the club, in my opinion, a very safe place to go.

Jack Roig: We controlled the streets. The only problems we had were the motorcycle gangs. Asbury was pretty tough. It was tough times. But there was understandings we had, or forced. Everybody had guns, everybody had them.

Tracey Story Prince: There wasn't a small guy that worked there. They were monsters.

Dube Sullivan: Shields was another notable one. He was a collegiate football player. He was a punter with Clemson, and then he became a kickboxer dude, but he was just playing nasty when he got into his cups when he started drinking. He was bouncing for a while. We had some big dudes in there. Once we started getting those crowds in there, you had to look formidable in there because there was guys coming down there, just like the bust-up places.

Pete Llewellyn: I met Jack in the gym. That's how I got the job. I was in the gym, lifting weights. I was eighteen years old. I guess he liked how much I was bench pressing. He said, "You want a job?" So me being young and dumb, I went up to meet him for the interview, and I brought a pint of Jack Daniel's in my pocket and I started drinking it in the bar. I got thrown out before I got to interview with him. But I made it back.

Bruce Springsteen: The bikers, they pretty much stayed to Mrs. Jay's. Mrs. Jay's was next door to the Pony at the time, and it was just a famous sort of outdoor beer garden that catered to the local biker community.

Pete Llewellyn: We would spot knives on them at the front door. They had to leave it at the front door, or a helmet. Couldn't bring a helmet in. Early we had a guy beat up three people with his helmet that had spikes in it.

Jack Roig: The bikers basically ran the beachfront. I couldn't live like that, so we started changing and they didn't like that, and it was a problem. I mean, you ever had anybody shoot at you? I ran into a guy in Reggie's at Belmar, in the mid-nineties, and he said, "You know who I am?" I looked at him and said, "Yeah." He said, "Do you remember the big problem in front of the Alamo?" The Alamo was a bar on Third and Kingsley, I think. He said, "I couldn't get a clear shot at you that night. That was my job."

Ernest Carter: They could be rough. There was one time I was loading out. This was with the Fairlanes. This biker was pissing on my car. I said, "Hey, man, what are you doing?" All of a sudden, my friend Billy Lilly, who was a biker himself, came out and all his other biker friends came out and just beat the crap out of the guy.

Tony Pallagrosi: Live music, particularly the kind of music that the Jukes played, and the Shakes played, and Cahoots played, and the Asbury bands play. Bikers loved it.

Pete Llewellyn: When I first started working at the Stone Pony back in '79, literally it was a bucket of blood. We didn't let bikers in, per se, or patches or colors or other clubs' insignia anywhere on them. We sure had our hands full. They sure wanted to come in, but they weren't coming in.

Southside Johnny: I'm sure there was a lot of grease being splashed around. I'm sure the fire chief and police chief, lieutenant, this guy, they all got a little something, so we could call them.

Dube Sullivan: The rank-and-file police, they were our boys because they would come in and party up big-time. I could tell you in the winter, fall of '74 going into '75, there were a couple cops that used to come in and drink in uniform on duty incognito because there was nobody down there. There was a hundred and fifty, two hundred people, and they'd do it on the side. They wouldn't be chugging beers, but they'd have a glass in their hand. But they had our backs big-time because they didn't like the bikers either. They were just champing at the bit anytime they could run the bikers out of town for sure.

Jack Roig: The police were unbelievably great, if they were around. There weren't many of them. We ran benefits so they all got [bullet-proof] vests.

Dube Sullivan: One night I was working, I was on the floor. It was just Butch, and we had a skeleton crew. This was going on, I guess something happened previous, a couple of weeks before something, they had a run-in. Butch comes up to me about ten thirty and says, "Do you notice anything about the crowd?" I'm looking, I'm like, "Well, there's a couple of dirtbags up here." He goes, "Yes, look, look." I'm looking, he goes, "They're bikers, but they're not wearing colors. I'm going to call the cops and have them roll a black and white up here. I don't feel comfortable." Then he comes busting out of the office. He goes, "The phone lines are dead. The phone lines are dead." When you look around, and sure enough, there's ten of these guys. And I was one of three bouncers.

Judy DeNucci: The Jukes weren't playing that night and the bikers had gotten kicked out a number of times because they would come out and look like they were going to start fights or push people around. They would get kicked out regularly. They decided that they were going to come in, take over the Pony, and they cut the phone wires, which meant Jack couldn't call the cops. They all surrounded the Pony. The employees actually went into the walk-in in the back because they started coming in and then somebody found that the phone lines were cut off.

Dube Sullivan: Just before something was going to break off, the black and whites rolled in. There had to be four or five Asbury cops. Back then, the Asbury cops used to come in and drink and to drink for real, cop drinking. So they rolled in with the lights flashing boom, boom, boom, man. Then Butch just went around with the cop and they're pointing him out, out, out, out. That could have been pretty scary jumping off something like that. They did it on the sneak because they wouldn't wear their colors because they knew they couldn't get in the door.

Jack Roig: A fight never started, because before anything could happen, the lady working the front door recognized it and got to Butch and said, "Get the cops here." And they backed the wagon to the front door, came in, walked them all right into the wagon.

Judy DeNucci: Then all the police showed up with the paddy wagons and arrested them all. That was crazy. They had guns. Nobody got shot, but the cops brought their guns out and arrested a bunch of them.

Jack Roig: Another time they were supposed to come and burn us out. I told the staff, "Nobody comes in." One other guy wanted to go up on the roof with me, and he didn't work there. I was up there in the morning. It was like something out of the Alamo. I had a shotgun, automatic weapon, Molotov cocktails. And the state police turned them back at the state line and at the county line. And then the locals came by and said, "You can come down now."

Southside Johnny: There were incidents where I think they threw out a member of the Pagans, or one of the motorcycle groups, and there was a big rumor that they were going to come in and so here's Butch, Jack up on the roof with shotguns, and all the bartenders are carrying pistols and I'm like, "Oh, great. Are we playing tonight? No? Okay, I'm going home. I didn't need to be in the crossfire here."

Jack Roig: It was my life. And I was going to lose. I knew I was going to die up there. You knew it. If a hundred bikes come up, you know you're going to lose. Except, not by myself I wasn't.

Pete Llewellyn: It's not a gun state, so very rarely did you ever see a gun on someone, but we saw a lot of knives. In fact, I got stabbed in there one night by a guy. I got stabbed right in the chest. Knives were to fear but if you were going to get it, it's either a bottle over the head—I saw Jack get it with a full beer bottle over the head. You were either getting hit in the head with a bottle—they should have had only cans—or you were going to get stabbed. Rarely did we see guns. In the thirteen years I was there, maybe two guns, but almost never guns. Almost always a beer bottle or a knife, and that was your enemy. It was a violent place.

Jack Roig: You were in a liquor establishment, and you've got young people, you've got a lot of the hooch, you know? You're gonna have problems. You always knew you were going to have problems when the floor man would say, "We got Bayshore people," which means Keansburg, Union Beach, up that area.

Dube Sullivan: Most of the stuff they jumped off in the Pony wasn't with the bikers. It was just rowdy-ass guys. We always used to call them the Bennies from up north. These guys would come in and get all fired up, whatever they were doing that night. They wanted trouble, and we had a bunch of big guys walking around the Pony, and it was like a contest. They wanted to break up a place and they started going at it. There were some knock-down drag-outs.

Pete Llewellyn: You were going to be in four or five fights a night. That's just the way it was. You get guys going in there looking to pick up girls and they wouldn't be successful; they were either going to fuck or fight, take your pick. If they didn't hook up with a broad, they were picking a fight.

Dube Sullivan: You're talking about the late seventies. Everything was going on there. They had a lot of drugs going on, guys getting really fired up and stuff. The combination of alcohol, some lines. The guys were ready to rock. There was powder going around all at the time. You knew the guys that were in business out there, and there was the local connections too. Hey, we weren't angels. None of us were angels in there. We were right there with it. You couldn't be overt with it with Jack and Butch, but actually, my first bartending gigs at the Stone Pony was when Butch and Jack back then used to let all the bartenders get breaks, a twenty-minute break, and that's how I broke in. I would leave D'Jais at nine o'clock on Sunday night and I'd go to the Pony and then I'd start breaking all the bartenders. There was six bartenders. I'd go around and each of them would get their twenty minutes. They go out and do their thing outside. Most of them would puff some weed or stuff like that, but I'm sure they were doing other stuff, and I'm sure they're also bringing their ladies out there for whatever they can get from the ladies real quick.

Tracey Story Prince: I never felt unsafe. I walked home from the Pony. The few times I had a problem and I had—when they had the old phone booths, I would lock myself in there and I'd call somebody up and say, "There's these guys trying to drag me out of the phone booth." They're like, "Oh, shit, we got to go get Tracey again." John Simon was the one who used to come and save me most of the time. They chased me around the park like, "We're giving you a ride." I said, "I'm walking." Yes, it was a little bit of a problem. It's three in the morning when I would leave. How many people are really going to wait around to mug a drunk bartender? Probably a few. When I think about it, it doesn't even make sense. Yes, a drunk lady walking around a lot in winter. What dummies, they should have got me.

Tony Amato: We're never worried about anything at all. Because in the Pony, what's going to happen? You got Big Erick working there, he'll kick the shit out of anybody. And then you got Jack and Butch and one of them would have a gun on them. So there was nothing to worry about. Most of the guys back then, we all moved to Asbury and lived in Asbury. And we were within walking distance from the Pony. And we'd always be together, two or three of us. So yeah, there was nothing security-wise that we really worried about.

Southside Johnny: My birthday party at the Pony. This was back in the seventies. I don't remember which year, and they kept feeding me drinks. I'm up onstage and I wear prescription sunglasses, and I jumped up in the air and my glasses fell off and I came right down on them, crunch. And I had to walk home, which fortunately I lived down on Eighth Avenue, or whatever it was, and I was drunk and blind walking home. You know, those are the kind of nights you would have. It was your club. You could be completely drunk and you knew you were safe. Or you could be angry or you could be just quiet and people would leave you alone.

Harvey Leeds: Southside, you know, everybody got a nickname. So I was Harvey TCB Leeds. Taking Care of Business Leeds. Southside came up with that one.

Southside Johnny: The nicknames were Steven and Bruce. Everybody had one, Funky E for Garry Tallent, and I became Southside, because I played Chicago blues and that was known to be from the south side of Chicago.

Bruce Springsteen: It was just a local, very classic sort of street thing in Asbury Park and all around the world. It's like, parentless people come up with nicknames. Why that is, I'm not sure, but some way of divorcing yourself perhaps from your actual family and joining these little street communities where, "Oh, there's Southside, there's Miami." And anything too. You didn't have to do very much. You had to like the blues to become Southside Johnny, you had to have been to Miami to become Miami, and you simply had to pay some of the band members to become the Boss. That was all you had to do. There was nothing else to it.

Richie "La Bamba" Rosenberg: It wasn't immediate that, oh, we're going to call you La Bamba. No, it was a little time had gone by, a couple days at least, or a week, and we were all in the back bar of the Stone Pony huddled back there. Place was packed, and Gary Anderson was a roadie for the Jukes. And they were thinking, oh, when are we going to come up with a name for this guy here? I had a Fu Manchu, I had a short Afro, very dark from tanning, whatnot for some reason. And instead of giving me a Jewish nickname, Gary Anderson yelled out "La Bamba" and Bruce jumped up on the bar and with a shot and "All right, give me an *L*. Give me an *A*. Give me a *B*." So I was christened La Bamba by Bruce. Thank you, Gary Anderson.

Mark Pender: Almost everybody in the E Street Band had a nickname. Mighty Max. The Professor. Yeah. I can't remember what they called Danny. It might have been Wild Man because he was wild when I first met him. He was wild. He could throw back a few. And then he got sober. One of those guys. Probably saved his life at the time. He was so crazy, it probably would have eventually killed him.

Southside Johnny: Steven was Miami Steve, Bruce is Dr. Zoom, later the Boss. Dr. Zoom came from Dr. Zoom and the Sonic Boom.

Joe Prinzo: That's a story.

Southside Johnny: Bruce had come back from California, went to visit his folks, who had moved out there, and he was broke. And this guy Fisher, who ran the Sunshine Inn, which was the old hullabaloo, a big garage, terrible acoustics, said, "I want you to play. You're a big draw. I'll give you X amount of money." So he started this band Dr. Zoom and the Sonic Boom because he didn't want it to be Bruce Springsteen. He was starting the Bruce Springsteen band or something at that point. But this is just a one-off, we thought. So he starts to hire everybody he knows. He hires me. He hires Bird as the announcer. We had a Zoom choir, we had baton twirlers, we had a Monopoly game onstage. I had a chair and a little nightstand, and I put a bottle of Jack Daniel's in one thing and a bucket of chicken in the other thing. And every time they took one of those long guitar solos, I sat down and ate chicken. And then Bruce would go over and get Big Bobby, I think, was playing Monopoly with somebody else. "How's it going over here?" "I just took Boardwalk." "Great." And the others just looking, and we ended up opening up for the Allman Brothers. And they had just made the *Live at the Fillmore [East]*, I think it was. And I think it was that tour or the tour after that. So they're sitting, and I remember Duane Allman sitting in the audience just baffled, baffled by us. We played three farewell gigs.

Al "Doc" Berger: Bruce gave a lot of nicknames out and we all had nicknames. And Steve put them on. I think all of them are on the second album. We all had stuff on there. And that's another Jersey thing. It's almost like we're Jersey mafia musicians here. Steve put on the second album liner notes, "Al Doc Berger, Jewish stomach." I always had stomach problems, nerves and this and whatever. So I always carried Tums, Mylanta, aspirin, all over-the-counter, all the medicine things that anybody could need or want. With eleven guys in the band, there was always somebody who was sick. I was the doc. I had the pills.

Judy DeNucci: I was Jaws. I used to change the sign on top of the Pony. Now it's on the side of the building, but back then, it was on the roof. I'd have friends come and hang out with me and we'd go on the roof and smoke a joint and hang out. Well, this one day, I was by myself and I was coming down the ladder, and one of the rungs broke and the ladder fell and I landed right next to the dumpster in the back and broke my jaw. But some people said they called me Jaws because . . . I would put my elbows on the bar and talk to all my regulars that would come in. I would watch the bar. It wasn't like I was talking and not working. Some people called me Jaws because I talk too much and some people call me Jaws because I broke my jaw.

Mark Pender: My nickname, the Loveman? We were playing with Little Steven and the Disciples of Soul. One of our first concerts was at Big Man's West, Clarence's club [in Red Bank], right next to the Count Basie. I'm in a hotel. I have a Walkman in and I'm singing along with Marvin Gaye. Steven came by the room to ask me a question, but I'm singing so loud, I don't answer the door. I was singing some love song. He loved to give everybody nicknames, so that night, he goes, "And tonight on trumpet is the Loveman." He starts calling me that, Bruce starts calling me that, and then it kind of sticks. A couple of times I tried to walk away from it, but that's a pretty good nickname.

Erick W. Henderiks: James Brown actually gave me my old nickname. He saw me one time handle a couple of angry people and then he just said, "Damn, you must be the Payback." So James gave me that, but of course, Bruce backed it up.

Judy DeNucci: We were like a family in those years though. We always did stuff. We would close the Pony on one day and we'd rent one of those little buses and we'd go up to Action Park and spend the day on the water rides and do all that. We always did everything together. We would do the same thing right around Christmastime. We'd rent a bus and we'd ride around, look at Christmas lights and drink tons of whatever people brought on the bus and just have fun. We were like a family for so many years.

Jack Roig: I really believe that the Pony kept Asbury Park alive in the seventies. It was the only thing that kept them alive. There was nothing else. It was bad. And I really believe Asbury owes that building a lot.

9

National Attention

Rock clubs have a draw to musicians and fans alike. As the Jukes toured internationally and Springsteen and E Street became house-hold names, national icons passing through Asbury Park wanted to experience the Jersey Shore scene at the Pony for themselves. But eventually the Jukes outgrew the Pony; the audience was too big and the pay too small to keep up any regular rotation of performances.

Billy Hector: When Johnny and the Jukes just started taking off, all the bands that would play at Convention Hall, since there was such a buzz on the Jukes, they would come over and jam with them. Loggins and Messina did. Boz Scaggs was over there and they sang. They did "Loan Me a Dime."

Billy Rush: Loggins and Messina were real big I think around that time and they did a gig at Convention Hall. But Jim Messina came over and jammed with us, and I remember Clarence was there too. Clarence used to come down and play with us a lot. And Jim Messina got up and was like—oh my, that guy was a monster guitar player. I don't know if people realized what a monster he was, but he was really fantastic. And he got up and really broke loose in a way that he wasn't able to do on his own, playing the pop songs that they did. He and I were trading licks back and forth.

Al "Doc" Berger: We're playing and people are coming into the Pony, jamming with us. We had Mitch Ryder on the stage. We had to throw him off; he was drunk. It was like a Jim Morrison thing, where he is drunk and he is going crazy and sounding obscenities. And so we had to throw him off the stage.

Vini Lopez: It was always a crowd. And then, there were always the folks from out of town, and then the people from Europe started catching on. And when they would come over, they would come there because that's the birthplace of . . . whatever it was, which I kind of disagree with because the Upstage was the birthplace of what I know is rock and roll in Asbury Park. But the Pony became that symbol.

Southside Johnny: We played in Knebworth with Led Zeppelin. And I'm walking through this crowd of 150,000 to 200,000 people. This outdoor field kind of thing and I'm just kind of wandering around before our set and I hear someone going, "Hey, Southside! Asbury Park! Yes! Stony Pony!" And I'm like, "Oh man. I can't get away from it." It's a blessing and a curse.

Steve Schraeger: One night, it was a Sunday night and Boz Scaggs turns up. The place is supposed to close at three, they kept it open. He did three or four songs with the Jukes.

Butch Pielka: Boz Scaggs was here when one of his albums turned gold. We partied in the back room. Bruce was there.

Southside Johnny: They started bringing in national acts and people would come to jams and I remember a jam Boz Scaggs was playing at the Convention Hall, or something like that, and he came in and jammed.

Judy DeNucci: Boz Scaggs after we closed, and Bruce was there, they got up and played with the Jukes until four in the morning. Everybody left, we closed the doors, and then they did their own little show.

Bob Santelli: I remember talking to Butch and Jack the owners and saying, "Man, guys, there's new bands." And they said, "No, we're sticking with our people. We'll stay. We'll be fine." I don't know why they did. They brought in some bands, like Graham Parker. He was a big fan of Bruce's.

Graham Parker: In '76 I did two tours; the second tour was later in the year. And that's when, I guess, I got wind of this band Southside Johnny and the Asbury Jukes, and they were a New Jersey thing. And apparently they were a soul-type band, so the soul revival more than anything with a horn section, a four-piece horn section. So by then I'd said to my manager, because we had horns on the *Howlin Wind* and the *Heat Treatment* record, I believe. And I loved the idea of powering my songs with a horn section.

Tony Pallagrosi: We had a tour bus. It was like the shittiest tour bus known to man, the first one. Basically, two guys, Doug and Dennis Gallagher, owned this bus company called Coast City Buses. And they build buses for clients. And basically they took the standard old beaten-up passenger bus, took the seats out, and screwed bunk beds into the floor. And that was our first tour bus. Now of course the screws and the washers and the nuts and bolts that are holding the bunk beds got loose. So at a point the bunk beds were wobbling. We had a driver who was blown out of his mind on blow every night. . . . I'd sit up with him because there was no fucking way I could sleep knowing how wasted he was. I don't think I ever slept unless we were in a motel.

Graham Parker: December 1976, me and the Rumour played at the Stone Pony as it says "Guests of Southside Johnny." In other words, my manager had finagled it that we go on in the middle of the night after Southside Johnny had played to a home crowd at the Stone Pony. I don't know what time Southside went on, but I know it must have been about, between twelve and one a.m., that we went on. Because the bar people kept holding you up saying, yeah, a few more minutes, because they want to sell more drinks. The place is round, so they keep selling drinks, and it's like dawn will be coming soon. And you're young, you can do it. Anyway, I was full of beans and strong and whatever, and I just accepted this is what you did.

So on we went and I remember walking out the dressing rooms through a very, that narrow space towards the stage, like running the gauntlet, and was—I could feel the hostility in the air and as I'm walking past one guy he says, "Why do we need this while we got the real thing?" And I held my fists down to the side, said don't smack him, there's way too many people here who might kill me. So I gave him a cursory "Fuck off" and kept walking. And there's the crowd saying yeah, whatever, impress us. And we did, and they loved us. They would have been hearing mentions and comparisons to Bruce Springsteen and people don't take kindly to that. We've got our Bruce Springsteen, man. He's the Boss. Who's the interloper from England? You've got to be kidding me. So, I totally understood a little bit of hostility there. But they stayed. They didn't go anywhere and they listened. Before long, they're fucking roaring.

Tony Pallagrosi: I was friends with Graham. So Graham and I used to sit on the bus all the time together. We all got along really well, and we had a great time. And we basically opened for them all over Great Britain for almost two months. And I was basically sitting with Graham all the time. And I found out why, because nobody could really sit with him because he would roll these hash-and-tobacco joints. He would just smoke three or four of these joints on the ride and he'd be fine. Now I would be a zombie. So finally, I couldn't sit next to him anymore because it was too tempting and I couldn't say no. But he'd listen to music and our little recorders and talk about the show.

Huey Lewis: I was in a band called Clover before Huey Lewis and the News, and we were signed to Phonogram Records in England, and we were there when Southside came over to Britain and played shows. And I played shows, and we jammed a bunch, so I knew Southside, and I knew La Bamba, and I knew all them cats from the Jukes, you know, because Clover and the Jukes were same deal, kind of like. They were a little more successful than us, but we did the same thing; went over there and supported rock, and supported Thin Lizzy, supported Lynyrd Skynyrd, supported . . . did all that, and got shit thrown at us, and booed off stages and stuff. And then we would play a club, there was a little club called the Nashville in London, which was London's version of the Stone Pony, and that's where all the roots music was happening. That's where Elvis Costello would play, it's where the Jukes played, it's where Clover played, and we'd sit in with each other. Me and Southside playing harp, and then there's La Bamba and a few of the horn guys onstage, and then Scott Gorham from Thin Lizzy with three feet of hair hanging down. The strangest bedfellows.

Tony Pallagrosi: Coming back to the Pony, there were more out-of-state plates. More girls trying to find out where you live, and wanting to stay with you or them wanting you to stay with them in their hotel room. Suddenly our world, the world of the band and our personal worlds, expanded exponentially. They're coming to Asbury Park because of Southside Johnny and the Asbury Jukes. And they want us. That dynamic was cool. I mean, suddenly, you know, I'd wake up in the morning and there were four or five girls from Cleveland in various states of undress, hanging out in my apartment. And being very nice to me and my roommate, who was the other trumpet player. We had this two-bedroom apartment on Fourth Avenue, I think it was 410, and I woke up one morning, and there were just all of these naked bodies, strewn on the couches, on the chairs, on the floor and the beds. And I'm just walking around looking at it. I'm like, man, life is fucking great. This is incredible.

Southside Johnny: The thing that knocked me out was when they started bringing international acts like Elvis Costello and, of course, the Ramones and all the rest of these people would come and play and go, this is great. I live maybe a half a mile away, at one point I lived within walking distance in Asbury Park, and if they're going to play and I've got the night off, I'm going to go see these bands.

Jack Roig: We definitely weren't looking for national acts. It came in through an agent. Because in all honesty, we didn't know the national touring scene really existed; it was above our pay scale at the time.

Pete Llewellyn: Cheap Trick was climbing. They came in, they started cursing. Cursed the crowd. It was a little crowd; they didn't draw a big number.

Jack Roig: [Cheap Trick] were so loud. They were so loud the staff wanted to quit. I went to the sound guy and I said, "You got to turn it down . . ." Just looked at me. Said, "Fuck you." I went up to the stage and I told him, "Turn it down." Another "Fuck you." I went up to the stage, grabbed the two of them, took them, threw them out the side door. That was it.

It took about three weeks later, and their record was number one. They never came back. Ha. Part of growing up.

Stevie Van Zandt: We kept coming back for years, really. Sure felt like years. Right up until I left the entire scene when we moved to New York.

Pete Llewellyn: The Jukes had some dispute with the owners and that went south. They didn't even come in as customers. There was bad blood that made up later, and that was with Southside and Jack and Butch.

Southside Johnny: We had a love-hate relationship with the Stone Pony. I was grateful to them for giving us a job. When we started they paid $135 a night for five guys. For the band. I mean that was it. Split it up. And after we started selling out the place, I said, "We need more money." It became this ongoing thing and then later when we started, it really started happening, I said, you can't charge, I think it was fifty dollars a ticket. I said, "I won't play." There's an interview with Butch said, "He thinks he can tell us what to do in our own club." I just said, "I won't play here." It's just one of those things. I'm more loyal to the audience than I am to the club owners.

10

That Other Bar Around the Corner

When the Jukes left the Pony's regular rotation for national tours and larger venues, cover bands again became core to the repertoire at the Stone Pony in the very late 1970s and early 1980s. Local bands playing original music and some nationally touring bands started playing at the Fast Lane, a bar around the corner from the Pony. A large part of the Pony scene soon followed. Erick the Pony bouncer became Erick the Fast Lane manager. Tony Pallagrosi left the Jukes and booked shows at the Fast Lane. Soon Springsteen and E Street were hanging there too. And a young kid from Sayreville, John Bongiovi, was drawing a crowd.

Bob Santelli: By 1979, the Fast Lane opens up. The Pony now is not as significant or as hip as it was, because now the new wave is happening. And that whole new wave sound is going to the Fast Lane.

Jean Mikle: The Pony was not doing as much national music as the Fast Lane in the early eighties. And that's why the Fast Lane was kind of where the cutting-edge music scene kind of migrated over there. And then Bruce started going to the Fast Lane.

Bruce Springsteen: Fast Lane is where I saw Sam & Dave. Absolutely. It was Fast Lane. I cried my eyes out. I cried my eyes out in the back of the room, because of how good they were and how small the crowd was. Sam & Dave were at their greatest.

Sam Moore: I didn't pay him attention. I didn't know he was coming. I didn't even know nothing about Springsteen. I knew this rock and roller at one time, he was who he was. But I didn't know, before he started going to the stuff that he does today, I didn't know anything about that. And he didn't know at the time, when we locked eyes, he did not know at the time that I was on drugs. He really didn't know. Just to show you: as time went on, he had a song he wrote for me. And the word got back that I was, let's call it like it is, a junkie. And they said it hurt him so bad, so he gave the song, which was a hit, to Gary U.S. Bonds.

Bruce Springsteen: Stevie and I happened to catch them both [at the Fast Lane] and at the Satellite Lounge in Fort Dix, New Jersey, at the same time. And they were just still at their peak. So I cried from the fact that they didn't have any audience, and they should have. And it was simply majestic. That stayed with me.

Sam Moore: Years later, I found out that every time we played here— and if you ask me how many times, I don't know, it was several times, I believe—but I found out that there were times Bruce would just stay at the end of the bar and watch Sam & Dave. I didn't know that. Most of the time, we would do the show. We were not that popular at that time.

Billy Hector: The original scene moved over to the Fast Lane for a little bit when the Fast Lane was happening. That was a different story over there.

Tony Pallagrosi: Fast Lane was the real original-music nightclub. The Pony wasn't. The Pony was a Top 30 club after the Jukes left. The Pony would have a national act on occasion. But the Fast Lane was really purely a national act, regional music club. And I started booking bands there in the eighties.

Willie Nile: I played the Fast Lane, that was after my first record, in 1980. And it was fascinating. That area around the shore, it was fascinating to me. It was a real music community. You know, my record was on Arista Records. And there was a lot of hype around my record. Next Big Thing kind of nonsense. And you could tell it was a music scene down there. They cared about the music.

John Cafferty: We were playing in New Haven and a guy came to see us play, and asked us if we wanted to play down in Asbury Park. And we said, "Yeah." And he booked us at the Fast Lane, which was next to the bowling alley. We started out at the Fast Lane, and I know Johnny played at the Pony.

Eileen Chapman: The Fast Lane were the first ones to really do national touring bands. They had U2. Elvis Costello. They had bands on the way up. Pony was doing a lot of cover bands or original bands that had an R&B flavor. So it was really a different kind of mix, but the clubs were open till three in the morning, so most of the people I know, we'd come out, we'd hit the Pony, we'd go over to the Fast Lane, we'd go back to the Pony.

Tony Shanahan: Memorial Day weekend in 1981, U2 played the Fast Lane. I saw them, I think one of their first shows they played at the Ritz, so me and a bunch of my friends, we went to the Fast Lane to see them play [again]. They played what was their big hit, "I Will Follow." They played that at the beginning of the show and then they played it again at the end. That was their thing, I guess, back then. It was like, "You guys want a hit." When the show was done, we hung out with them. We walked over to the Boardwalk with them. They were all in a station wagon. We drove them out of Asbury so they could get back on the parkway.

Erick W. Henderiks: I remember the night that I told Butch that I was leaving the Pony to manage the Fast Lane. I said, "I just wanted to be fair and give you two weeks notice." He said to me, "You can leave right now." I said, "You want me to leave right now?" He says, "Yes, get the hell out of here. You're a traitor." I said, "Why am I a traitor?" I said, "I have a better opportunity, work creative." He said, "You can leave right now." I started to leave and then Jack came out and I said, "Oh, geez, now I'm going to have to deal with Jack." Big Monster Yeti, the Yeti from the Asbury Jetty. Jack was actually very nice. He says, "You know what, Erick? I understand. I wish you all the luck in the world."

Matt Pinfield: The Fast Lane was this club that was down the street, and that was where I saw everybody from U2 to Joe Jackson to . . . I mean, I saw Stray Cats where Bruce actually came over and sang "Fever" with them that night.

Pete Llewellyn: The Fast Lane had as many famous people as we did, I'll guarantee you that. That helped us. If they had someone big, that place was small, it'd probably be full. The overflow would go, "Well, let's go to the Pony and see what's there," if they couldn't get in.

Peter Mantas: This was the land of dreams for John Bongiovi. We were sixteen-year-old kids coming down here from Sayreville, thirty miles. We used to just come down here on nights there was no gigs, hang out, Fast Lane, Pony, Jefferson Hotel. My first gig in Asbury Park, with Atlantic City Expressway, was at the Stone Pony. One gig and one gig only because the second gig, the bass player got caught with a fake ID. So we couldn't play that night. Went to the Fast Lane. So, that's why John's career was basically Fast Lane.

Erick W. Henderiks: John Bongiovi came to me [at the Fast Lane] with the cassette tape. I think he gave it to me or it was his mother. His mother was very concerned about her son. It was probably annoying to him. He gave me a cassette. I listened to it with Jim D'Antonio. We said, "Hey, we got nothing else going on." I think it was Wednesday nights. "We got nothing going on. Let the kid play." You had a band like Atlantic City, or the Expressway, some local kids. Some kids from Sayreville, yes. They played and I liked it. We said, "Okay." Then slowly over time, he built a little bit of a crowd. They started building a crowd.

Stan Goldstein: I was on break from college; it was a cold night during the week. [A friend] said, "Go to the Fast Lane, check out this band, Atlantic City Expressway. They play Springsteen and Southside Johnny covers." I went with a few friends. Bar was maybe a hundred people in there, and I just remember this young, energetic singer running around the stage, and Bruce was in the bar that night, but he was hanging in the back. All of a sudden, the band did "Promised Land," and Bruce jumped onstage maybe for a minute and sang part of "Promised Land," and then jumped off. That's all he did. There are pictures of it though. It wasn't until six, seven years later, Billy Smith said to me, "You were at the Fast Lane that night when Bruce played with Atlantic City Expressway." I said, "Yes." He goes, "You know who the lead singer of Atlantic City Expressway is?" I said, "No." He goes, "That was John Bongiovi in high school."

Peter Mantas: Three summers every Sunday, always opening up for all the big acts, whether it was John Bongiovi and the Wild Ones, because the Expressway didn't last that long. That was a ten-piece horn band. It was the Asbury Park sound. Horns, doing Bruce and Southside Johnny songs and "Mustang Sally," and you know, all the R&B. Sweet soul music.

John Cafferty: When we first started playing there, there weren't that many people there, the first couple of times. John Bongiovi was opening the show. He had a band called the Atlantic City Expressway, big horn band, but he was a kid. And that's what was going on the first couple of times we played there. After that, the word got out that the local stars like these guys from up the street, and they might be in to say hello, and get up onstage. So after that, the places were packed. And it really didn't hurt to have the endorsement of those guys with the local fans. And they came to see us as part of the scene down there, so to speak. We were the long-lost cousins from up the road.

John Eddie: The Fast Lane, we played every Wednesday night for one summer. There was a time where the Pony went this way, and then the Fast Lane was the place for original music and stuff. We played every Wednesday night with John Bongiovi and the Wild Ones. We used to have a double bill there. I never got as big as those two guys, but it was that era, there was a lot of interest on the shore, and it was all because of Bruce.

Tracey Story Prince: There was a different set of people that were at the Fast Lane. . . . There were some other really good musicians that used to be more at the Fast Lane. That's where Lance let Bon Jovi open up for him in the Expressway.

Jack Roig: Bon Jovi, he was mostly at the Fast Lane, he started over there. Unfortunately. That's one we missed. U2 played over there too at the Fast Lane and we missed them. But Jon would come and hang out in the Pony, and his wife, Dorothea.

Erick W. Henderiks: I watched out for Jon and told his folks. "Don't worry. He's sixteen, I'll watch him. The kid won't go wild here." Saw him drinking a Heineken he had snuck in one night. I punished him by locking him in a cold box for a while.

Peter Mantas: We were friends with all these people, you know. I still see these guys nowadays, the older guys, and you know, "Hey, you guys were nice to us." Some of them weren't, but some of these guys sort of took us under their wing. The George Theisses, you know, Vini Lopez, Garry Tallent, Johny Luraschi, Steve Schraeger, Billy Hector. There was a whole scene going on down here. We were sixteen. These guys were probably twenty-seven, twenty-eight.

Bob Santelli: There was a signal where, when John Bongiovi was like fifteen, sixteen years old, if ABC [Alcoholic Beverage Control] people came in, he knew where to go, and they knew how to get him the hell out of there. But the women loved him. I mean, they loved him. And that was a Jukes cover band for crying out loud.

Tracey Story Prince: I hung out with Bruce and Bongiovi in the Fast Lane dressing room once with Lance, and there was a bar called the Jefferson. They rolled, they did tumble-saults from the Fast Lane to the Jefferson. Bruce and Lance. All the way across the street through traffic. Yes, that was a fun night. Just because they decided to stay drunk and decided they were going to do somersaults.

Richie "La Bamba" Rosenberg: The Fast Lane was two blocks over on Fourth Ave. That opened up . . . I was already in the Jukes for a year, maybe close to two years before that opened up. But that started to take some business from Jack and Butch.

Lance Larson: We used to play the Pony and the Fast Lane. I told Butch, "I need more days, I got to earn." He goes, "Yeah, go ahead." And he never gave me no shit for it. I did the Fast Lane, then we'd walk down the street and play the Pony, and back and forth. Jack really didn't like the idea that we had to do it. But it got to a point where he understood what I was saying.

Tony Amato: After we played a concert at Monmouth College, it was time to go to the Pony to go get a drink. I didn't make it past the front door until Jack grabbed me and planted me on top of the cigarette machine by the door, asked me if I was trying to start a war. I asked him, "What the fuck are you talking about?" Next thing I know, I was thrown through the door. Remember there was a piece of wood on the

Stone Pony door at the bottom? Yeah. Well, I made that. Jack threw me through there because supposedly there was an ad saying that we were going to go play the Fast Lane. I never said we were going there, but one of the guys in my band said, "I don't know. Ask Tony. He runs the band." So we got fired from the Pony. "You guys will never fucking play here again!"

Bob Santelli: By 1981, '82, new wave is the music. And the Fast Lane owned that. They just owned that.

Dan Beck: I was still renting the place down in Belmar, at Belmar with my friends. So Steve [Forbert] came down one weekend and hung out, went to the beach. It's drinking and cards and parties and the whole thing. So the next weekend, I'm down there, and there's a knock at the door. It's Friday night, dinnertime, and it's Forbert. He said, "Hey, I just happened to be down here." He said, "There's this girl playing at the Fast Lane. You've got to see her." So he said, "She's playing at such-and-such a time." So my friend Tony and I jumped in the car after dinner, and we drove back up to Asbury Park and went to the Fast Lane to see Cyndi Lauper. So I went back to the office the next Monday and went straight to Lennie Petze, who had taken Steve Popovich's place as head of A&R. I said, "Oh my God. I saw this girl. You've got to sign her." He said, "You're kidding me." He said, "I'm talking to her." I said, "Well, if you sign her, I'll be the product manager." That ultimately is what happened.

Tony Pallagrosi: When [the Fast Lane] kind of went down the tubes, I had to stiff Beaver Brown one weekend. Our owner Phil, who passed away, he used to take all the money. He'd come in, take all the money. Leave me with a little bit. And this had been happening and been getting worse. We'd been hit by the Monmouth County marshals, had our registers emptied because of bills that were owed. It was pretty crazy. When I was running the place, I'd have to put my money in to open the doors. I used to have to go buy liquor from liquor stores because the liquor distributors wouldn't do business with us. So you go to Buy Rite, or whatever. Go with a van. They'd throw cases of beer out the back door, load them into the van, whatever we needed. Take it back to the Fast Lane and get it loaded in. I'd pay him in cash. This was all illegal.

Tony Pallagrosi: When the Fast Lane closed, John Eddie and Beaver Brown went to the Pony. And then the Pony started doing the national acts on the club level that the Fast Lane had been doing.

The House That Bruce Built

A bar, just like a stage, can be a sanctuary. A refuge where comfort comes from the familiar. Bruce Springsteen, Pony regular. A moniker first stamped in the mid-seventies, waltzing across the dance floor and belting out "Havin' a Party" with Stevie and Southside. For a brief era in the late seventies, Springsteen was at the Fast Lane more frequently. But in the early eighties, with his fame soaring after *The River*, that reputation as a Pony regular resumed, as did his spot at the back bar. "I Heard Bruce Might Show Up" became the town motto. His surprise jams onstage became almost routine. But the frenzy never faded.

Bruce Springsteen: Where I grew up meant something to me. I liked the clubs, I liked the little towns. I liked the characters that were there. I felt safe, I felt appreciated. People kind of watched over you, and it was just a lovely atmosphere, I found. I was still young. I was in my thirties. *Born in the U.S.A.*, I was only thirty-four. And so I was going out, I had my white pickup truck, and I hopped in that old junker and I took it down to the Pony. And that's where I spent my Fridays and Sundays and I had no interest in what was going on in New York City or LA. I always said, "No, no, no." This is interesting. This is interesting to me. These people are interesting to me. This place is interesting to me. What happens here, I think, matters. What we do here matters. You're sustaining a local scene. Even though you've had tremendous success, you are still part of the local operation of a local band, serving its community, which I always thought was a great thing to do, and a lot of fun. And I enjoyed remaining a part of that. So it was a no-brainer for me. It was just what I wanted and liked to do and what I felt safe, comfortable, and like myself.

Bobby Bandiera: I broke off from Holme to go in a band called Cats on a Smooth Surface. And that's when I started playing the Pony pretty much every week, whatever night. There was some Wednesdays, there was some Sundays.

Glen Burtnik: I had done this stint with the Broadway show *Beatlemania*. I did a Paul McCartney thing. I was done with that, I left that, and I came back home to New Jersey. I needed a gig and this cover band Cats on a Smooth Surface called. I thought it was a cool place. There was this Bruce thing about it. This is post–*Born to Run* and stuff. There was the Bruce and Asbury Jukes connection. It seemed it was a cool place.

Bobby Bandiera: Now I'm doing my thing with that band, and we're trying to get some more original material together. It didn't happen for us in that regard, but Bruce started popping. This was 1981, and I remember the first night I met him, and it wasn't the first night I'd seen him there, but it was the first night I met him. I said, "Hey." He says, "I'm Bruce." I said, "Yep. How you doing, brother?" And he says, "You mind if I come up and play?" I said, "No. Sure. Come up." It's the summer of '81. He started coming up, having a good time, having a blast. Crowd was always electric when he showed up.

Bruce Springsteen: Cats drew a lot of people. A lot of people. A lot of the second-tier bands, other than Southside, drew a lot of fans. I mean, the Pony was full very often, for just local groups. It was a scene. Everybody knew everybody else. It was a real legitimate scene. There was a group of people that went to that club and they went there pretty exclusively, with the rare exception. And it was very valuable to have at the time.

Bobby Bandiera: He would come, if it wasn't every week, it was almost every other week.

Bruce Springsteen: There was a small group of songs we knew and would tend to sing together, or just really easy stuff that came out of the blue. "Hey, let's do 'Long Tall Sally.'" I just liked to play, go down to the bar, go and sit in. And they played very well. And so I just always liked playing. Played every weekend there almost.

Glen Burtnik: Bruce would call whatever the hell he wanted to call out. The first time I played with him, it was "Twist and Shout." This was my first time meeting him, and he sang a verse, and then he pointed to me. It was my turn to sing a verse, which now when I look back on it, I think it was just his way of checking me out or something.

Ernest Carter: Bruce used to come down to gigs with the Fairlanes and jam with us.

Eileen Chapman: On the nights that Bruce or somebody played, there was this whole line of people at that phone right next to the restroom doors, because there were no cell phones then.

Tracey Story Prince: The pay phone, it was in or next to the ladies' room, so you didn't need a crowd when you're trying to get to the bathroom then. It was right there in the ladies' room hallway.

Joe Prinzo: Before the internet, there was a phone booth in the back of the Pony, that everybody would use to call their friends and you'd call one or two friends and then they'd call one or two friends. "Hey, man, he's here tonight. Let's go."

Stan Goldstein: There was also a phone booth on the boardwalk, Second Avenue and Boardwalk, right across from the Pony. That's back when they would stamp your hands and let you back in.

Jean Mikle: The phone tree, I found out about it from a bunch of girls that would go to Cats every week and we would do Dance Till You Drop every Sunday. We used to call the one girl Kitty. I don't know if that was her real name, but that's what we were told. She was one of the people that started the phone tree. I remember I had the number and I would try constantly.

Kyle Brendle: Those Sundays, Bruce was just there. He didn't have extra people with him or nothing, no. He'd just be there.

Bruce Springsteen: You'd come in through the kitchen. Well, they have a sort of a kitchen. It's sort of a kitchen, but you'd come in through the back door. They never had any real backstage space.

Pete Llewellyn: It would be a Sunday night and there'd be a hundred and fifty people in there all mainly in the back bar, all locals, waitresses, bartenders from other establishments. Bruce would come in, and within forty minutes there'd be four hundred people in there. How that happened, it was a mystery to me. If Bruce didn't show up, it would stay the same hundred fifty, two hundred people. If he showed up, in one night when it happened, I watched the pay phone. That pay phone in the ladies' room right before you walked into the ladies' room, when he showed up, was in constant use. From the second he walked in, it would stay in use. The only way they were communicating was through the pay phone, and it worked. One pay phone, there's no beepers, there was no cell phones. Somehow they knew and that place will get packed. People would walk to other bars and say, "Hey, Bruce is at the Pony," and that bar would unload. There was a bar called the Golddigger, it might have forty people in it. If Bruce walked in the Pony, it's going to have zero people in it in a minute.

Jean Mikle: I'd see him, and I'd run in there, waiting for the phone, and you're like, "I got to get on the phone."

Eileen Chapman: There was a clock in the kitchen of Mrs. Jay's, and it was like eleven o'clock, and I took the clock and spun it around, and I said, "Okay, two o'clock, last call." And everybody's like, there's food falling out of their mouth. They're like, "Wait a minute. Wait a minute. I just saw what you did." I said, "No, we're closing up." And so we threw everybody out, we all closed up, and all of us went into the Pony to watch the show, to watch Bruce play with Cats. And then it turned into a just about weekly thing. And we would shut early, and go on over and hang out in the back bar and watch the show.

Tracey Story Prince: He'd play every single Sunday and hang out at the back bar. One Sunday, I was sitting with him and I wanted to dance. I said, "Could you just stay here and watch my pocketbook?" I danced for four songs. I came back and he was still sitting there. I was like, "Aw."

Stan Levinstone: Bruce played on Sundays. He's playing almost every week or at least a month or whatever. When he wasn't here Butch was still charging ten dollars to get in. It was a potluck. "If Bruce is here, great; if you're not, you're screwed."

Judy DeNucci: I had a bouncer all the time. He would stand at that back door next to the bar, so if I had any problems or if I needed stuff, he would call somebody to go get the beer or whatever, but there was always somebody stationed there. And when Bruce would come into the back, especially the later days, he would always have his own. Not his own, but one of our bouncers would be assigned to just follow him just because.

Tony Shanahan: In the early eighties, I had a band. We played at the Pony and we got a few better gigs, I think. We opened for either it was Joe Grushecky or John Cafferty. We were in a little room in the back. All of a sudden—we were sitting there after we had played. The door just opened and Springsteen stuck his head in. He just went, "Good set, guys." Then he just closed the door and he walked off. That was our big thing. I remember we were on a buzz that night because he had said that to us.

Tony Amato: Anything after '79, it's every night, it's all Bruce. Bruce, Bruce, Bruce. Go to Asbury to see if Bruce will come in and jam with them.

Eileen Chapman: Those nights were crazy. People were dancing on chairs, and on the Stone Pony fireplace, and everywhere else. It was a lot of fun. And that was a time when Asbury Park was really starting to go downhill. Things were closing down on the boardwalk. All the business had moved out of downtown, because Seaview Mall was built. Everybody went. And so it brought people back to Asbury Park in a time when crowds were starting to diminish. So it was a really good thing for the city, and for the music scene. And brought the attention back to the music scene and to the Stone Pony.

Bruce Haring: Whenever he'd show up at a club, it was big news. That's what we would write about, and that's what people liked. You're chasing a phantom. It was all up to his whim as to where and how he showed up. It wasn't like there was an internet site where you have a calendar of potential sightings or anything like that, but there were always rumors that Bruce was going to play there that night. It's like a Kenny Rogers Roaster, where they always said, "Kenny is coming in next week." That sort of same thing. I'm sure a lot of that was the clubs themselves trying to get extra bodies in there, hyping it up.

Butch Pielka: I never advertised Bruce's name and I've never paid him a penny to play here. It's funny. A lot of people even think he owns part of the Pony.

Jean Mikle: When Bruce was playing, a lot of times he wouldn't go on until one thirty. So you couldn't never leave. If he was in the bar and you knew he was there, you couldn't leave because heaven forbid you left right at one o'clock or one thirty. And then he went on at ten of two. And now you've missed it.

Tracey Story Prince: I've worked many of those Bruce and Cats nights. The only thing I didn't like about it was because they would play until four in the morning. I was supposed to be done, and I'm like, "I can't leave the bar." It's every Sunday, so I was like, "I'm going home." Thank God my bosses were cool and were like, "Okay, just have a drink and just sit back and wait it out." I was able to get up on the bar. They say, "Don't let anybody on the bar," so I would stand on the bar and make sure they didn't get up. I always had the best view.

Eileen Chapman: E Streeters came. Clarence would go. Max would occasionally show up.

Ernest Carter: One night he came in with his band. Max had a problem getting in or making it down on time or something. And Bruce was like to me, "Okay, let's do this." He'd just show up, do his thing, and everybody would crowd the stage as soon as he shows up and it's on.

Bobby Bandiera: Bruce even came to a rehearsal. "Where do you guys rehearse?" I said, "We rehearse over at the airport, on Route 34." He says, "Well, I'll come by." I said, "What?" He did, and it was some kind of anniversary night at the Pony. He says, "I'll come up and play that show with you, but let's rehearse." I said, "Okay." He was doing the Detroit

Medley thing, the Mitch Ryder thing, when he was on the road. "Let's do that." I said, "Yeah, sure. Sure." So we learned that.

Bruce Springsteen: Most of these bands were cover bands. Southside played originals, but almost everybody else . . . Well, some of the other bands played some originals too, actually. There was still a lot of covering going on.

Kyle Brendle: They did some national acts, some tours here and there, but not a lot of them. It was mostly filled with regional bands and the top cover bands. There's Farm, Nines, Holme, Baby Blue. I could go on and on. Salty Dog. There's so many of them. Cahoots, Lance Larson. It wasn't a concert venue at that point. It was a bar with a great stage.

Richie "La Bamba" Rosenberg: In I think it was '82, I wasn't with the Disciples; Steven let the horn section go. And I was just hanging around the area and I didn't have a band. I wasn't in the Jukes either at that time 'cause I was with Diana Ross for a couple years, and then Steven called to do the Disciples. And then after that period, I was hanging at the Pony and Butch came up to me and said, "Hey, I'm going to have Wednesday nights open if you want to put a band together. Just what do you want to do?" I said, "Yeah, it sounds like a good idea." And Lee Mrowicki came up with the name the Hubcaps. So we called it La Bamba and the Hubcaps and started playing on Wednesday nights. I think we eventually got moved to Thursday nights.

Glen Burtnik: I left Cats and I joined La Bamba in the Hubcaps. Cats was a four- or five-piece group, guitars, keyboard, drums. La Bamba, he had come from the Jukes and it was horn players. It wasn't the first horn band I was ever in, but it was a pretty good one. Because it was an offshoot, so to speak, of the Asbury Jukes, it was a little higher on the rung, a cool factor or something. Musically, we weren't doing any Eurythmics or John Cougar or any of that. It was more R&B stuff.

Gary U.S. Bonds: I think Kyle booked me in with La Bamba and the Hubcaps. When I got there, they gave me all the history and I went, "Oh, that's cool. I didn't know what it means, but that's cool." Jersey has always been great for me. I don't know what happened. I would imagine because I was supposedly very, very good friends with Bruce and they just took me in as "Okay, you are welcome." In fact, a lot of people still think I'm from Jersey.

Mark Pender: Bruce would show up and sit in with La Bamba and the Hubcaps. And suddenly, I remember, there were a couple of bands. When Bruce showed up, guys who weren't good players could sometimes magically become good when he hit the stage. It was this, "Man, I've never heard you play that well. You usually kind of suck. And tonight you're like . . . You've got your shit together. What happened?"

Glen Burtnik: There was one story I recall playing with the Hubcaps, right next to the stage, there's a door that goes onto the sidewalk. I don't know if we took a break or what, but I walked offstage, opened the door, and there's Bruce walking down the street. I said, "Bruce, come on. You want to play?" He said, "Yes."

Nils Lofgren: Jamming with La Bamba, Ed Manion, Mark Pender on horns, was exciting. A few years later, they joined E Street on the *Tunnel of Love* tour, which was wonderful.

Erick W. Henderiks: Bruce was cool, though. He never just hopped on. He always asked because I think a musician thing is you don't want to share your stage unless you invite somebody on. You don't want to share your stage. Bruce knew that. He was always very polite about that. People say, "You want to come on?" "Yes, you sure it's okay? I don't want to—" "Yes, Bruce, come on."

Lee Mrowicki: That's kind of like, you know, that's going back to the Upstage days, where everybody knew the same songs, or you could learn 'em real easy and they were good enough players to be able to do that, and that kind of transferred over to the Pony too, the late-night jams. That was kind of unique to every place, because no other place really had that except the Pony. And especially like, Sunday nights was a night where musicians mostly didn't work, so they would be coming here to see their friends and to see their friends play. And some of them even went onstage, like Bruce. And that was kind of unique in the industry. We used to have people that come from Washington, DC, drive up and drive back the same night, and then go to work the next day. I always thought that the song "Dancing in the Dark" is actually written about going to the Pony.

Jack Roig: I came off the train one night, and I'm walking down the street. It's a weeknight. Nobody outside. It was early. And I walked in. Who's behind the front bar? Bruce. He's behind the bar, just ripped, and he's the bartender. The actual bartender, who was my special lady, she walked out behind the bar and let him bartend. I don't know how much money he cost me, but it was worth it. It was fun. Yeah, I mean, he had given the house away and he was having a ball. I don't think he got up and played after that though. I think he was smart enough not to try.

Bruce Springsteen: I started to jump behind the bar and I wasn't much of a bartender, but I'd serve up the beers and just have fun with the fans, and just enjoy myself. [My signature] was beer. With a Jack Daniel's on the side, maybe.

Southside Johnny: Bruce guest-bartending meant all shots of tequila. And I'd scoff and said, "I don't drink tequila." And then Eileen would come and bring me a shot of whiskey.

Max Weinberg: I do remember Bruce buying shots for the whole place, standing on top of the back bar at one point.

Judy DeNucci: One night, he was playing with Cats on a Sunday night as he used to do often, and it was my birthday. He said, "This goes out to Judy for her birthday. Happy birthday, Judy!" from the stage. Then he came behind my bar and started bartending. I said, "What are you doing? Look at all these people." It was like five deep around the bar and everybody's got their own hands raised and everything. I'm saying, "Nobody wants me to give them the drinks. They want you." He's yelling, "I can only make beer!" People that regularly drank mixed drinks were ordering beer. I just stood at the register and he said, "Where are the Budweisers?" I was showing him where the different beers were. He was just handing people beer and handed me the money and say, "This is for two Buds." I'd bring it up and I'd hand him the change, and he goes, "Don't you want to give this to Judy for her birthday?" Well, they wouldn't say no to Bruce, so I'd put it in my tip jar. He would be on my bar I'd say probably a half hour and I made five hundred dollars in a half hour.

Erick W. Henderiks: He could only make maybe four drinks: gin and tonic, a rum and Coke, a vodka and something, a glass of water, and a beer. That was his repertoire. You were getting something, but it could've tasted like rocket fuel or it could've tasted like water. He wouldn't charge you or he'd charge you the wrong price or something. He felt at home and we laughed about it. It's just another sideshow in a circus.

Butch Pielka: It's a place he can come to and not have girls rip clothes off his back. It's comfortable for him, with no security problems.

Erick W. Henderiks: We let him do whatever the hell he wanted, pretty much, unless he was breaking the law. He felt comfortable there and we wanted to make sure we had a place that he could do that.

Jack Roig: He never asked for anything. But one night, it must've been crazy. I don't remember why. He said, "I got to go hide in the office, okay?" I said, "Yeah, go ahead." And then I thought, Oh no, the dog. I had a big dog. About a hundred and five pounds, fully trained Dobie. So I ran back and I said, "Ramel. He's okay." That was his name: Ramel. I came back maybe half an hour later, and he was just sitting on the couch. He's got his legs out and crossed. And the dog's chewing on his boot. I said, "What the fuck are you doing?" He said, "Just enjoying myself."

Bruce Springsteen: It's the old thing Dylan said. "Where are you most comfortable?" He says, "Well, anyplace nobody's reminding me of who I am." So there's some of that, and I thought it was pretty good for that. Some people came up and at times were crazy, but so what? It's part of the job.

Jean Mikle: It wasn't that unusual to see him out and about in those days. He was out and about all the time. But the big thing is you want him to play. I was in there one night, Gary U.S. Bonds show. I think that was '84, and he actually came in the back door, and apparently, some girl jumped on his back, and he turned around and walked out.

Eileen Chapman: Then we started to get the Bruce watchers. You'd watch them walk in and they'd walk from the front to the back and they'd look around, look around, look around. Walk back to the back bar, look around, look around, look around, and then go back up again. So you could definitely tell a Bruce watcher. And there were times when Bruce would come in and he'd come back to the back bar and this whole group of people would just follow him pretending they weren't looking at him but looking at him out of the corner of their eyes. And it would be this whole mass of people. There was this drummer Steve Schraeger, who kind of resembled Bruce. If you don't know Bruce that well, you would think Steve could be Bruce. Bruce might go back in the dressing room. He'd take Steve and say, "Go up to the front bar," and Steve would go up to the front bar and this whole mass of people would follow him up to the front bar so they'd get out of our way and we could have our back bar again.

Steve Schraeger: They all thought I looked like Bruce. My hair. My beard. For some reason, they thought I looked like him. I mean, I was even at a bar in Long Branch one time, and people thought I was him, they were buying me drinks. Bruce said he won a Steve Schraeger look-alike contest. I even had to show a guy my driver's license one time. He didn't believe me. I said, "I'm not him. Here's my ID."

Jack Roig: We used to get mail from all over the world. Bruce Springsteen, USA. And it'd be delivered to us. Yeah. I bet we would get fifty, a hundred posts a week. And he'd come in and we'd say "Here's your mail."

Jean Mikle: I was working at the Freehold weekly, which doesn't exist anymore, called the *Colonial Free Press*. That was the first time I ever saw Bruce tourists. So I was working there in '84, and Bruce was on the *Born in the U.S.A.* tour, and some guy walked into our office from Germany with a camera asking where Bruce's houses were. And the only one I knew at that time was 68 South Street, which was right down the street from our office. And I'm like, "I really don't know anything else. You can walk down there." I'm like, "Holy shit. People are coming here for Bruce." Traveling here. That's the first time I noticed that.

Pete Llewellyn: He had a garage apartment deal and he was writing *Born in the U.S.A.*, and about the time, maybe early [1984], I don't remember if there were five people sitting there that were with me. The Pony closed, Sunday night, three o'clock, we threw everyone out. Bruce, it was a snowy night, got his guitar, and we sat by the fireplace, there were ten of us, and he played songs that he was going to put on the *Born in the U.S.A.* album. He played it just for us. Now if you want to talk about a true, real unplugged, it doesn't apply anymore, and I know every single person who was sitting by the fireplace, and he would play a song and then we would talk about it.

Lance Larson: The red hat on the cover of *Born in the U.S.A.* was, the red hat was a gift that was given to me by a friend of mine. It came with a Rembass fishing rod, or reel. And Bruce and me were out one night and we came back to my apartment in Wanamassa so I could show him some new guitars and amps. And when we left, me and Bruce were leaving and Bruce said, "Man, I like that hat." And I said, "Here, you can have it." The next thing I know, it was a few months later or maybe a year later and he came in and said he was looking for me. And he came into the place up the street from the Pony, and he goes, "Yeah, I've got a surprise for you." And I said, "What?" He goes, "The red hat that you gave me," he said, "it was on MTV." I didn't find out until later that night. I went home and I turned on the TV and MTV was on, and they showed him in "Born in the U.S.A." He had it in his back pocket.

Richie "La Bamba" Rosenberg: Cats on a Smooth Surface was always, that was always fun to get up and play with them. And then we started doing that on Sunday nights with them, and then Patti would come in and Patti and I would sing a couple duets together.

Patti Scialfa: Bobby said, "Let me learn a bunch of songs so we can, on the weekends, do a bunch of songs together." So they learned a bunch of songs that I could sing, some old-time girl-group songs, and some R&B. Not that much, but enough to go down and have a lot of fun. We got into the Ronettes songs, the Crystals, all of that kind of stuff. Some Carole King stuff, some Etta James, "Time Is on My Side." Did it like her. She did it before the Stones. Just stuff like that. Whatever was floating around that was fun and sexy to sing. Just picking them out and learning them; there's no great thought behind it. Let me put it this way: You're not rehearsing. You're jamming.

Southside Johnny and the Asbury Jukes, with Billy Rush on guitar, playing one of multiple sets during a 1977 show. (Michael J. Brazinski)

The scene at the Stone Pony bar in the later years of the Butch and Jack era. (Keith Meyers/*The New York Times*/Redux)

Ronnie Spector and Southside Johnny share a mic at a show in 1977.
(Michael J. Brazinski)

Bruce (*center*) joins Southside Johnny and the Asbury Jukes for their famous live broadcast in May 1976. (Richard E. Aaron/Redferns)

Stevie Van Zandt (*right*) with Donnie Bertelson, lead singer of the
Shots, backstage at the Pony, 1977. (Lewis Bloom)

Bruce joins Bob Campanell and
the Shakes to sing "Sea Cruise"
in 1977. (Peter Howes)

Lance Larson playing with Cold Blast
and Steel in an undated photo.
(Lewis Bloom)

Bruce and Southside Johnny share a microphone during a 1977 concert. (Peter Howes)

Bruce backstage at the Pony, 1977. (Lewis Bloom)

Bruce Springsteen, Clarence Clemons, and Nils Lofgren at the famous *Born in the U.S.A.* show at the Pony in 1984. (Lewis Bloom)

Bruce and Patti dancing at the Pony in the summer of 1987.
(Debra L. Rothenberg)

Bruce corrals Stevie Van Zandt at a surprise appearance in 1987.
(Debra L. Rothenberg)

Springsteen returns to the Pony in 1987 in his guest role with Cats on a Smooth Surface. (Lewis Bloom)

Patti Scialfa joins Levon Helm at the Pony to sing "The Weight" in 1987. (Debra L. Rothenberg)

Bruce joins the 3M union activists onstage at the Stone Pony.
(Stanley Fischer)

An oversold Stone Pony crowd for the 3M benefit show. (Stanley Fischer)

Cyndi Lauper at the Pony in 1989. (Danny Clinch)

The Smithereens return to the Pony in 1987. (Danny Clinch)

Warren Zevon at the Pony in 1989. (Danny Clinch)

Bruce Springsteen (*center*) and Joe Grushecky (*left*) return to the Pony in 1995. (Danny Clinch)

The Warped Tour, set up behind the Pony, in 1997. (Mark Sullivan)

Courtney Love of Hole on the Pony Big Top stage in 1994. (Mark Sullivan)

The final Fury of Five show at the Pony in the late 1990s. (Mark Sullivan)

Bruce (*center*) and Southside Johnny (*right*) return to the Pony for a fundraiser in 2011. (Danny Clinch)

Bruce and his mother, Adele Springsteen, in 2011. (Danny Clinch)

Patti Smith donning a "Happy Birthday" crown at a show at the Pony in 2001. (Danny Clinch)

Patti Smith at the Pony in 2001. (Danny Clinch)

A young Jonas Brothers play at the Pony in 2005.
(Robert Garbowsky/Jonas Brothers)

Michael J. Fox (*center*) joins Bruce and Joe Grushecky at a Light of Day benefit concert in 2003. (Michael J. Brazinski)

The Gaslight Anthem headline at the Pony in 2008. (Ricardo Saporta)

Pete Steinkopf from the Bouncing Souls is joined by Frank Iero from
My Chemical Romance at the 2007 Home for the Holidays show.
(Ricardo Saporta)

Slightly Stoopid plays the Summer Stage. (Doug Hac/Slightly Stoopid)

The Gaslight Anthem on the Summer Stage in 2013. (Danny Clinch)

Mike McCready (*right*) and Danny Clinch play the Ocean Avenue
Stomp superjam after Sea.Hear.Now. (Michael Ryan Kravetsky)

A sight that would be
unimaginable years ago:
the sold-out, packed
beach of Asbury Park
during Sea.Hear.Now.
(Kevin Doherty)

Richie "La Bamba" Rosenberg: We'd do "Ain't No Mountain High Enough," "I'm Gonna Make You Love Me," like that.

Patti Scialfa: Delving into all those catalogs with all the great girl groups, I'd never gone there before. That was a introduction for me. And so it did, when I did my *Rumble Doll* record, my first record, I had this song called "As Long as I (Can Be with You)." That was a couple nods to that kind of girl-group thing. So it did influence me. Well, I always liked those groups. They were the first women that I heard on my transistor radio when I was a kid bicycling. You could take your radio and put it around your handlebars. And that was magical and mystical to me. Again, it's like, "Okay, I love what they're singing about."

Lee Mrowicki: Patti was good friends with Bobby Bandiera and with Richie Rosenberg. She would play with Bobby's band, Cats on a Smooth Surface, at the end of the night. She used to do "Boy from New York City" and a few other songs, oldies.

Bruce Springsteen: I met my wife [at the Pony]. We actually bumped into each other on occasion a few times previously, but not significantly. I saw Patti before the *Born in the U.S.A.* tour, and that's how she got in the band.

Patti Scialfa: Do you know how many times I have corrected that, when he's telling this story? Even to our friends, sometimes I'm going, "I got in the band? You asked me to be in the band." I wasn't knocking on the door of the band trying to get in.

Pete Llewellyn: He was sitting at my bar the night he first laid eyes on Patti. He was just about to go to the back bar. I can even remember what he was drinking. He was drinking kamikaze on the rocks and I was talking to him a little about, I think, softball or something insignificant. Cats called up, and said they were going to have a special guest. Of course, everyone thought it was Bruce, and it was Patti Scialfa. She went up and probably did three songs with him. Bruce was just fixed on her; he couldn't get his eyes off her.

Bruce Springsteen: She came out and played onstage with, it might have been Bobby Bandiera or, I forget which local band was playing. But she came out and played the Exciters' hit "Tell Him," and she was very striking right from the beginning.

Pete Llewellyn: When she got off, she went to the back bar—zoom, there goes Bruce. He followed her right back there. He took his drink with him. He was gone, he followed her. When she went off the stage, he followed her straight to the back bar.

Patti Scialfa: I got offstage, and it was further towards the back end of the stage, walking back there, and I had a drink. Somebody handed me a drink. And then I saw all these people kind of walk up. I'm going, "What's going on?" Just like a little bit of a slow swarm, and I'm going, "Gee, what is this about?" And then he taps me on my shoulder from the back. He was standing behind me while I was talking to some of my friends, and that's why people swarmed up in front of me. I was like, "Oh, I get it." And he reintroduced himself and just said that he liked the way I sang. And then we became friends. We went back, had a couple of drinks together. Oh, God, I remember that night. It's funny. We had a couple of drinks together. Anyway, we got to know each other a little bit. And so when I'd come down on the weekends, he would always drive me home from the bar after just hanging out with the Cats. We'd go out for a hamburger down at the Inkwell, just stuff like that.

Max Weinberg: Bruce went down to the Stone Pony. La Bamba, the trombonist, was playing with his band, and Patti was singing with his band. And of course Bruce knew Patti. We all knew Patti. And that was the night he said, "Well, I got the guitar player, we'll get Patti." So she joined the E Street Band the next day.

Patti Scialfa: And then he called me up one night and said, "Can you come up? We're in Lititz rehearsing for the tour." I guess Steven had left the band, Little Steven. And Nils was there, but Nils had laryngitis, so he needed somebody to sing. I came up there for a couple of days. I thought I was only going to be there for the afternoon. That was a week before the tour, and then he called me three days before the tour and asked me to join.

Max Weinberg: I think they drove up together to Lititz, Pennsylvania. We were already there. We stayed at this little Route 66 motel. I remember while we rehearsed for that tour, and the rest is sort of history.

Nils Lofgren: Other than being born, the most important day of my life was meeting Amy Aiello at the Pony, sometime in the early eighties. She wasn't there to see me but I saw her and was smitten. Talked through the night at the Empress Motel, where I implored her to come to Boston with me on our tour bus, which had to leave at six a.m. She said she had a job in the morning and her mom wouldn't allow it, so no. I offered to call her mom and boss at four thirty a.m. and square things. She laughed and said that was not going to happen! We said our goodbyes as my tour bus departed. I was playing a club in Jersey every few months, so I assumed I'd see her soon. Wrong. It was fifteen long years before I got a second chance at the Rockin' Horse Saloon in Scottsdale. I got her number that night and we've been together since. Whew!

Max Weinberg: It was at the Stone Pony that all of us became aware of the girl who would later become my wife of forty-seven years. Becky, my wife, was a student at Monmouth College, and she and her brother, her younger brother was like a year younger, would go there, and Becky would dance. She still does. She'll dance by herself. But she was gorgeous and still is gorgeous. Looks virtually the same as she did then. But you'd sit in and you'd see this gorgeous girl, she wasn't following the bands, she just was blowing off steam from going to college all day.

And she dated Billy Rush of the Jukes for a couple of years, maybe two years. I didn't actually meet her at the Stone Pony, but I certainly recognized her. We all did. And truth be told, everybody had a bit of a crush on her. There used to be this stage rap that Bruce would give. I forget what song it was in, but he talked about the Mystery Lady, and that was her. I don't think any of us, I didn't even know her until later. We never even knew her name. But she was like a fixture there just dancing, blowing off steam. She didn't drink and she just wanted to dance.

And then she started dating Billy Rush, who was going to law school at the same time as he was in the Jukes, and it was a college kind of thing. And they broke up. And then I met her in LA and she was visiting a friend who became actually our maid of honor at our wedding. But there's distinct memories of watching her dance. There's a song on the Jukes' second record called "When You Dance," which I believe was inspired by Becky.

Mark Pender: To me, that's really what the Pony was. It was actually more those kind of bands like Cats, La Bamba. It wasn't really the big names that made the Pony. It was the local musicians that had good bands with a good enough following to fill the Pony. Taste changed over time. It used to be people would go out in droves on a Monday or Tuesday night, on a Sunday night. It seemed to change over time, where it became Thursday through Saturday more than anything.

John Eddie: Obviously our goal was the Stone Pony, but there was steps up to the Stone Pony. The Brighton Bar, the Fast Lane, and so we started playing the Brighton Bar first and Big Man, obviously Clarence had Big Man's Club.

Bob Burger: John Eddie, everybody thought that he was the second coming of Bruce at that time.

John Eddie: Obie Dziedzic, who was his friend from very early on, and then she worked for him and stuff, and she brought him to see me. She had seen me play opening for Beaver Brown, and she liked our band and we struck up a friendship. She was really helping us. The first time we played there, there was eleven fans. It was a Sunday night, it was eleven fans. And then a couple Sundays later was Easter Sunday. And Bruce came to see, and she was printing up these little flyers that said "11 screaming fans can't be wrong." A take on the Elvis thing. And then every week we would up the flyer to forty-three screaming fans. And then Bruce came on Easter Sunday and he got up and played a couple of songs with us and then that got us, all of a sudden people started looking at us in a different light, because Bruce gave us his benediction, his stamp of approval. So all of a sudden we started drawing more people, and I'm sure it had to do with my great songs. In fact the people were waiting to see if Bruce showed up, but that was a challenge for us, and that was our thing. We knew that, but we were like, "Fuck that. We're going to try and be as good as we can, so people aren't disappointed if Bruce isn't there." So it really helped us in getting attention to me and my music, and getting better gigs and stuff like that.

Tracey Story Prince: Of any show I've ever seen there or any big act, I love watching John Eddie play. He is one of the best performers. His music is great. He has a thing. We were called the Faithful. He was just so talented. He'd throw water on the crowd.

John Eddie: We had built such a cool following that we ended up getting a residency at the Pony on Friday nights. And that was around the summer of when Bruce was about to release *Born in the U.S.A.* And we were part of that whole Bruce phenomenon. So we were sold out every Friday night and it was packed. It was crazy, it was just like being part of the scene, so it just worked out that we were there at that moment.

The most famous show is when Bruce played before the *Born in the U.S.A.* tour. It was the first show that he did before the tour. I got a phone call from Bruce, and Bruce doesn't call me. I'm sure he doesn't have my number. Obie probably gave him my number. And he was very sweet, and he was like, "Hey, John. Listen, I want to play a show at the Pony, and I know it's your night." And he could have said, "Fucking fire John Eddie." And they would've done it in a heartbeat. He was like, "I want to play a show, and I know it's your night. Would it be cool if me and the band came down and opened up for you?" And I was like, "Dude, you can play all you want, but I'm not going on after you." And so it was very sweet and it was ridiculously cool. And we got to open up for him. And Eddie Testa was opening for us, and he got bumped. "Sorry, Eddie, but this is my time, brother."

Pete Llewellyn: That was the first time he played with the whole band after writing the album. That was the first get-together, the band playing before his tour at the Stone Pony. He didn't charge a dime. He had the whole band there and they played for maybe two hours, three hours for free. He came in and played the whole night unannounced; it just happened.

Bruce Springsteen: I wanted to get the guys playing locally and I just wanted to run through the show. And John was headlining that night. I just asked him if it would be okay if we came down and played, at some point during night. So of course, John's always been great and he's just like, "Come on down."

John Eddie: I imagine that had to be seeing the Beatles at the Cavern for everyone in the audience. Because it was the first show of the *Born* *in the U.S.A.* tour and that whole phenomenon. And I got to open it, and I got to stand on the side of the stage and watch it. And then afterwards we went to Bruce's house. It was just a pinch-yourself type of moment, and probably won't be topped in my lifetime.

Nils Lofgren: Playing a warm-up gig with Bruce and E Street at the Pony before the *Born in the U.S.A.* tour was a momentous night, also. As I didn't get the gig until four weeks before opening night, it was an overwhelming, beautiful experience. Being at the Pony with Bruce's audience on our side was a huge help that night.

Max Weinberg: We had rehearsed because we had two new members, Nils and Patti, and we had rehearsed up in Pennsylvania at this soundstage and came back and there were pictures of that night. So my distinct recollection is playing that material in the Stone Pony, the *Born in the U.S.A.* material. And in those days they didn't have air. They may have had air-conditioning, but it didn't work, and it was unbelievably hot. And at one point, Bruce just said to the crowd, "Game called on account of heat." I almost passed out on the drums. And I was young. I was only thirty-one at the time. Well, it was hot and humid, of course, and I think it was even just May, but it was mainly because it wasn't air-conditioning and the crush of people that was in there.

John Eddie: I'm sure we surpassed fire marshal numbers that night. It was wall-to-wall, hanging-off-the-ceiling type of crowd. It was sweaty, it was hot, it was rock and roll. It was what you imagine a Little Richard song is.

Nils Lofgren: Playing the Pony after I joined E Street did give me a bit more confidence and a feeling I belonged, even more than usual.

Bruce Springsteen: It was an event. It was a big thing at the time. We were one of the biggest bands in the world at the time, if not the biggest, but it was our place and we didn't think much about it. We just went down there and did it.

Tim Donnelly: The Pony for us was always, was like having fucking Yankee Stadium up the street in a way where legends were. I graduated high school in 1985. Bruce Springsteen was the biggest star in the fucking world in 1984, 1985. So Bruce Springsteen, Michael Jackson, and fucking Prince. And we had one of them.

Chris Barron: One of the coolest kids in my high school, my middle school, was a kid named Ian Magar. And Ian was just a huge Bruce Springsteen fan. *Greetings from Asbury Park*, we listened to that record a lot, and wore bandanas around our heads and back pockets, and all that kind of thing. And I always say to people, about New Jersey and Bruce Springsteen, was like, "He wasn't the Boss, he was our Boss." We looked to him.

John Eddie: Whenever Bruce would play with us, it'd be random. It was never a phone call or anything like that. You'd be playing and all of a sudden the energy level in the crowd would rise, and you might not even know, and it's because someone spotted Bruce. One time inside the Pony, we started playing "Suspicious Minds." And I'm in the beginning. I don't know that Bruce is going to play with us at all at this point. I'm closing my eyes, I'm singing, I'm getting into the beginning that we have this long intro, blah, blah, blah. And then I've got my eyes closed, and all of a sudden the crowd goes crazy. And I'm like, "Yeah, I'm fucking really killing it. I'm killing it." And I didn't realize Bruce had walked onstage and then got a guitar and got up to join us.

Gary U.S. Bonds: I used to go there and Bruce would come in and that was it. It was pandemonium from then on in. We'd get up there and we'd sing something. Half the time I didn't know what we were singing. You just make it up as you go along. But he'd do that at the Pony and at stadiums to me. We'll be in a stadium and he'll do that. What are we talking about? There's fifty thousand people out there. Are we going to make up shit?

Pete Llewellyn: Bruce could walk in there any given time and not a single person would walk up and pester him, for his autographs, "Please go up and play. Come on. We want to hear you." No pestering. He'd come in, chill. He always had a baseball cap on. He would chill out, he knew everybody, who were the bartenders, who were the owners, who were the bouncers. He was at home and he knew he was safe because we had every bouncer making goddamn sure he was safe, because if, God forbid, something happened, we had to get to him quick.

Jack Roig: He didn't want people watching over him. You watched over him, but from a distance. Bruce knew how to move and how to take care of himself. He didn't want the Secret Service all around him.

Pete Llewellyn: He was being watched, but not pestered. There's a big difference. He was at home. He could get drunk. He liked drinking, like everyone else who was in there, and he'd have a good time, a great night, he'd go home. He was at peace in there. He even played. He even put a bag on. He'd get four or five kamikazes in him and he'd go up to the band and play for an hour.

Bobby Bandiera: Playing the Pony as much as I did on whatever night during the week, a Wednesday or the Sunday, weekend, a lot of the guys from the Jukes would come in. Kevin Kavanaugh lived a couple of blocks away, so he used to be there all the time. And he used to play with me in Cats from time to time. I would get him up and play. And he'd say, "Mark Pender and La Bamba are around. Why don't you call them to play horns?" I said, "Yeah. Yeah." So I put this thing together on Sundays. It was a revue, where I had a lot of those guys come up and play in the band, and Patti Scialfa was around. I'd have her come up and sing. Bruce would watch; he'd come up and sing. And then that Sunday turned into a crazy night. It was one of those things. It was a fun time just to be in the mix, with an area that was so overflowing with talent. Bruce, Steven, Southside, Patti Scialfa was hanging around. Somebody was always coming around.

John Eddie: We were witnessing the last glory days of the fantasy version of Bruce's songs, that *American Graffiti* vibe where it was fast cars, hot girls, all is good in America. We saw the last vestiges of that.

Max Weinberg: They call it the House That Bruce Built, he and the Jukes. We always kind of thought it was like our Cavern Club in a way, at least from my point of view.

Jean Mikle: Everything changed after *Born in the U.S.A.* And then I think he didn't feel as comfortable hanging out. I still saw him out quite a bit.

Tracey Story Prince: After *Born in the U.S.A.*, that's when he got real big.

Stan Goldstein: There was always a rule. We didn't bother Bruce. You wanted him to play. You didn't want to annoy him or he would walk out. That was always the locals' rule. Leave him alone. Maybe you'll get to see him play. That was always our rule.

Eileen Chapman: Bruce had a really keen sense of when his presence could make a difference in something or somebody. The way he gave money around town. Computers to the Boys and Girls Club, and jackets to the marching band, and a roof for the Stephen Crane House. I mean, just things that people didn't notice, but that just made a difference and an impact. And the Pony was the same thing. I mean, there were times in the summer of '82 or '83, I'd have more people in Mrs. Jay's than would be in the Pony. And I don't know why. I don't know why people stopped going as much for a while. I don't know if it was the bands or just that other clubs were popping up. There were new shiny pennies, Key Largo, Pier Pub, and all these sort of dancey clubs were opening up, and the Green Parrot, and places out of Asbury Park that were drawing people, because they were new. And so I think that impacted the Pony for a few years.

Southside Johnny: It made Asbury Park—between Bruce's *Greetings from Asbury Park*, Jon Bon Jovi's *New Jersey* when that came out later, and us and the Asbury Jukes, and all these young acts, rock-and-roll acts coming to play, it made Asbury Park, as you say, a destination. But it also became a hip town in a sense. It was still a blighted neighborhood. It was worth your life to walk the streets at night, but for Friday and Saturday night, the cops would be there helping people park, and there'd be a police presence so people felt safe. It really was a real beacon of light for New Jersey and Asbury Park.

Bruce Springsteen: I would say at the time, 1975 to 1985, the town was kind of on the last of its blue-collar legs. And it would really become very desperate shortly. But my recollection was the boardwalk was still open and there were amusements and rides, and that part of the town hadn't shut down yet. But it was post the riots and so there was a noticeable closing down of a large part of the town in those days. So, it was just a little, hanging-on-by-a-thread, blue-collar beach town that happened to be our home.

Eric Deggans: Bruce going to the Stone Pony and checking out who was there, and sitting in with the bands, and it became this whole thing. I can't even imagine an analogy nowadays, like if Taylor Swift decided to go to a club where she lives and sit in with the bands every so often, imagine that, imagine the masses that would come just for the possibility of seeing her do that. He did that, and it made international news, and it turned the Stone Pony into this brand that people heard about all over the world. They heard about it in a way that was just the most romantic rock-and-roll kind of way to hear about it. This superstar is so down-to-earth that he'll come in and have a beer, and if he has enough beers and is feeling like it, he'll fucking get onstage and play for people. You can pay your five- or ten-dollar cover charge and get to fucking see Bruce Springsteen. It also feeds into the mythology of the area because the area has always prided itself on these down-to-earth, working-class, bootstrap-type rock stars. That's what Bruce was, that's what Jon Bon Jovi was, that's what the Smithereens were. Right? It wasn't Taylor Swift, it wasn't like somebody who's off on a hill somewhere isolated from people. These were folks who were other people. That just built into the legend and became this powerful story for rock fans, and then the Pony could build on that and become this venue that hosted a bunch of great shows. That's really how you become a classic venue. You create a scene and you become home for a bunch of great musical moments. That's what the Pony did.

12

Speedball Games

A common refrain among Pony People is that they were family, from the famous musicians to the locals to the bartenders to the back-bar regulars. While there were countless manifestations of these deeply intertwined relationships, the softball games between E Street and the Pony crystallized the shared experiences. And the spoils of a rock star—trashed hotel rooms and celebrity-soaked clubs, lofts in Tribeca, and penthouses in the Los Angeles hills—did not appeal to Springsteen. It was more fun to be at home in New Jersey, playing pickup baseball with the bartenders and bouncers of his local bar.

Bruce Springsteen: We were kids and we wanted to play games. We wanted to play baseball. We were all baseball freaks. And so we said, "Hey, man, it's Saturday. We can have hot dogs or get some beer. And let's meet out at the Holmdel baseball field." And there was enough guys in the band, and then there was enough guys in the crew with the Pony, there was some other bar. And we just challenged them.

Pete Llewellyn: We were the Pony Express. We used to always meet somewhere else first and then call the game when everybody was there.

Jack Roig: I mean, some days you found out, "Okay, we have a softball game on Sunday, eleven o'clock. A field to be announced."

Max Weinberg: We had a team called E Street Kings, a baseball team, which was organized by Steve and Bruce. It was Steve's idea to get the red satin jacket, which I still own.

Bruce Springsteen: The E Street Band had a team. It was pretty good. And we would play the Stone Pony and other bars in the area.

Richie "La Bamba" Rosenberg: Those softball games. That all started before I came in. And then once I was in, and hey, I was playing games and the whole deal. The Pony would have a team and the Bruce would have a team, and it involved Jukes and E Street members and whatnot, friends. And then there would be a couple radio stations, I think like WNEW. And in Cleveland, WMMS, I think they had a team.

Eileen Chapman: I think Jack played. I don't think Butch ever played, but all the bouncers played, all the floor guys, all the bartenders.

Jack Roig: We didn't have any good players. The whole team sucked. Well, we were terrible. I was a pretty good pitcher because I played a lot of softball before that. They had one very good pitcher, and that was it. Oh, Lee was pretty good.

Erick W. Henderiks: Bruce was a decent player, but he hired a couple of ringers back then. He hired a couple of guys, but we still beat him. I was in the rah-rah section. I was too big to be competitive in that sport. Can you see me running around bases and shit?

Bruce Springsteen: We had in our pocket an excellent fast-softball pitcher, Barry Bell, who has been my agent for fifty years. Barry could really pitch a mean fast-pitch softball and we'd beat a lot of people.

Pete Llewellyn: The guy could throw a fucking softball like most Major League Baseball players throw a baseball.

Dube Sullivan: The great leveler was Barry the pitcher because he threw fast underhand. He kept a lot of guys off the base. He kept it competitive. I considered myself a little young, punk jock. It was the musicians against the bar, and they had a couple of other ringers come in. Bruce had a friend named Matt Delea. He had a couple of brothers, Tony, and then the other brother I forget his name. The three younger brothers were good athletes.

Lee Mrowicki: Some of them were good players, some of them they brought some ringers in, like Barry Bell, who used to be Bruce's booking agent, was a semipro fast pitcher. And we had a bunch of guys who used to play slow-pitch softball, so when Barry comes on, and all the sudden these guys are seeing sixty-mile-an-hour fastballs, it's like holy shit. Now, I had played baseball, so I could hit stuff like that. So the first time Barry gets up, I'm like hitting third. The first two guys are like, phhww, just looking. What the? So, I'm the third man up, and all the sudden I let one go by. I said okay. The next pitch, I hit in the gap, and Barry's looking at me, he says, "Who the hell are you?"

Max Weinberg: Bruce, of course, up until he discovered the guitar, wanted to be a baseball player. I mean, he was really good, fantastic batter. And he played second base and shortstop, and he had a great arm.

Bruce Springsteen: We were pretty good. Everybody hit and everybody fielded pretty decently. But like I said, we were only in our thirties at the time.

Richie "La Bamba" Rosenberg: Bruce was probably the best. I would think he was. I was terrible. They were probably happy when I wasn't around. Oh, is the ball coming on my way? I got, oh, I'm going to take off my glove 'cause I caught with my left hand and I threw with my left. And then they probably scored.

Tony Amato: I played with Bruce's team once in a while, and Mrs. Jay's or the Pony's team. Bruce was good, great little second baseman. But while Bruce is good, Clarence was fucking great.

Bruce Springsteen: Clarence could knock ball to the frigging rings of Saturn. I mean, he was just amazing at the bat. I used to be able to hit in those days a little bit.

Tony Amato: One game, I'm standing playing right field, outfield, and Clarence gets up. So I think, let me back up a little bit. He looks over at me, he starts laughing, and I'm thinking, what's this big motherfucker laughing at me for? Pitch. Holy shit. He hit this ball right over my head, over the fence into the sticker bushes. I looked around and said, "Yeah. Well, you're such a man. You're going in there because I ain't climbing any them stickers now."

Max Weinberg: I was never a very good baseball player, but I was game. Steve was good. Steve was a real good athlete. We had a good team. Of course, I think I got always stuck in right field. Baseball was not my sport. I was a very, very good placekicker. I loved football. I did hit a home run in high school softball once, which was the high point of my sporting career. After that, it was all downhill.

Tony Amato: Federici, he didn't play. He asked me, "What are you doing playing sports?" I'm like, "Shut up. I look good. How else am I supposed to get laid?"

Jack Roig: One of those games, Bruce, he was playing second base. And I was on first, and I'm about as fast as the hedge. And somebody hit a ground ball and it's going to be a double play, and I'm going to go down there. And normally I would try to kill the person. And I'm saying to myself, "I'm going down." I'm saying, "How's that going to look? Owner of Stone Pony breaks Bruce Springsteen's leg." And I stopped, probably one of the biggest decisions of my life, and it was a good one.

Tony Amato: One game, we were playing Crosby, Stills & Nash. They were good. And Van Zandt and Bruce was running around looking for ringers. They said, "Dress crazy, dress crazy." So I got a pair of knickers, green knickers, green socks, and green shirt. Look, I thought I looked more like a leprechaun. And then they started calling me "Boccigalupe."

Max Weinberg: Crosby, Stills & Nash had, I think it was called, well, I know it was, parts of that band had a band called the Hoovers, so-called, because they would suck up coke, and they were called the Hoovers. We played them in Holmdel.

Bruce Springsteen: I do remember playing Crosby and them, but all I remember doing was beating them badly. They had a pretty decent team, but several of them simply did not know how to play baseball.

Erick W. Henderiks: Crosby and them were all fucked up.

Bruce Springsteen: But we had a great time and they were game. They were playing at the local amphitheater and they all came out. Crosby and everybody came out and they were really great sports and they played on this funky little ball field with us and we had a lot of fun.

Pete Llewellyn: The softball games were an important part of the pie of the Stone Pony and Bruce. That was unique. How many famous rock-and-roll musicians go out with their local bar and play against them in softball with their band? Not many.

13

New Music and "Metal"

Live music happened seven nights a week at the Pony. Seven nights. Even a club as stubbornly proud of its signature sound as the Pony has to adapt, experiment, and change. Or just fill the bandstand. So-called metal bands first cracked rock radio, and then Tuesday nights at the Pony.

Dave Wyndorf: The whole Asbury sound was going on, so it was like the Pony is a big deal. We went down there. I was a punk rocker at that time, so we weren't buying that jazz. We went down there to check out the place. Boys looking for girls, and eighteen years old, had driver's license, and legal to drink. Let's go.

Dave Sabo: I'm from Sayreville, and I grew up right down the street from John Bongiovi, so he started going down there as a teenager. I remember just being awestruck by, well, you could sense the history, put it that way. And I was aware of Springsteen and Southside Johnny, and David Johansen would play down there. And then they'd have punk bands like Shrapnel and the Reds. And I can remember I had tickets to go see Black Sabbath and Van Halen, at the Convention Hall. And I sold them and snuck into the Stone Pony with a fake ID to go see Shrapnel. And I was like, "Oh my God." I was fourteen at that time. At fourteen, I'm in a club and it was amazing. I felt like an adult. But then the promoter of the club, Jimmy D'Antonio, threatened to break my thumbs if he saw me with a drink. Or the promoter of the club. I wasn't so mature-looking. I didn't start shaving until I was twenty-two, for God's sakes.

Dave Wyndorf: Asbury closed at four o'clock in the morning, so you had these really, really late calls. "Four o'clock, last call." We hit every place, and the Pony, we would go into. But we weren't, at that point, it was so, well, let's say they had found their thing, and their thing didn't include guys like me. We were eighteen or nineteen, but we looked like we're fourteen and we looked like assholes. We had leather jackets on. I had a Johnny Ramone haircut and they didn't like that. It's just the minute you go in and you know the whole Jersey thing. You know what I mean?

If a bunch of guys don't like you, it's immediate, like, "I don't like your face." I'm like, "Oh, no." They're hanging around, not playing the game. Go up, wait for a beer, have the barmaid or the bartender not get to you, and then drunk, I would say something like, "Oh yes, how you doing? I've only been here for a couple hours." That would be enough for them to go, "What the fuck did you say to her?" That kind of thing. "What the fuck? Did you say something to her?" Then I'd rise off more and the next thing you know, kicked out. They threw me out. Literally, it looked like a 1930s movie, like, "Get the bum out of here." They took me by my arms, like an arm under each armpit, their arms under each armpit, two guys, and then picked me up by the back of my jeans and threw me out face-first. Opened the doors, and happy to do it.

David DiPietro: T.T. Quick played on Tuesday nights at the Stone Pony. The only hard rock band, they called it "metal." I'd never thought of us as really metal, but I guess a lot of people did, to ever play the Stone Pony back then. The reason that T.T. Quick was invited to play at the Stone Pony was because at one time, before I joined them, they were pretty much an AC/DC cover band. They were known for that. It's not all they did, but that's what they were known for. I think they had an AC/DC show that they did. And back in the eighties, tribute bands were huge. You could be a nobody player, but if you were in a tribute band that was sought after, you would be playing big rooms and doing big numbers.

CJ Ramone: I had always heard Asbury Park was a giant carnival, kind of not unlike Coney Island. Like that it's a Coney Island of New Jersey.

Except that Asbury Park had the Stone Pony, Asbury Park had a music scene, a major music scene, with Bruce Springsteen, Johnny and the Asbury Jukes, and Gary U.S. Bonds, you had all these bands. Before I played in the Ramones, I went down to see a couple of shows. A friend of mine was like, "Hey, I'm going to go down to Asbury Park and go see T.T. Quick." And I was like, "Man, I would love to go." So I jumped in with him and went down and saw T.T. Quick there. They were so good. I was blown away. To me, they were the best club band that I had seen at that point because of their originals.

David DiPietro: Nobody ever said you can't play original music. It was not very regulated. If you had a crowd, they didn't care what you did. And if your bar tab was big, and T.T. Quick's bar tab was exceptionally big because it was a little rougher-around-the-edges crew that used to come out. They drank, and they drank a lot.

Zakk Wylde: T.T. Quick, they were regulars there because obviously they had a following and they brought money. If me and you own the Pony, we want people drinking in there.

Tracey Story Prince: I was a cocktail waitress and T.T. Quick was my first night. That was a heavy metal band feature night. There was air guitar contests.

Rachel Bolan: The first time I was actually in the Pony is the first time I played the Pony. It was in a band called Godsend. We were kind of glam, kind of metal. We didn't know what we were, but we knew that we were the only ones in the club. The whole staff just treated us like, you are wasting every second of our time today. They could not wait until that set ended so they could push us out the door. It was a random weeknight that they put us in. I think it was kind of a favor to this guy our drummer kind of worked with at a booking agency and they put us in and yeah, literally it was us and the bar staff, were the only people there. So it was just one of those gigs. I was like, "So this is it? This is the world-famous Stone Pony? Awesome." And we have bragging rights. It's like, "Well, how was the turnout?" "Yeah, there were people there for sure." The people I was talking about was us.

Dave Sabo: I hung out with a group of people that were all older than me and played in different bands, and so I was able to go down there and it was definitely . . . You could sense there was something special; it was hallowed ground because its reputation preceded itself. But going to the Pony, I can remember seeing T.T Quick there and Dave's guitar playing was just so through the roof. He's such a talented guy and they were such a great band and they played around the area so much. But going to see them at the Pony was something special. And back then too, there was a place that was right next to it. I think it was called Mrs. Jay's. So I used to sit there and go get a cheesesteak and get . . . There were quarter beers or fifty-cent beers or something. And I'm a fourteen-year-old kid drinking beer by the ocean and there's T.T Quick, and I'm on Tuesday night and my mother thinks that I'm doing homework or over at a friend's house, and here I am being a decadent little punk.

Zakk Wylde: We'd be opening for T.T. Quick . . . But I never saw shows there because when I was playing there, I was seventeen, eighteen years old, I couldn't get in. If I wanted to go back then just to go check out T.T. Quick, if I wasn't opening for them, they wouldn't let me in.

David DiPietro: We were so out of the box for that place, but we then would have opening acts, so they would be more our genre. And Zakk's band, Zyris, was one of those bands. But we used to ask him, we'd be backstage and we'd be like, "Hey, can we get you a beer?" And he'd be like, "No, no. I have to go to school the next day." And our drummer, Eric, said, "Well, how about some milk and cookies?" And so we dubbed him Milk and Cookies.

Zakk Wylde: I was never rolling around with a beer in my hand or anything like that. That was just out of respect because it's just, you don't want that club shutting down and putting them out of business. It's just have a smidge of respect for the guys that own the place.

David DiPietro: So Zakk would come in and I just remember watching this kid play and just being like, "Wow, this kid is tearing it up." And he was a big fan of us. And so he and I got to be friends and we'd talk, and he would ask me about different little things I was playing and how I was doing certain things. I would show them to him, and he would come back the next week, he'd go, "Is this it?" And I'd be like, "Yeah, that's it. Slow down."

Zakk Wylde: A couple of my buddies went to Berklee College of Music. For me, the Pony was a huge part of my education. Seeing Dave playing every night and seeing Kenny. It was just phenomenal. It really was a huge part of my development. What I got from them was like firsthand cooking in the back of a kitchen and cooking for Gordon Ramsay. And being his assistant and watching how he cooks . . . I was a sponge, just taking it all in.

David DiPietro: It was a weird thing because back then, and I don't know if they still do this now, but you played a weeknight every single week at the same place. We'd never heard of that in Connecticut, playing a weeknight. I thought, don't people get sick of coming out and seeing the same band? And Mark and the guy, Walt, were like, "No, no. It's the opposite. You build a night, it gets bigger and bigger and bigger."

Zakk Wylde: Everyone was going out on a Tuesday night, the street would be packed. For me, it was only the one night a week or whatever we'd be going down there.

David DiPietro: I thought, that's weird that people would come out and see the same band every Tuesday night. But I'm telling you, Tuesday night at the Stone Pony was a mob scene. It was incredible.

Tracey Story Prince: People with their heads and headbanging. These people probably cannot hear and probably have brain damage right now. They would stick their heads right in the speakers. I don't know if you've seen the stacks at the Pony. You couldn't even stand close. Used to walk by and your clothes used to do this, like vibrate. Heavy metal people were a whole 'nother breed than the normal Southside SOAP crowd.

Eileen Chapman: I was managing Mrs. Jay's when T.T. Quick was playing, I think, on Tuesday nights, and that's the night I would take off because my office was backed up to the DJ booth at Mrs. Jay's, and the noise was so loud I couldn't stand myself. That would be my night off from managing Mrs. Jay's. It was so loud.

David DiPietro: T.T. Quick was a big attraction for bikers because think about the music. That's what they would come to see. And we were friends with them and it was never a problem, man. And I think back to it now, and I don't know how there wasn't. But there wasn't.

Rachel Bolan: When we first got together, it was always like, "Oh, let's play the Pony." Of course, in our head it's like, "Let's play Madison Square Garden someday." But we wanted to play the Pony because we were in Jersey, we were from Jersey, and that was the place, that's where you played when you had a name for yourself.

Dave Sabo: As we were about to tour with Bon Jovi, we wanted to play the Pony before we left to go on the road. It was like it was the right way to send the band off onto the next step in our careers. And we felt like there was no other place that would be the same other than the Stone Pony, just because it played a significant role in our lives. Rachel and my lives as individuals, and Scotti's I guess, to a certain degree. But the band's for sure.

Rachel Bolan: We parked the van really close to the door. We got the stuff in as quick as possible, and when we loaded out, we got it loaded and didn't just leave the car running outside to say goodbye to friends. We said goodbye first, and loaded and then took off. It wasn't like we felt like we were in danger for our lives; it was the only gear we had. And we would just hear horror stories about bands coming into town and playing and their van getting clipped. So that was the one thing that always concerned us. We never really feared for our life. It was just that we didn't want our gear getting stolen and we didn't want to be one of those stories that you hear about.

Dave Sabo: We rehearsed pretty close to the Pony, and that area really, really was not the same area of our youth. It really had gone downhill.

Rachel Bolan: I just remember being so hot that our drum tech was like, "I need something to drink." And he looked at me and he just took a full Solo cup of ice water and just threw it right at my chest. And I was like, "What the fuck are you doing? That's going to mess my bass up." And then I was like, "Oh my God, that felt so good."

Dave Sabo: If you can draw at the Stone Pony, you knew that you were doing well. There was a feeling in the room like, "Wow, these guys actually have a shot. They might do something. They really might have a shot." And we did have a shot.

Rachel Bolan: The Stone Pony was our CBGB. It was like the pinnacle for a new band out of New Jersey to play the Stone Pony and do well there. Every city has its place, its venue, that everybody wants to play. New York has CBGB. California has so many. And every city or state, I should say, has their place that everybody wants to play and do well at, and Stone Pony was ours. There's other places in Jersey, but Stone Pony was definitely ours that we wanted to do. We were like, "Man, if everything ends right now, we pack the Pony." That's all we gave a shit about, man.

Rachel Bolan: It was crazy, because we went directly from playing the Pony, to four or five hundred people, whatever it held. And our next show was in Dallas at Reunion Arena on the first day of the Bon Jovi tour in front of twenty thousand people. We were like, "Wow, this stage takes a lot of energy to run across."

Dave Sabo: We kept saying, this isn't the Pony anymore.

Rachel Bolan: We compared everything to the Pony. It's like music is compared to the Beatles. For us, every venue was compared to the Pony.

Jim Babjak: We started the band the Smithereens. And I just had a feeling that . . . It's easy for people to say now, but back then I just had a feeling that we would do something, that we'd be able to make a record and be able to play at places like the Stone Pony, because I just felt it. The only thing I owned back then was a car. And it was a nice car. It was a Trans Am, and it was kind of new. I bought it in 1977. Only thing I owned. All of a sudden now, I'm unemployed, playing in a band that's getting twenty-five dollars a night. And we were playing at the Bitter End in New York in the Village. And my car got stolen, because I couldn't afford the four dollars to park it in the fucking lot. So, I used the insurance money from that to open up a record store in New Brunswick [New Jersey], where I was living at the time.

Dennis Diken: We were just four guys from Jersey. The band took shape in early 1980. Our sights were certainly on the Pony, but we thought that that was so remote because we were really just an infant band. Good songs and good band, but we still had a lot to learn about our craft.

Jim Babjak: Lance Larson paid us to play every Thursday night for two months. And yeah, twenty-five dollars. And I remember having to pay for, and I said, "Oh wait, got to pay for beer?" And then there went all my money. It was gone.

Dennis Diken: They were kind enough to let us open for them for at least a month, maybe more, and that was a huge break for us because that place was off-limits.

Jim Babjak: In the old dressing room, there was a little window where you could get pizza. And it was good pizza. I've never been in there. I only know in *The Munsters* or *The Addams Family*, Thing. A hand coming through with pizza. I'm like, "Whoa." And I think we didn't have to pay for it.

Vini Lopez: Now they have the actual back room. You go out the back door and then you get to that other club or places there. Because that used to be a pizza bar. And when you went into the back room at the Pony, not that place, but they had a hole in the wall where you could go, "Hey." And somebody would come over and you'd go, "Two slices," and they'd put the slices through the hole in the wall.

Dennis Diken: It put us on the radar a little bit in that neck of the woods. I think that after that stint ended, I think there was a long gap between then and the next time we played the Pony. I honestly can't remember. I don't know if Jimmy has a better recollection of it.

Jim Babjak: It was a learning experience . . . I didn't know how to stand onstage and all that stuff. And it felt to me like a clique that we didn't belong to. And I always felt like an outsider back then. But Lance was, like I said, our champion. So, he made us feel at home, so I'm always grateful to him.

Jesse Malin: The band I had called Hope came down on a winter night and did an audition down there or played the slow Monday or whatever. We were psyched just to get on that stage. It meant something to us to go down there. . . . Me and the band at the Pony, we got there, and it might have been nobody there, and it's snowing outside. To look at the walls and see all the stuff that had gone on and see what was going on and stand on that stage and whatever with the logo behind you.

David DiPietro: No question in my mind what happened at the Stone Pony, keeping the band alive and in circulation and on everybody's mind, and that logo being in the paper constantly, every Tuesday night, every Monday night. So if you're a record company in New Jersey and you're looking for a heavy metal band, you didn't need to look very far. You just had to know what you were seeing.

Jesse Malin: We're playing on a weird night with the bored staff, nobody's really paying attention, but it was empty, and it had that feeling of like, "Oh, wow. The world is hard. The road is hard. You get out there, it's not all like can we jump up and be Springsteen or Bon Jovi," but it was definitely a thing of standing on that stage and looking at those photos and looking at the guitars on the wall and looking at the wood and the building and seeing like, "Wow, this building has seen a lot of stuff. These walls have been around a lot of great jams and a lot of great crazy shows." That's something.

Zakk Wylde: It was a huge part of my education. Like I said, my friends went to Berklee, and me, I went to the Pony.

David DiPietro: Using the restroom, I met Bruce in there and he was real nice. We were just signing a record deal, this Megaforce [Records] thing. And I didn't understand anything about publishing. And so I asked him, I said, "How do you know if you're getting a good publishing?" And he said, "Well, what are you giving?" And without getting into the minutiae, I told him. And he said, "Well, then you're only getting a quarter percent." I'm like, "Why?" And he explained why. And he said, "Let me explain this to you." And he took some time in the bathroom. So I got schooled on the basics of publishing from Bruce Springsteen, in the bathroom of the Stone Pony.

14

National Acts Arrive

Jim Messina may have wandered over in the seventies, and Cheap Trick and Elvis Costello, the rare national booking amid the Jukes' boom times. But the Pony's renown rose with Springsteen's fame. Following *Born in the U.S.A.*, he was probably the most famous person in the country. Bands wanted to play there. And with costs rising, booking national acts instead of relying on local and cover bands became a means of survival.

Tony Pallagrosi: Butch actually came to me because he saw us [at a new club called Xanadu] do good with a couple of national acts. And so I gave them a national act that wasn't going to work at Xanadu, and that was Gregg Allman. And that sold the Pony out. . . . They did like eight or nine hundred people, and they drank their asses off.

Stan Levinstone: I used to do stuff at Xanadu with Tony, and Tony had actually booked Gregg Allman, but he thought that Gregg Allman had the early R&B sounds and he had that thing about the Pony. So I went down to the Pony. I walked into the Pony, where we're doing beer bar in the back. Butch said all local bands are in the back. I said, no, I'm Stan Levinstone. And it's, "Oh! Come in!" I walked in and I said, "Let's try to figure something out." I got Gregg to play for two thousand dollars versus one hundred percent of the door up to four thousand dollars. We get twelve hundred people. That was my welcoming to the Stone Pony.

Jack Roig: I remember that show. I remember that because Allman got onstage. He was up there maybe thirty seconds, and all of a sudden blood squirting out of his arm. And he says, "I guess I sprung a leak." Roadie comes up. He must've just shot up. Roadie comes up, duct tape, what a show.

Stan Levinstone: Gregg was the beginning of a whole new slew of national artists. Pretty much every artist that played in the Pony from '84 until the time Butch closed it, I booked everything.

Lee Mrowicki: When the Fast Lane started going downhill, we were getting more and more into the original music, although, you know, there were bands that were playing cover tunes that were just packing the place, so there was no need sometimes to spend all that money on a national act when you had other bands that were making $300 to $400 a night, when you had to pay a national act $1,500 to $2,500 or so. So, in that respect, you know, they were bands that were great bands, but mostly cover bands, although they would be allowed to do their original music, as well.

Jack Roig: Bruce and the locals kept it going, and then we'd get into the national acts later on.

Max Weinberg: During the eighties, it was always packed. No matter who was playing there, I mean, it was going great guns. And then, it did change. It became a showcase for national acts. I saw Graham Parker there.

Eileen Chapman: I had a compact disc store in Belmar. I opened the first all-compact-disc store in all of New Jersey in Belmar. And I was lending Jack the money for the deposit for the national acts.

Jorma Kaukonen: It's a venue that did national acts a lot, but it was a local venue. So there's a lot of that community stuff that was going on. And that sort of feeling was a lot different than going to, let's say, a performing arts center in Long Island or something like that where you probably never even get a chance to really talk to anybody in the audience because the backstage is another world entirely.

Huey Lewis: In our day, you would release the record, and then you would go play each town, and you'd invite, obviously, the radio station and the critics . . . the newspapers, whoever they were . . . to come to the show, and then when you left, hopefully the radio station would say, "Oh, what a great show last night," and play the record, and you get a nice review in the newspaper, and then you go to the next town. And that's how you broke a record, right? And so, you go from one end of the country to the other end of the country, but interestingly enough, even if the record didn't work, you played eighty shows. And so that's how we honed our craft. That's how we learned to do what we do, is in places like the Pony.

Marshall Crenshaw: I thought that it was the sweatiest, hottest place that we played. The stuffiest. 'Cause it would get packed when we were there, it'd just get utterly packed. And lots of places would, but in that place it would just be hot breath, nowhere to run, nowhere to . . . Yeah, there was really no escaping from the heat and the hot breath in that place. It stood out in my mind. I used to call it a pizza oven with a stage. I think I said that to the crowd a few times. Because it popped into my head one night, I'm up there dying of heat.

Dave Wyndorf: I remember the Ramones show, when we opened up for the Ramones. Walking down on the stage and looking at the crowd, really seeing how far punk rock went outside of New York City, and it didn't. There were a lot of people, but nobody really got the fashion. It was just basically guys who had just gotten their haircut, but not short enough. Jean jackets and stuff. Just with that kind of fuck-you attitude that the Ramones sold that no one had really sold to anyone before. You had a lot of guys who were just there to go, "Fuck you."

Stan Levinstone: The first time the Ramones ever played there, people were white as ghosts. They had never seen anything like the Ramones. Their early founding was not the kind of people that moshed, stage-dived. But the Ramones started getting a following of the hardcore kids. When I got down to the Pony, Little Butch [not Butch Pielka] was the assistant manager. He was biting his nails. He said, "Stanley, I've never seen"—Joey was hitting people with the microphone. There were people peeing behind the speaker stacks. They were freaked. They had never seen such a phenomenon. That kind of opened up some eyes over the years.

Monte Melnick: Early on, I guess we weren't big enough for the Pony, so that the Fast Lane I guess got us in there first. People didn't know the

Ramones that well, so we started off with smaller places. But eventually, you know, they got a following and then the Pony picked us up.

Lee Mrowicki: The Ramones loved playing in Asbury. All right and 'cause Joe's from Brooklyn, like Rockaway Beach area and everything like that. This is just like it. Back then you know the punk movement is just starting to really blossom. That's the first time we saw a mosh pit.

Monte Melnick: They loved going down because it was such an easy trip. They like to come back to New York all the time. So it's like a quick trip down, quick tour back right after the show. A lot of times that we just get there to play, you know, we wouldn't even do sound checks. So we really didn't get a chance to slip around the place much. It seemed okay driving down there, made sure we parked near the club so we're okay.

Jack Roig: The Ramones were characters. Absolute characters. But man could they draw.

Dave Wyndorf: [Someone in the crowd] threw a cigarette at me and I caught it and smoked it, and they loved it, so I got a pass. It was ready to smoke and in one of those one-in-a-million chances of luck. After getting pelted with, I think, a bottle, because they were still serving bottles. I think I got pelted with a bottle and hit in the head or something and people were like, "Fuck you." Just because they're enjoying the whole fuck-you attitude of Ramones, of just the thing. Being able to say fuck you at a show as part of the show was very new. You hadn't seen that at the shows, that kind of attitude. Nihilistic attitude or celebrating rage for rage's sake and stated as such, was just not part of the culture back then for white kids anyway. They were enjoying it. "Yes, yes. Fuck you. We'll boo these guys off the stage, and gabba gabba hey, I want to beat on you with a baseball bat." That's what they were saying and I'm out there like, "Okay, I'm trying to do my thing."

Jorma Kaukonen: It was more than a venue. It was a good neighborhood bar. And that's a whole different thing altogether. Especially for a guy like me who'd just gotten divorced after twenty years. I had no place to go anyway. So you could see how it would be perfect.

Tracey Story Prince: Mink DeVille did the shortest concert ever at the Pony because he was on something. He strummed his guitar once and fell into the audience. That was the end of the night. That was it. He went bling and went face-first into the audience.

Butch Pielka: Agents are more anxious to book now because we've become as big as the Ritz and the Bottom Line.

Jack Roig: Cyndi Lauper, she's one of the greatest people I've ever met. She came in as a paid act. She was booked there, I think she played, I'd say, three or four times at least. But what a character. We were open until three, and you'd put the lights on and it didn't matter to Cyndi. "I'm gonna keep playing." What are you gonna do? You can't pull the plug on her. I mean, you could, but, you know? So I told the bar to just stop serving and let her go. And about three thirty she knocked off. How that little body produces that sound is amazing. And the second time Cyndi was there, it was a Saturday. They were doing their sound check on a Saturday afternoon, and I walked in there. I was just hanging out and watching. "Ehhh," she talked like that. Walks over to me. "Ehhh, I know you, I don't remember your fuckin' name, I don't remember your fuckin' name, but I know who you are." I said "Jack." She goes, "That's right, you own the fuckin' place, yeah? How you doin'."

Pete Llewellyn: Joan Jett. I took that as a prank phone call when she called the place. I told her manager to fuck themselves. At two o'clock, me and Butch were coming in from the beach. This guy calls up and says, "Hey, I'm Joan Jett's manager. We lost our gig tonight in New York. And she wants to play where the Boss got started." I told the guy to go fuck himself. Then he called back. That was on a Thursday. And I finally got Butch and he got on the phone and said yeah, come down, and she showed up on her tour bus. And she ended up liking it so much that at the end of the night, at three fifteen in the morning, she said, "You know what? This is pretty fucking cool. I'll see you all tomorrow night." And she played the next night.

Chris Layton: We had a chance while we were doing a tour and our manager asked we want you to play there, and we were like, hell yeah, let's go, man, it's the Stone Pony.

Stan Levinstone: Stevie [Ray Vaughan] and Double Trouble, they wanted to play at the Pony. I think they wanted to get in a warm-up show. I don't remember the exact scenario. A lot of people that played at the Pony made my life easier because I was looking for shows, but at the same time I got calls. They knew I was booking the Pony.

Jack Roig: Stevie Ray Vaughan, special guy. I don't know how this happened, we sat in the office after he got paid, for two hours, just talking. He had a bad rep, but he had been sober for a couple of years.

Chris Layton: Springsteen's talked about this stuff in song, about the rusting of America, and I'm paraphrasing here, but we were thinking was there one time where this place was like the happening locale in that part of town, all of it? I've seen so many places in America that at one point in time, you knew that this was like the epicenter of things, shiny and new and bright. I think everything has a season and its time.

Rich Russo: One Tuesday or Wednesday night was two shows billed with a band called the Sports Section. Because I've been going to the Pony so much, I got to know the bartenders and everybody there. They said, "Oh, make sure you buy tickets for that Sports Section thing." Like, "Okay." They said, "Do you want to know what it is?" I said, "Okay." It was Huey Lewis and the News, they're doing a warm-up and they're playing. At that point, Huey Lewis and the News is multiple number one hits, playing arenas. And there were max five hundred people there.

Huey Lewis: The Sports Section was, well, between records, we'd write songs, and it's really good to road-test those tunes, and it's fun to play them live. You learn a lot. You mainly learn not from the reaction of the crowd necessarily to a new song, because after all, it's a brand-new song. But you learn how you feel selling that song to those people. At some points, we'd write songs and have them, and they'd seem great, but now you go and you perform them in a club like that close up, and at a certain point you think, "Oh, man, this is going on a little bit. I need to cut this." You learn to edit your own stuff. So, it was really helpful, before we record, to go out and road-test these tunes, and we wanted to do all of them. We had ten or twelve of them. You can't play a concert as Huey Lewis and the News and play ten or twelve new songs, you know? That's not going to happen, so we changed our name to the Sports Section, and it was an excuse, really, to go play the Pony.

Tracey Story Prince: Huey Lewis hung out with us all night; we had a big party after.

Huey Lewis: Word was out that the Sports Section was actually us, for the most part. We sold it out. It was a busy night. And, well, because the 49ers were resurgent, and it was the 49ers and the Giants, and I knew a bunch of the 49ers were kind of pals of ours and stuff, and it was a playoff game coming up. And so I got in their face about how much better of a quarterback Joe Montana was than Phil Simms, in a real kind of lighthearted . . . I thought . . . West Coast way, you know? And then it turns out some of the audience didn't take too kindly to my comments, and they had to kind of escort me out to the bus. They were afraid somebody was going to try and beat me up on the way to the bus. It was a Jersey crowd, you know what I mean?

Tracey Story Prince: We had a suite in the Berkeley-Carteret, and Huey Lewis and his whole band hung out until like six in the morning with all of us. I was in the elevator with him, and he goes, "Am I making you nervous?" Because Kevin Buell, Bruce's guitar tech, was supposed to get in the elevator with me and he walked away at the last second and I kept yelling, "Kevin!"

Jack Roig: KISS played one night. KISS called up and they said . . . I happened to answer the phone and I said, "I can give you like twenty minutes. Right?" Well, we settled on an hour. To this day I don't remember if they were in costume or not.

Tracey Story Price: It was a basic band with no makeup and playing KISS music.

Jack Roig: KISS went on and they were on I guess about forty seconds and the power blew. And then somewhere or another I found what was wrong, turned it back on. They went back on and they played one hour to the second. That's how professional they were.

Jorma Kaukonen: I've been in this game for a long time, but I have to laugh whenever somebody goes, "Well, I can't believe this gig. You had to walk down through the crowd." I'm going, "You have no idea." But in a way, there's something kind of cool about it too. You sort of became part of the family for that night.

Gary U.S. Bonds: I kept coming because they kept booking me. I enjoyed doing it and they always had a crowd. It fit. For some reason, man, like I said, I lived in Norfolk, Virginia, and during that time, all my bookings were in this area and Long Island. I go, "Why am I living in Virginia? I'll just move up here."

Dennis Diken: We had been struggling for six years and now we're playing all over the country, and then all over the world eventually on the tour for the first album. Playing in Asbury Park to a hometown crowd or home-state crowd and to have all that love come from the audience, and then to be able to headline the Pony, that was a big deal. That was really special, and it meant a lot to us. It meant a lot to our fans, I think too. Then we continued to play there. We play there to this day.

Jean Mikle: They'd still had the local bands. Cats only played every Sunday. They were still playing Sundays. The Diamonds would play. Was that Mondays or Wednesday? I can't remember. So that was still going on. But then maybe Friday, Saturday, they'd have national acts. And that was cool. I remember seeing Wilson Pickett there, maybe '87. It was interesting too, because Bruce would get up and play with the national acts. I remember him playing with Marshall Crenshaw, Jimmy Cliff, Levon Helm.

Marshall Crenshaw: I really debated with myself whether to ask Bruce to come up or not. Somebody told me he was there. And I'd met him before. We had mutual friends. I met him backstage on the first night of the *Born in the U.S.A.* tour. But I still felt funny. Am I supposed to bother him this way, or is it a bother? I couldn't make up my mind about it. And then finally I just thought, "I got to do it and see what happens." So I called out to him, and it was late in the set, and he slowly came up. It was an exciting night, but then when he got onstage, forget it. Then it's just something else, like I didn't even expect. People went nuts. They already were going nuts, and then it was really nuts, when he got up there.

Marshall Crenshaw: As soon as I thought about having him come up and realized I was going to page him, for some reason I thought of that old song, "You Can't Sit Down," by the Dovells. I had this feeling that he would want to play it, and I knew he would know it. And so we played it and we'd never played it before. We just kind of faked it, but it worked great. And then after that, it was "La Bamba," because *La Bamba* was out right then. Number one movie in the country, and I'm in it, you know. So we did "La Bamba." I forget who sang it, because I don't think I attempted to, since it's in Spanish. I don't remember that. Somehow "La Bamba" turned into "Twist and Shout." It was just bar-band rock and roll, just exactly right on the money.

Max Weinberg: A very, very dear close friend of mine was Levon Helm. And Levon in early '87 was playing Frank James in a movie about Jesse James. And in one of the scenes, he had to twirl a gun and put it into a holster. Long story short, he was practicing with a loaded .45, and he shot himself in his right leg. And it went through right above the knee, but it didn't hit anything vital. But he couldn't play the bass drum. So he called me and he wanted to put a band together, Levon Helm's All Stars, and he wanted me to play bass drum so he could play the top parts. One night we got booked at the Stone Pony. I have a picture of the marquee, and it was Levon Helm's All Stars featuring me, Max Weinberg. So I called Bruce and I said, "Gee, I'm playing at the Stone Pony with Levon Helm." "I'll be there." So him and Patti came down.

Patti Scialfa: Levon Helm, who I'd met earlier in Woodstock one time. I don't know, somebody brought me to his house, and he had a lot of people over, very lovely, lovely gentleman, and one of the most amazing musicians. And I ended up singing with him in the Pony, "The Weight."

Max Weinberg: Bruce had the hand-printed words to "Cripple Creek." He couldn't wait to sing "Cripple Creek" with Levon Helm at the Stone Pony.

Dennis Diken: It's funny, in all the years that we played there in the area, Bruce never sat in with us. We thought that would happen, but we did become very good friends with Garry Tallent early on when we started playing there. He would often come and sit in with us.

Stan Levinstone: I had Warren Zevon down here, and his agent came down with him. It was right after Warren got out of rehab, and the Pony just got a beer delivery. Their dressing room is L-shaped. So, they had drapes over the beer. In the rider it clearly said no alcohol or anything around Warren, and then they get a beer delivery, and I'm like, "Holy shit." Warren was walking around like he was going to kill somebody. I did not talk to him the first night.

Rich Russo: Got to see Warren Zevon here, which was great, but also sucked because the Pony had that flat floor with very limited sight lines and at that point had these two giant pillars. Warren Zevon, who's sitting there at a piano or electric piano, whatever it was, if you weren't in the first or second row, all you saw was the top of his head and maybe the top brim of his glasses because he was then sitting down on a low stage on a flat floor.

Stan Levinstone: I don't think Warren ever played a full band gig of all the shows I did with him. It was always him and his piano, and his chicken and ribs and black coffee.

Rich Russo: But Bruce was there and he was in baseball hat, and he had a couple days' growth, and he was standing next to me pretty much unassuming and I recognized him, and he looked at me like "Nobody knows I'm here, so . . ." And I said, "Are you going up there?" And he goes, "Nah, Warren doesn't even know I'm here." "You should do 'Jeannie Needs a Shooter.'" He goes, "Yeah."

Stan Levinstone: Warren and I got to be really, really close. He used to make me get up onstage. We had a DJ, he would let the DJ go off, and then he'd make me go up onstage and emcee. He would write a script out that I couldn't read till I got onstage.

Danny Clinch: My buddy growing up, Mickey, his brother and sister were several years older than us, Billy and Kathy, and they talked about coming to Asbury Park, I think, and they would go to the Stone Pony and stuff like that. Those two were big for me because they turned me on to Warren Zevon, Cat Stevens, and Allman Brothers, Bob Seger, Springsteen, Led Zeppelin. And when we became teenagers, and then we would try to go to see a show at the Pony. The Stray Cats might have been one of the early shows that I saw there, Del Fuegos, Tommy Conwell and the Young Rumblers, Cyndi Lauper early on. And I always was hoping I would see Springsteen or something, and I was always bringing my camera.

Mark Pender: You'd never know when Bruce was coming. He'd just show up. At that time, he'd just drive himself over and come and hang out. We had done the *Tunnel of Love* tour in 1988. After the tour was over, Bruce invited a bunch of us over to his house over there. We're all hanging out and he goes, "Yeah, yeah, let's go to the Pony." I'm like, "Cool." I'm looking at his Corvette. I said, "I always wanted a Corvette." He says, "Well, why don't you drive it?" He throws me the keys. I drive the Corvette, him and Patti get in the back of Ed Manion's pickup truck, and we all head down to the Pony. It might have been Cats that was actually playing. But we just all go in there on a whim. That's, I think, how he always did it, and that's what made it magic too. But I remember there was a point in the night where I had to have both arms out to get people to stop rushing him. I felt like I'd become a partial security presence. Because he just wanted to come back there and throw back a few drinks with the rest of us.

Tracey Story Prince: It was funny because you'd have Joe Grushecky, Bruce, and then you had Nils. They all looked like each other. They're all wearing bandanas and it was like big me, regular me, and mini-me. When they walk in together, it was really a funny thing. They all resembled each other.

Lee Mrowicki: Nils used to have a trampoline on the side of the stage. He's really a gymnast. He would use the trampoline to do backflips with guitar in hand on the stage. There's this one album called *Flip*, a picture of him that's from the trampoline.

Jesse Malin: I was looking for other things musically as a writer and player. I started to get into songwriters, like Billy Bragg and Elvis Costello and the Replacements, Paul Westerberg. Then the *Nebraska* record came across my hands and suddenly I became a Bruce fan, really believing. It just seemed to be the next step after punk for me and where he was at. When *Born in the U.S.A.* came out, I was in. A lot of my friends didn't get it. I was like, "You better read the lyric sheet, man . . . this is not some patriotic Rambo thing. This guy is really talking the real truth here. It's amazing that it's out there on such a big level with these songs, even the title track."

I was down. I took a ride down there with a girlfriend. I had a van, I was a moving guy, and I had just broke my band up. I always went down there, and we didn't have enough money to get in. We just drove and looked at the beach and stood outside and slept in the van and just hung in that area. I was amazed that this club with all this energy and was similar to CBGBs. I would go back with a friend of mine who was digging in deeper after the Bruce thing, and we would go see somebody like Gary U.S. Bonds.

Mark Pender: *Better Days* [with Southside and the Jukes]. We did that record, and then they put together a huge reunion at the Pony. Steven, Bruce, Bon Jovi. The *Better Days* show that they filmed. It was just such an incredible show. "It's Been a Long Time," that's a song that Steven, Johnny, Bruce, and Bon Jovi all traded verses on. There's a DVD of it. I did something really stupid. They had a camera set onstage, like at sound check, and I didn't realize it was still continuously recording. And I took my dick out and started waving it in front of it. I thought nobody will ever see it, but then I heard somebody did see it.

Pete Llewellyn: We had famous people walking in all the time. I almost got fired one night because I proofed a girl, and I wouldn't let her in. And I almost got fired because it was Christie Brinkley and Billy Joel. And he says, "She don't need ID." And I said, "I don't give a fuck who she is, she needs ID." I didn't recognize him.

Jack Roig: But we always needed the locals. You needed them during the week because you'd only get the national acts on, say, Saturday/ Sunday/Friday.

Huey Lewis: We were very much into the jammy thing, because we all came from bands where you'd play three or four sets a night in a club, you know? And when you did that, man, you wanted somebody to come up and jam and give you a break, you know? And you're sick of playing the same stuff over and over again, but that's all you know, so, we were more than happy to invite people to jam, always.

Jorma Kaukonen: The Pony was probably the first time I played with Dickey Betts. I'd known the Allman Brothers guys for a long time since the Fillmore West. But I can't remember what kind of format Dickey had back then. But we were both doing sort of solo things, however you want to look at it, and it was, "Hey, man, how are you doing?"

Bobby Bandiera: They were crazy days, I'll tell you. Oh, drugs were off the chart. More cocaine than anything. People were always getting busted. People were always on the street where you can park head-on, you know, right around the Pony? Getting busted. So, it was a learning experience. You know, you don't come to a place like that where you're supposed to have fun, and lose your fucking mind, and thinking that you could actually do drugs in the car outside and not get busted. It was all cops though. Pony security were involved more on the other end. It was like, "I'm not telling anybody what we're doing, and we won't tell anybody what you're doing." But it was that kind of world back then. And a lot of people didn't make it through. Died of an overdose here, died of an overdose there. Crazy times.

Glen Burtnik: I had heard about there being some after-party things that you could join. You have to be a member and then you'd be able to go into a place and drink till five a.m. or something. There was a lot of drugs. There was a lot of cocaine at that time and alcohol, is how I would call it. Usually, after a gig, you would either go home to your wife and kids, which is what I had, or stay out and somebody would have a hotel room and there'd be a party there.

Stan Levinstone: People partied hard. Bouncers, bartenders, everybody. You go in the office, cocaine. Thank God I never developed a habit. Everybody partied down there. It was part of the times. The bars were open late.

Pete Llewellyn: I would catch a drug deal happening, we'd break it up, and we'd throw them out of the bar and they weren't allowed back in. We'd mark them and they were never allowed back then.

Huey Lewis: We, in our day, needed somewhere to hone our craft, and these benevolent music-loving club owners provided that for us, and the crowd. And the crowd, the audience, it let the audience in on something, an acquired taste, which is a band that plays synergistically, a Rubik's cube thing, the interplay between the musicians, and that kind of stuff, which you don't see a lot of in Taylor Swift's show, you know what I mean? And the audiences were schooled on that kind of stuff, and it helped to develop their musical taste, and it helped us to become better musicians and better players and better performers, because we performed with audiences, and interact with audiences. Look at how Bruce interacts with audiences. Forget about it. So, those clubs were incredibly valuable to us coming up.

15

The 3M Show

Boarded-up factories. Small towns in decline. The slow unwinding of the American promise. It was dubbed "heartland rock" by the *New York Times*. Springsteen was its godfather. But the grand orator of the workingman had never himself worked a shift in factories or mills. An effort to save a manufacturing plant in 1985 and 1986 would bring Springsteen close to the union and factory hands he sang so frequently about.

Stanley Fischer: This whole thing started in September of 1985. That's when 3M first announced to us that they were going to phase the plant down, shut it down.

Jean Mikle: It was part of the last of the industrial legacy of Freehold. You had the [Karagheusian] Rug Mill, you had Rockaway Glass, and you had 3M.

Bruce Springsteen: I lived through the closing down of the Rug Mill, and it was a tremendous job loss in town. And then 3M, in Freehold of all places, decided they were going to shut down.

Stanley Fischer: There were four hundred and fifty jobs at the plant, it was a three-shift operation. Actually, they would have a seven-day-a-week operation where you work six days on, two days off, different times. Majority of the people—half the factory were women, single moms, and working.

It was a situation where we were so busy that they literally just ran us into the ground and they didn't upgrade any of the equipment while they're working us seven days a week, twenty-four hours a day.

Jean Mikle: It was after the steel mills had gone down. And here's these manufacturing, blue-collar jobs, well-paying jobs, and I think it was symbolic of a lot of the industrial decline. Then Freehold, it was another blow because they had lost so much.

Patti Scialfa: Factories were closing down in different areas, and that was just horrifying. It just disrupts the whole community and people lose jobs and they're displaced and it's terrible. As they did everywhere at the time. The place where Bruce's dad worked, they shut down. They shut down the coffee place there. It happened everywhere.

Howard Saunders: There was a record on *Born in the U.S.A.*, one of the cuts was called "My Hometown." The cut refers to a rug mill, a textile mill actually, in the song that closed down and workers lost their jobs. And we immediately started wondering, was there a way to find out if that was a real textile mill? Was that really in Freehold? Did it really exist? And what if they were workers in the textile mill that were actually working at 3M? This we didn't know. Immediately phone calls were made. And we found that in fact four workers from the original rug mill, it was a rug mill, the Karagheusian Rug Mill, were now working at the 3M plant and many parents and grandparents of workers currently in the 3M plant had worked in the textile mill.

Stanley Fischer: We came up with the correlation between Bruce's song "My Hometown," which was the closing of where his dad worked and the Rug Mill, and that this was now happening again to his hometown. We wrote letters to everybody and his brother and we did our research. Bruce donated to steelworkers in Pennsylvania and Pittsburgh and California, and the closing of Lady Beth out there, that steel mill.

Bruce Springsteen: I went to Pittsburgh, I met a man named Ron Weisen. Ron Weisen was a union activist. And of course, the steel mills were shutting down all through the Monongahela valley. And they had developed food banks, to attempt to assist themselves and service themselves. So when I found out a little bit about this, I tried to give them a hand. And then when I left, they said, "Hey, there's these guys in LA, you should check them out." So I went to LA and I went to South Central LA and there was a whole group of union guys there. People didn't know that that part of Los Angeles produced a reasonable amount of steel, and they were going under. So they had a food bank. So I got involved with them.

Stanley Fischer: Then eventually we got a call from Barbara [Carr from Springsteen management] saying, "What is it that you want Bruce to do?" We talked about it and then she invited us up on, at that time, [Jon] Landau had an office in, I want to say it was near the Hard Rock on Fifty-Seventh Street.

Bruce Springsteen: I knew a union spokesman in Freehold, Stanley Fischer, and Stanley said, "Gee, is there anything we can do about it?" I said, "Well, I don't know. I'll throw my two cents in for what it's worth."

Stanley Fischer: We talked to her about it and I guess Bruce was in the back room and then he came out and, "Hey, anything I can do to help?" What we wanted to do is we wanted to take an ad out in the *New York Times*. So he had to pay the *New York Times*, which he did. It was pricey back then, it was like twenty-five grand.

Jean Mikle: It was a huge deal because all these people got involved. Not just because Bruce got involved. The *Hill Street Blues* cast and Willie Nelson, all these people signing huge newspaper ads, "3M, don't abandon my hometown."

Stanley Fischer: It started getting more critical in the press. We were criticizing them in our ads, that this is going to create more suicides and homelessness. Then it got ugly.

Howard Saunders: What happened is Springsteen's involvement has galvanized the local. This was a local that was really quite frightened of the company. Not a militant local—historically they've been fairly passive—and a lot of people in the plant were very scared, reluctant to do anything to make the company angry. They did not want to shake anything up. Some people would have probably been very happy to take a good severance package and think they were getting, you know, getting off of something good. Springsteen's involvement made them feel valid. They sensed that people cared about them in a way they couldn't possibly have imagined before that and it really empowered them. It gave them a sense of their own spirit.

Stanley Fischer: When we finally decided we were going to have this event at the Stone Pony, we had no idea initially that Bruce would call at all because that's not something that they're going to publicize or else the walls would've burst open.

Eileen Chapman: Lee was always putting benefits together at the Pony. It made sense that they would do it there for visibility reasons.

Stanley Fischer: The Stone Pony event was a way to make money. Naturally we hoped that he would come, and certainly, I would say we orchestrated it with press and stuff like that, that it would be very inviting to him to come, but we never sat down in an office with Barbara or anybody to say, "Hey, we're going to put the benefit together and Bruce could come." Then when we did find out that he would come to the Pony event, it was the type of thing where nobody can know. We didn't tell anybody else on the union committee. Nothing. We didn't let it out. It was just me and Les, and Barbara, Bruce.

Eileen Chapman: That was a pretty incredible show and mobs of people. It was just a high-energy show. I just remember, it was insane. People were dancing and screaming and yelling and standing on tops of everything. And Bruce spoke about the 3M plant and spoke about the impact to workers, and you didn't always get that in the Pony. In fact, I don't know if we had ever heard anything like that before where people actually got up and had something to say. It was not just to play music, but there was a meaning to it.

> **Bruce Springsteen (speech from the stage):** Before we play a little bit, I'd like to say a few things about why we're down here tonight. Mainly, I'd like to say that I think that the marriage between a community and a company is a special thing. It involves a special trust. I think that four hundred jobs is a lot of work lost in a small town. What do you do when after ten years or twenty years, you wake up in the morning and you see your livelihood sailing away from you, leaving you standing on the beach? What

happens when the jobs go away and the people remain? And, I guess I'd like to say what goes unmeasured is the price that unemployment inflicts on people's families, on their marriages, on the single mothers out there trying to raise their kids on their own. Now, the 3M company, it's their money and it's their plant, but it's the 3M workers' jobs. I'm here tonight to just say that I think that after twenty-five years of service from a community that there's a debt owed to the 3M workers and to my hometown.

Stanley Fischer: Bruce probably played for maybe an hour and then I got to meet him again or see him backstage. We brought some other people back there to him and stuff like that. I couldn't tell you off the top of my head. It wasn't the full band. I don't believe the full band was there as it was constituted back in that era. Clarence was there. Max was there.

Eileen Chapman: I remember that night as people were dancing on tables and on the bar, it was insane. It was one of those classic Stone Pony nights that don't happen often or are so memorable. I remember he did the song "Stand on It" and I remember people were just absolutely out of their minds, dancing on every surface they could.

Garry Tallent: A good time was had by all. This was the first time we played since we've been off the road. It felt good.

Kyle Brendle: There was really good energy there. A lot of people were sympathetic to the 3M situation. You could feel just some real positive energy.

Stanley Fischer: We had that electricity that was in the air and everybody was jacked up, and Bruce came through. It was great. Bruce came through, and the place was packed and we got lots of press afterwards and then on the heels of that, then we had Barbara Walters doing a 20/20 piece in February, and South African workers going on strike.

Jean Mikle: It was really cool when Bruce came out and played that night with Clarence. I think it really lifted the spirit of those people. It didn't wind up being successful, of course, keeping 3M open. The plant closed like a month or two later. I did a story with another reporter ten years later to find out what happened to everybody.

Eileen Chapman: Everybody knew Butch and Jack were those kind of guys. You could go to Butch and Jack and say, "There's this cause." And they would embrace it and say, "Yeah. Come on in." And, "Here's the room." Everybody, all the musicians had relationships with Butch and Jack, and with the Pony. If you're going to some other club, they're going to charge you a room fee or they're going to charge you for sound, or they're going to charge you for something. And you didn't get that at the Pony.

Max Weinberg: There were always a lot of benefits being done at the Stone Pony. You could always, whether it was Bruce or anybody else, because it was such a tight scene, if there was a benefit going on, you didn't have to twist anybody's arm.

Butch Pielka: Bruce came in here a few weeks ago to do the 3M benefit, and I'll tell you, to see him play up there sent chills right through my spine. Here he is, now the biggest guy in the world, and he's on my stage, in my club.

Max Weinberg: Bruce had not yet really, except for his famous statement in Pittsburgh about Ronald Reagan, wondering if he listened to *Nebraska*, moving towards realizing that he had a political voice. And that may have been one of the first organized, other than No Nukes in the West Coast antinuclear movement. But this was a local thing. And he felt, obviously still does feel, very close to Freehold. It wasn't like we were out politicking, but it was to raise funds. So again, you get Bruce, even with a group of locals playing behind him, I happened to be playing the drums, you're going to get a crowd.

Bruce Springsteen: I was deep into the idea, like, okay, I had this sudden success, this great success. Well, what do you do with that? Where do you apply that if you can in any way? And so I was just basically interested in finding what the parameters of that kind of some success might give you. And it turned into that particular show.

16

Troubles

Greed. Corruption. Shortcuts. New liquor laws raising the drinking age to twenty-one would take full effect by 1985. Asbury Park was struggling, and the "Jersey way" of doing business was taking its toll. A local psychiatric hospital shifted care, leaving some patients to largely fend for themselves in the hotels of Asbury Park. Springsteen was basically on tour for two straight years, and though the Jukes were back playing the club on rare occasions, their star had faded. The Pony continued to pack out on weekends, but the drag of the town began to be felt on the bar tabs in the late 1980s.

Rachel Bolan: I don't know how many times I heard, "Oh, the Pony is closing," and you're just like, "Please don't be true this time. Please don't be true."

Kyle Brendle: Part of the thing was when the drinking age went to twenty-one and up from eighteen. That's the population that spent their income. When we lost them to the new laws, that changed the dynamic very visibly in New Jersey, not just Asbury Park, because you're losing people with expendable income. That's the way I see it. And it was noticeable after the summer season.

Eileen Chapman: Then as the drunk-driving laws started to change, again, another impact on attendance and how far people were going to drive. People weren't living in Asbury Park. Getting people to come to Asbury Park when they're afraid of being pulled over or they weren't the right age had a huge impact.

Bruce Haring: The drinking-age change was huge. Clubs were open seven days a week, and they were crowded for the most part. Kids at eighteen, they'd go out. Eighteen to twenty-three to twenty-four, twenty-five, whatever, that's prime age. It was a concert every night. . . . You can't state how much of an impact that had versus . . . the club scene even dropped off once it went back to twenty-one.

Glen Burtnik: Right around that time, when they changed the law, I do remember us feeling like, "Shit, there goes half the audience," or something. Although it wasn't dramatic.

Southside Johnny: Asbury Park was really getting kind of rough. And it was also the feeling that you don't want people hanging around in the area to see you play and getting mugged or anything like that. I didn't like the danger for the people.

Kyle Brendle: The drinking age went up to twenty-one and it went to 0.1–0.15, Breathalyzers. It was the end of an era. It was a twenty-year run of just pure madness.

Eileen Chapman: Things really, really started to hit the skids by '84, '85. [Patients from the Marlboro Psychiatric Hospital] all found boardinghouses in Asbury Park. And people who couldn't afford to keep up their big Victorian homes were making smaller apartments, and housing all of the halfway-house patients that came out of Marlboro. And you'd see a lot of people walking the streets that were definitely under heavy medication and going through garbage bins. Even some of the hotels. Hotels became refuges for halfway-house patients.

Southside Johnny: They started putting all the people from the halfway houses in the SRO hotels and things. And then the drugs started to kick in. And I think it was just plain cocaine and heroin.

Bruce Haring: It was lawless. It wasn't a place where if you were coming in from the parkway to go to Asbury Park, you wouldn't stop at the local stores or anything like that. The town had a lot of group homes back then too. Between that and the people wandering the streets and breaking into cars, it wasn't exactly a town that you would stay in.

Danny Clinch: Coming here was pretty scary. We would come down. I recall we would come in and we would go right to the show and to our car. We weren't hanging around. We had our rides.

Bruce Haring: Even though it was friendly inside the Pony, outside when you parked, it was a little bit shaky there. A lot of times there were car break-ins and equipment stolen, and things like that too. That was part of the mystique too. You were taking your life in your hands at least to go to your car, but inside was a welcoming beacon.

Glen Burtnik: There were less and less people coming to Asbury Park. It seemed like the rides were stopped. It became a ghost town.

Tim Donnelly: If you're coming to Asbury Park back in the day, you were coming for two reasons. You're coming to see music or to cop drugs.

Tony Pallagrosi: I'd heard things about the mayor and the town council taking bribes and all of that. I didn't really become intimately aware of those things till the nineties when I was a concert promoter.

Tony Amato: Asbury started to look like Beirut. Because some of the people on the city council were putting money in their pocket.

Bob Burger: It was just like a bombed-out city. . . . There was just nothing there. And I was thinking, boy, it can't stay like this because this property is too valuable. This beachfront property is beautiful. It can't stay like a slum.

Kyle Brendle: We would send bouncers to walk women to their cars all the time. It was becoming obviously a problem.

Vini Lopez: They were preying on people coming out of the Pony for a while.

John Cafferty: Playing at the Pony years ago, at the end of the night I was going to walk down to the Flamingo Hotel and Butch said, "I'll walk with you." And I said, "Really? It's right there." He said, "No." He goes, "There's some stuff going on. It's probably not good for you to be walking around with an instrument on your back, and whatever.

Because, they figure you might have a pocketful of money coming from the club or something."

Jesse Malin: There were a lot of problems and desperate people around. It was destitute in other areas, and there were these banged-out motels and people just all over the street. And I was used to sleeping in a van on Avenue B.

Dan Jacobson: There was a prejudice in the suburbs about Asbury Park that remained until recent days, which informs a lot of my work. I heard it through a lot of my life. I really combated that and have a real problem with it. Back then it manifested itself in people in the suburbs telling you it's dangerous there, got to be careful, lock your doors when you go through, all that type of thing. There was a sense if you were from suburban Monmouth County, that there was a problem with Asbury Park. Kids being kids, we went in and we had a great time. We liked it and we didn't care.

Henry Vaccaro: Since tourists were not coming here, you had vacant hotels that they would allow mental patients. And one time, I guess there were five or six thousand mental patients living at Asbury Park all along the beachfront.

Henry Vaccaro: That's how bad it was. And then when Johnny Cash— that's another whole story, how I got him involved. But there was an old antique store on Main Street, and they had a sign in the window, "We bought for cash. We sell for cash, but we need Johnny Cash and we need him now." And Johnny was with us that night. So we're driving from the Berkeley, which was under reconstruction. Johnny had an apartment in New York that he sublet from Liza Minnelli. He and June came down to check out the progress in the hotel and we're driving down Main Street and I showed him the sign. And June says, "Why, John, we have to stop here." So we stop and get out. I thank God I get a picture of him in front of the sign. So he knocks on the door. "Sorry, we're closed." Knocks again. This is about six o'clock at night. "Hey, buddy, I don't think you heard me. We're closed." Johnny knocks again. "You don't fucking understand, sign says place is closed." So Johnny yells back and says, "I see by the sign in the window, you're looking for me." He says, "Here I am." And this guy had a scream you could have heard in Nashville.

Bobby Bandiera: I know that when a few people were looking at the Berkeley-Carteret, Johnny Cash was one of them, to refurbish it.

Henry Vaccaro: Johnny Cash and June were the first investors in the Berkeley-Carteret Hotel. I saw an opportunity that the Berkeley-Carteret Hotel had been boarded up for five or six years, and they were going to demolish it. And I bought it for $325,000.

Things were so bad in town, the town was going to sell the entire beachfront, which included the Casino building, the Convention Hall, the Paramount there, the Marine Grill site, the swimming pool, and five pavilions, for two million dollars. I went to court and got a restraining order and stopped the sale. . . . They went out and hired a planner and they redesigned the whole beachfront, and they put it out for public bids. And the plan was very comprehensive. It divided the whole beachfront into ten subsections. Each subsection had a designation where you could bid on an individual subsection or the entire project. So my brother and I owned thirty pieces of property in town. At one time, every area that was to be developed, we owned a piece of property.

Lee Mrowicki: At that point they were thinking, well, we have to move the Stone Pony and we gotta maybe put it near the Casino. Down at South End and it used to be a real working power plant. They said, "Well, the power plant seems to be the only place where you know these condos are gonna take over everything."

Henry Vaccaro: One time they were talking about moving the Stone Pony into the power plant. And then it was scheduled to be demolished, just like the Palace Amusements was scheduled to be demolished.

Lee Mrowicki: They were talking and saying, "Well, it's gonna take it over by eminent domain and you know." The owners didn't want to put any money into the building because they didn't think they were gonna get any return out of it. If it's an eminent domain you're gonna get pennies on the dollar.

Bobby Bandiera: There was actually another building being built, and they took down the whole exoskeleton of it. It was being built. It was high up in the sky. And it stayed that way for seven or eight years. And it was an eyesore.

Henry Vaccaro: We started building this sixteen-story high-rise called C-8, because it was in a C-8 zone. Okay. The Bank of Boston gave us a fifty-million-dollar construction loan commitment. They advanced eighteen million. Now it's 1989, the nationwide savings and loan crisis. Fourteen hundred banks failed. Five banks I'm doing business with failed. Bank of Boston now refuses to honor their commitment and the job has stopped.

Dan Jacobson: It's a classic case of trying to force a big, bad, cookie-cutter redevelopment project. It's tremendously conformist on a town and expect it to work. It didn't. The mistake here that was made, the cardinal mistake of trying to redevelop the waterfront first. Because everybody around here said it's not happening until the waterfront's redeveloped. It's not happening until the families are coming back. It was total bullshit. So what happened was, they tried to force it up there first. It hit a recession. Before that, when people saw a little bit going on there, it was complete speculation of the housing stock west of there driving up the price, throwing out long-term people, tenants, homeowners, because they sold out and you really eliminated the neighborhoods. So, all of a sudden, you hit a recession in 1991, and the thing goes downhill. It fails because it was nonsense. It was too big. It was too ambitious. That's total conformity, which is what I hate.

Eileen Chapman: The boardwalk was empty for years, because then the developer defaulted, and it was a lawsuit that took forever.

Dan Jacobson: There was no good choices. As I always said, there was one side that later was proven to be corrupt; there was another side that was absolutely intolerant and out of control. One election I voted for the ones who ended up being pretty corrupt. But I always thought the corruption stuff was overstated because there were a lot bigger forces than corruption holding the city down at that point. There was a problem of the perception around everywhere, that you can't go there, it's dangerous, you'll never come back.

Eileen Chapman: They closed all of the pavilions here on the boardwalk. There were a couple of the pinball places open, but for the most part, there was nothing going on on the boardwalk. You'd just see people roaming the streets, eating out of trash cans.

Bob Burger: It didn't feel safe. I mean, I never was in a situation where I was afraid, but walking down the boardwalk at night, uncomfortable. Not too many people, but people in the shadows, things like that.

Bobby Bandiera: You knew not to drive down certain areas, if you were driving home and you got rerouted for whatever reason. I mean, it might have even been a checkpoint. Let's go this way. Well, we better not go that way because we're not going to be in such a good area.

Marshall Crenshaw: I didn't know at the time if it was the scene, or if it was me, or what it was. But yeah, the last couple times we played there, of course it was not the same at all as the early days. I guess that's what happened. We played maybe one show or two shows that were just . . . like nobody particularly showed up. It wasn't a big scene at all anymore.

Marshall Crenshaw: You could see that Asbury was a wreck. The big glitzy hotel they tried to revive had gone south. It was sad; it was really, really sad. And it just puzzled me. I thought, "Okay, there's the ocean, there's the beachfront, there's all the history and the beauty . . ." Just because it's got this kind of funky beautifulness to it. "And maybe there's another town, the next town down the shore where everybody's going, but this is not working." It looked really beat up and bad. And I think there were some unfinished construction sites too.

Pete Llewellyn: There was so much shit happening in the Stone Pony, and the outside was a fucking war zone. Prostitutes, heroin addicts, homeless, crime, and where were the cops? They were in the Stone Pony getting drunk.

Eileen Chapman: It was places like the Pony and the Fast Lane and other places that were featuring music; it's the only thing that kept people coming. And there were nights at the Pony even during the summer during the week that there would be maybe fifty people in there by the mid-eighties. So it started to really affect the clubs.

Billy Hector: Butch told me how much it cost to run the place and why he wouldn't hire me, basically. Because I would be going in there trying to get a gig. Especially after *Hot Romance*.

Eileen Chapman: Some late-eighties summers, when we were doing really good at Jay's, I'd walk over to the Pony and there'd be hardly anybody in there. Especially after Bruce went on tour, people didn't necessarily come to the Pony anymore because of course they weren't going to see him because they know these tours that lasted a year or two, and so all the Bruce watchers didn't come.

Kyle Brendle: I distinctly remember it taking a turn. I was sitting there talking with Butch one night. We had like three of their top bands playing all in one night, like the Fourth of July weekend, three cover bands. It was like, Cahoots, Cats, and somebody else, and there was like a hundred people there. Butch was looking out and there's no one around; you could see it was starting to happen quickly. This is like 1988 and already, that was when they started with—and the domaining of the oceanfront. Basically, most of the businesses north of Second Avenue were already closed, and the few that were left, they're closing up to eminent domain, and it was a stark, hard reality. It was coming down fast. It was very clear that something ugly was happening.

Eileen Chapman: It was a ghost town. It was derelict. It looked worn down. And people who came here expecting oh it's the Stone Pony, it's this great place, and they'd come to it the first time and they look around and they're like, holy shit.

17

End of the Ride

Liquor laws. Politics. Bad bets. A dying town. The life span of a scene rarely grows older than a teen. Although Springsteen still showed through the late 1980s, including almost weekly in 1989, and the Jukes were working with Stevie again, the scene had faded. Fans had gotten older, had children, and moved away. And the Pony, which had defied gravity for so long, succumbed to time.

Steve Schraeger: I knew something was wrong. I'll leave it at that. I didn't know the particulars or anything. I could just tell that things were getting worse.

Gary U.S. Bonds: I didn't think it would ever close. I couldn't figure out why. I said, "What did they do? What happened?"

Kyle Brendle: They had some financial legal troubles coming off of, I believe, lawsuits, injury lawsuits of people, and they weren't carrying insurance, so I knew it was going to be a problem. I wasn't being told this directly; this is just observation. I was a fly on the wall, knew that there was trouble burning.

Mark Pender: I was sure at one point, when those guys, Butch and Jack, things weren't going well, that eventually it'd just be over.

Stan Levinstone: The story I remember, I remember being in the office and Butch comes back from vacation when they got the bankruptcy papers. He had no idea that was coming.

Jack Roig: Then there was financial problems, because liquor law liability, one year they wanted $185,000. For liquor law liability. And that didn't count your normal liability, or your fire, or anything like that. That's a pretty tough knot for a place that size, you know? Especially in Asbury Park when you're charging four dollars to come in. So we ran with no insurance. And then we wound up with a million lawsuits. Boom.

Pete Llewellyn: There were so many lawsuits. I remember Butch crying about it. He was paying $10,000, which was a lot of money back then, a year or maybe $15,000, and it went up to $90,000 a year. He said, "Can't do it. It'll put us under." They did it self-insurance. They took a certain amount of money, put it away for lawsuits. That didn't last. The lawsuits piled up and they had to file bankruptcy from the lawsuits.

Bobby Bandiera: Everybody got sued. Everybody does get sued. The band, the venue, the guy sitting next to you.

Tracey Story Prince: Jack had to borrow the money from my father to put the sprinkler system in, because at that point, they were bankrupt. He made a personal loan from my dad. My dad put the sprinklers in.

Jack Roig: Lawsuits were killing us. Terrible. I mean, to get with all the liability, one year was 185,000 bucks. Just for the policy. Come on, ridiculous. And the lawsuits were killing us. So I filed on [Chapter] 11 for protection, and I think it would've still been open today. Only, Butch and the fucking attorney forgot to send in a form one month. That's when the marshal came in and said, "Okay, now we're in control." And it started.

Lee Mrowicki: One lawsuit was because of the Ramones. The Ramones love playing in Asbury. And to some people it was cool to spit on people. So this one guy spits on Joey Ramone. So Joey takes the mic stand and tries to remove the guy's nose. Bam. And this guy is bloody like you wouldn't believe.

CJ Ramone: When they spit on Johnny, or when they spit at Joey, that used to really piss me off because I felt like they were disrespecting the Ramones at that point. . . . That was not an American thing. That never was an American thing. So getting spit on here in the States was a whole different thing than getting spit on over in Europe. But it was part of the punk scene over there. It was part of the punk scene and something that the band had seen. Everybody was used to it and everything, but I was just not having it. Not having it. You're not spitting on Joey or Johnny when I'm onstage.

Lee Mrowicki: I saw the guy, the bouncers taking him outside to the, they called emergency, 911. Right out the front door and I said, "That's a problem waiting to happen." And you know first of all, we had bouncers that worked in the other bars and everything, they're pretty experienced but they never saw nothing like that. It was amazing and I knew that was a world of lawsuits that we're gonna face in the near future because it's like you don't just sue one person, you sue everybody in sight. So that was one of them that happened.

Monte Melnick: I don't remember that one.

Pete Llewellyn: The collectors would come in on a busy night and try to unload the money, but every hour Butch would walk around and sweep the tens and the twenties down the registers. They would come in and try to collect money for the lawsuits. Just a matter of time; it wore them down and they couldn't stay open.

Kyle Brendle: There was no more weekday business. The Pony prided itself on being open seven days a week. The weekdays were dead. Just nobody is coming. It was really, really hard. It was down to Friday, Saturdays, Sundays. The weekdays were done. Just, there was no more business to be had. Very hard times.

Eileen Chapman: It closed the night after we did a benefit for Billy Hector's girlfriend, Susan. That was the last night. That was a Butch and Jack night. It was a benefit for Susan. And nobody had any indication it would be closing.

Kyle Brendle: It was a Tuesday after Labor Day, 1991. Jack Roig came to open up and the county sheriffs had the lock on the front door.

Jack Roig: We ran a pretty good benefit. And then, bingo. Came in the morning, that was it. They changed the locks.

Eileen Chapman: Somebody started calling other people. Like, "What's going on? There's a lock on the door of the Pony. What's going on? What happened last night? Why is there a lock on the door?" It was all news to us.

Jack Roig: It was supposed to be a normal meeting. So I came in. For me, it was a normal meeting. For them, we were in the back of the building and the guy in the front was changing the locks. And I went into the safe. They wanted me to open the safe. I said, "Whoa." They wanted everything in the safe. I said, "No, some of that money isn't yours. It isn't mine. It's other people's." They had their guns. I said, "I don't give a fuck about guns. Guns don't scare me." I don't know. I must've thrown at least two cases of beer around breaking on the walls, just in anger.

Pete Llewellyn: They weren't paying their lawsuits off and the sheriff's department came in and put padlocks on the door. We couldn't get in.

Eileen Chapman: Lee Mrowicki had all his stuff in there, all his DJ equipment. He couldn't even get in to get anything. All his albums. DJ equipment and stuff, everything just got locked up. And that was it. And then people started calling everybody the next day, and there's a big padlock on the door, and the Pony's closed. I don't know what Butch and Jack knew, but whatever it was, none of us knew.

Jack Roig: I knew that was it. Lee wanted to fight. . . . It wasn't worth it. Yeah, it was just time. You couldn't fight them. It's impossible.

Jean Mikle: A lot of the clubs closed down. The beachfront was more and more deserted. Convention Hall and the Paramount were closed for a while. So there were no shows there for at least three or four years. But it just seemed kind of like Asbury was really going downhill.

Kyle Brendle: It was a miracle it lasted that long.

John Eddie: When it closed, it was for sale for $600,000 or something, and I had no money, but I brought some friends of mine who had money, and I was trying to convince them that we should buy it. And obviously it didn't work out, but I was surprised it was for sale, I thought it was a reasonable price at the time. I'm sure whoever did buy it made out like a bandit.

Lee Mrowicki: We had gotten a mortgage commitment through a business partner of Billy Joel's to be able to buy the Pony back for the employees, kind of like how employees will take over an airline. The trustee didn't trust anybody, let me put it that way. He was the guy who actually closed the place down. We went up against them in court. They had cash, which the trustee wanted, and we had a mortgage commitment. That was it. The trustee wasn't going to trust us anyway, thinking that we would continue to bring the old owners in to run the place.

Eileen Chapman: It felt worn-out. And, you know, Butch and Jack got worn out with it. How much money and energy can you sink into something that's foundering?

Jack Roig: In the state of New Jersey, you don't have to file a lawsuit for one year, three hundred and sixty-four days. Right? And by that time, who's going to refute what you say? You don't know what to say. People working this and all that. It's stacked against you, you know. And it still is. Especially if you don't have insurance, then you're done. That's what put us under. Just couldn't afford it one way, you couldn't afford it the other way.

When it was over, I didn't do anything for about eight, nine months. I didn't know what I wanted to do. I knew I definitely was not going back to work in the city. I knew I was not putting a suit on again. I knew I was not going to play coder again or kiss anybody's ass again. And after that, I guess it was like May of '92, I said, geez, I better get out. I gotta do something. So I said maybe I'll drive a cab for a couple of weeks, see what that's like.

Bruce Springsteen: All things must pass. It was sort of the end of an era and all that. But the town was straining and changing. So it wasn't a big shock.

Max Weinberg: For a lot of musicians at the shore, especially the E Street Band, the Stone Pony had once been like the great jazz clubs in Harlem in the 1940s. It was a joint where we could sit in with friends, try out new ideas and licks, and, most importantly, reaffirm our bar-band roots. When the Pony closed, that era ended.

Bruce Springsteen: It ended up being a little bit of part of the mythology of the town and those particular years, and that became a small part of the story of Asbury Park and spread around the world. If anybody had told me that somebody in Holland would ever even know the Stone Pony, I would have been shocked. I mean, at its height, it was really just a neighborhood bar.

18

Pony 2.0

The doors would not stay closed for long. The Stone Pony, no matter the environs, was too valuable a brand. But the version of the Pony that would reopen in just six months was substantially different, reflective of a changing of the guard and the growing influence of a local radio station.

Lexi Quaas: When the Stone Pony was for sale at a foreclosure, a guy named Steven Nasar bought it for $280,000. It wasn't a lot of money. He didn't see a purpose for the old seventies-leftover vibe where the Pony was falling apart. He gutted it and made it a new shiny club. It looked a little bit like the inside of an airplane hangar.

Kyle Brendle: Steve Nasar came out of nowhere. He basically was a local businessman. He owned a couple gas stations, and no background . . . no club scene, or music industry whatsoever. Nowhere. Came out of nowhere.

Stan Levinstone: Steve came and found me and said, "I want you to book the Pony." So I brought Tony and Jerry into the Pony.

Tony Pallagrosi: Steve Nasar had bought the Pony, Jewish guy, for a deal. Both Jerry and Stan are Jewish. So I said, "Guys, that's your guy. Talk to him." And Jerry really was the one who had a relationship with Steve, initially. And Steven opened up, he remodeled it. And much to the chagrin of all of the old-school Asbury people, who weren't all that old at that point, but they were getting crusty, instead of doing

Southside Johnny and the Asbury Jukes as the first show, or even in the first month, I did the Catherine Wheel. It did about seven hundred people. It didn't sell out. It did seven hundred people. Now, you have to realize that all of the Asbury Park regulars had no idea who the Catherine Wheel was. And most of them had no idea that this whole other musical world was happening.

John Eddie: We're playing a gig at a place called the Clubhouse in Plainfield, New Jersey. We noticed on the outer edges of the dance floor, everyone just watching, and it was a very stark moment in my memory. And again, we had our faithful there, so we were still doing good. But when we get done playing the first set, and the DJ plays "Smells Like Teen Spirit," and all of a sudden the dance floor was packed. Not slam dancing, just the undulating dance floor. And I remember looking at my guitar player, Joe Sweeney. I said, "We're done." It was that definite. It's like, "We're over. This is a new thing and we're not it."

Tony Pallagrosi: I hated the eighties in terms of the glam rock bands, couldn't stand it. But I always thought that if somebody came along with a pop sensibility of the glam rock bands, because they could write really good pop rock tunes, and the volume and the energy, but without the bullshit clothing and the shitty lyrics, if somebody synthesized that into something cool. And then I saw Nirvana. And I was like, holy shit, and I heard them and thought, this is fucking it. And I realized that John Scher, who was the dominant promoter in New Jersey, had missed it. He had invested everything into the arena show. And the arena shows evaporated like overnight. And everything devolved back down to the clubs and venues like Convention Hall.

Eileen Chapman: Steve, I think his vision for the Pony was not the Butch-and-Jack vision for the Pony. He was younger than Butch and Jack, and I think that he had a different audience in mind.

Kyle Brendle: When Nasar took over, the Pony became more of a venue. They were pursuing a lot of touring acts, definitely way more than it was prior to that.

Eileen Chapman: The night he opened, they were still painting the floors of the Pony on opening night. While people were still lined up outside. He changed everything. He changed it. And at one point he put the stage on the other side. So when we did the closing party, the stage was actually over where the sound board is. He just wanted to be different. He wanted to have his own identity.

Jean Mikle: It was now a concert venue, not really a neighborhood bar. It wasn't open seven days a week anymore. So you couldn't just go and have a beer, which was the way it used to be.

Tracey Story Prince: In the early nineties, it was a little tougher to work there and it wasn't the same. I might have been the only bartender he brought back. As far as I know, he brought a few bouncers back. I think he wanted to make it a younger thing. He didn't want to be that much associated with the older Pony.

Vini Lopez: According to him, we were dinosaurs. They didn't book us there, and he went out of his way to make it hard for guys like us to work there because we were dinosaurs. They want the new stuff; they want new stuff, new stuff, new stuff.

Tony Pallagrosi: I wanted to establish another facet of what was going to be the Stone Pony. And so the Stone Pony became the home of alternative rock.

Lexi Quaas: It's not everybody listens to Bruce. You know what I mean? It is very popular and I respect it tremendously, but there's a generation of kids that wanted to rebel against what their parents were listening to and they had pink hair, and blue hair, and nose rings, and tattoos, and spikes and listened to the Ramones.

Tim Donnelly: When Tony took over and he started booking, as he said, the Connells, which got a lot of airplay, the BoDeans, the Hooters, the Del Fuegos from Boston. So all that kind of stuff was bubbling under. And Tony really tapped into that stuff. And then with 106.3, HTG, so you had this really amazing synergy. This culture that was bubbling under that was starting to rise up. And it was separating itself from the Springsteen stuff, from the hair metal stuff.

Matt Pinfield: As the radio station became more influential and more part of the fabric of the Asbury–Jersey Shore area, it became more of a force and then linked up with the Stone Pony in a big way. So by the time I became music director, we had a great, unbelievable relationship with the Pony. So we were promoting all the shows there. And music had shifted quite a bit too. I mean, I think one of the bands who's great from New Jersey, the Smithereens, were a big part of what that's about. One of my favorite bands, and they were friends of mine. I used to play them on my college radio show, my first college radio benefit that I put together. So the Smithereens played that; so I love those guys and still do. And they were a big part of that Jersey Shore scene.

There was a band from New Jersey, Dramarama, that became huge in California thanks to Rodney Bingenheimer and KROQ, that their song "Anything, Anything" became a classic that everybody from Blink-182 to Linkin Park have covered.

John Easdale: HTG was playing modern rock, what they called it before it was called alternative. It created a scene in that central Jersey area and Asbury, in particular, because Asbury had venues and people knew where Asbury was. Obviously the city was dying, but they still had concerts.

Matt Pinfield: Put it this way: when Bruce Springsteen covered "Just Like Fire Would" by the Saints, I'm guessing he heard it in the eighties on HTG because he listened to the radio station. He was a fan. That was a known fact. And it was a place to find out about new music. And Little Steven, he was also open to finding new artists, absolutely loved new music. Steven was like that too. So you've got two guys right there that are amazing forces of nature and of love of music history and future things. I think HTG just became more important.

Lexi Quaas: It was a free-form radio station owned by a little old lady named Faye, and basically had a bunch of late twentysomething-year-old DJs who were in charge of the radio station, and it was really Matt Pinfield who had this real connection with a lot of these English artists. It's like every scene will have their big connector like LA had Rodney Bingenheimer and New Jersey had Matt and he was friendly with all these artists and spinning them, so they would come to New Jersey because they had an audience here.

Michelle Amabile: We would have artists come into the station before they would play the Pony. I interviewed Joan Jett before she went to play. I had Joey Ramone on for five hours. He came by, did a show for five hours. He came on, the first song he played was "Do You Remember Rock 'n' Roll Radio?" We want the airwaves. It was awesome. He had Ronnie Spector call in.

Lexi Quaas: The people that liked alternative dance music and alternative rock liked grunge, liked punk, liked acid house. They didn't like the mainstream Z100 crowd. And the mainstream Z100 crowd did not go to Asbury Park.

Rich Russo: Vintage Vinyl was key. The fact that you would be able to buy tickets at Vintage Vinyl for these shows. If you heard a song like "The Red House" or something from New Jersey that was going to play the Pony and you went to go buy the record or the CD and then they had the big wall of all the tickets that were available, then you would get them at the same time. It was very synergistic, where you would be able to hear the record on the radio, go to the record store to buy it, and the record store also had the poster or the thing of saying when they were playing at a really important club down here.

Al Schnier: If you have good radio DJs, which we did in the seventies and eighties, who were informative and told you about those things and why this song was important, or why this band was important, and how it was related to some of the other things that you may know, then you got a bit of an education either through your DJs or a really good independent record store owner who were equally passionate about those things. So I just grew up with this sort of awareness of Asbury Park being a legendary hot spot on the map, just as much as Haight-Ashbury was on the West Coast.

Michelle Amabile: One of Dramarama's last shows, and Johnny Easdale was up there like a huge rock star. It was mobbed. And that had everything to do with HTG. Because we didn't just play anything, we played so many of their songs. . . . We went deep on Dramarama. It was so deep that the people believed that lots of these songs were massive hits because we played them all the time.

Christopher Thorn: One of the first times we went out to visit the station, it was out kind of in the woods and there was a trailer, and that's where we hooked up with Matt Pinfield. I think they were maybe starting to play some of our songs, and it was us going to kind of kiss to the radio station, but it was Matt. So we immediately were like, this guy's the best. It was just a weird place. It was a radio station in a trailer in the woods.

Michelle Amabile: I had my Friday night frenzy show. I turned it into a punk show. I was playing Pennywise and everything. You should've seen the night Bad Religion played at the Pony. I played an hour straight of all Bad Religion songs. On a Friday night, it was like priming people for the Pony.

Matt Pinfield: There was certainly a faction of people that didn't want that change and the other stuff to come in because they used to say, "Well, that's the Fast Lane's music. Those are the bands. . . . That's for the Fast Lane." Those English artists, those kind of new alternative artists, postmodern, whatever they wanted to call the music at that time, alternative, there was some resistance at that period of time.

Kenny "Stringbean" Sorensen: Those were also the years that in the Blackberry Booze Band we opened up for Male Revue. Like male strippers. A weekly gig of us opening up for male strippers on a Wednesday night or something like that. It was an old crowd. The crowd was women. Butch and Jack were gone and they were trying anything. That was a low point for everyone involved.

Tony Pallagrosi: We were the first in New Jersey to actually do eighteen to enter, twenty-one to drink. All ages to enter, twenty-one to drink. We got away with that because, well, actually, because of me, because I made a distinction. I said, "Well, if you go to an arena, people can drink there. That's a concert. We're not a bar. We're a concert venue, just like an arena."

Lexi Quaas: The problem with the promoters that we've had at the Jersey Shore through all those years is they had no idea really what grunge was, what acid house was, what alternative rock was. I think that's where I came in because I had been in California for a few years and they'd been throwing raves out there. I used to go to a rave in [California] once in a while called Mr. Friendly and it was a very professionally done rave. . . . That rave culture had become very popular and it was a very peaceful, sort of like, maybe like Limelight back in the day. . . . So you were just sitting there going, "What do we do with all these nights at the Stone Pony?" I took a Thursday night and I threw a rave on Thursday nights called Vinyl.

Lexi Quaas: Ecstasy had made its second coming. You had ecstasy and then you had ketamine. . . . I used to bring DJs down from New York out of the Limelight. Guys that were popular up there. I used to bring Dave Kendall down from *120 Minutes*. I'd put guys in car services and just bring them down on those nights. I don't remember having a strong enough DJ culture where a DJ could take a night at the Pony. We weren't there yet.

Eric Deggans: Asbury's struggles, in a weird way, it fed into the rock-and-roll image, right? It wasn't this well-manicured area. I think there was also a sense that they could do what they wanted in that area because there weren't people around that complain about it. If they wanted to, if a band like the Ramones wanted to come in and turn it up to 12, they could do it and people wouldn't bitch.

Rich Russo: They did this thing before the summer stage that was called the Stone Pony Big Top. Which was literally like, who is that guy in Arizona that got arrested for the sweat lodges and the sweat boxes or whatever, where people would go in there and die? So picture that parking lot that's now the summer stage with this giant unvented tent. You didn't have vents, so it was just this big stretch of plastic or vinyl, whatever it was. It was so unbearably hot in there when it was summer that literally you felt like you were going to die.

Lexi Quaas: We were running out of room to have these bands. We can only hold, I think the inside of the Pony might've maxed out at about nine-something inside, and then you saw this desire that you could do two nights or three nights with some of the alternative rock artists, and the state and the town wouldn't let you build a permanent structure out there, but they allowed us to get a circus tent, and that's how it became the Big Top because it was a legitimate circus tent.

Tony Pallagrosi: So Mrs. Jay's was in the middle. And that space then was only about 85 feet wide. And then we went back 125, 130 feet. And that was what I called the Stone Pony Landing. We first called it the Stone Pony Big Top because we put a tent over it at first. We were trying to do shows all year-round in the tent. We got these big heat pumps. But it was rough. The storms are pretty intense. And that was a big fucking circus tent, held about 2,500 people. And now we could book much bigger shows.

John Easdale: We did the Big Top. We did the inaugural concert. Matt Pinfield introduced us there.

Rich Russo: I saw the Ramones there and it was lawless.

CJ Ramone: Easter Sunday show was completely chaotic and oversold. That show was definitely wild. That was probably the most people we played to in New Jersey in a club.

And I mean, our Jersey shows were always wild. They were always wild. We used to get a lot of hardcore kids come out to the shows. New Jersey was one of those places that really got the Ramones.

Tony Pallagrosi: Having the Ramones in the Big Top. Yeah, selling out the big time on Easter. Easter Sunday. You know, and you have to remember, Asbury was empty. Empty in the summertime, everywhere it was empty. You could be Donald Trump and shoot a gun down the beach. You wouldn't even hit anyone.

Lexi Quaas: It was a desolate, dangerous, dark, scary place, Asbury Park. It was the perfect place to throw a rave. It was the perfect place for kids to go see a punk rock show because none of them were scared.

Billy Hector: In the early nineties, man, there was nothing. When you went outside, there was only the Pony, and the Student Prince was now a hardcore go-go bar. Those were the only businesses up there. The Empress wasn't even happening yet. And people started getting jumped. But the only people they're preying on are drunk guys coming out of the go-go bar. They would get rolled occasionally.

Dave Wyndorf: By the nineties, it looked like something out of *2000 AD*, the comic book. Just like, newspapers blowing across empty streets, half-built buildings, squatters in there, and the scariest fucking homeboys you've ever seen in your life. Fuck. Scary guys, man, driving around in cars and they would carjack your car, jump out of the car, jump in your car, throw you out. It happened to a couple of friends of mine. No cops to be seen. Cops, they'd be like, what are they going to do?

John Easdale: There was a drug scene. I know that from firsthand experience, because I also was a drug addict. There were crack hotels, and I know that because I would go be a customer. I've never been shy about talking about it. I think half the reason why the band broke up the first time was because I was fucking up. And so, a couple of those last Pony gigs, I think I was going there, and then going there, and then I was a mess.

Jesse Malin: There were people turning tricks that were really low-level hookers out hustling and just scary people just drifting towards you like an apocalyptic zombie movie where these people, suddenly you've got to picture it with dust and wind. It was like that on a lot of nights, just physically the elements of it. There was probably nobody really looking out. There wasn't a lot of police presence or anything like that. It was like these people, this was this town they walked the streets of and they were looking for whatever they could, drugs, doing what they did to get by but you could get easily mugged or robbed in a sec.

John Easdale: In Asbury, more than most other places, drugs were the only other business, at least that I was aware of. After you drove in, there was a lot of empty buildings. There just really wasn't much going on except the Pony and a couple of crack hotels that I knew. And then, the Berkeley Hotel was not a crack hotel, but most of the other ones that were still standing were. We'd stay at the Berkeley, but I'd go spend time at some of the other places.

Billy Hector: Then they came and they took all the copper off of the Casino and sold it. It looked wasted. There's grass growing in the middle of the fucking street. There's grass growing in the fucking Circuit. It's just like, "Wow." I mean, it was that way for a long fucking time.

Eileen Chapman: I used to do a lot of the shows in Convention Hall. And I remember promoters saying to me, "I've never been in a town this dirty before where I've had to pay absolutely every department in order to get into the city." And I was so embarrassed to hear that one. It's my city.

Tony Pallagrosi: There was only one person who actually had his hand out to us. And I'm not going to say who he is. But it basically got us exclusivity at Convention Hall.

Eileen Chapman: When I heard that, I was floored. I had no idea. I had no idea it was that bad. I knew in City Hall, or I suspected and everybody talked about City Hall being corrupt, but I had no idea it had gone beyond those boundaries.

19

New Pony Music

Change was everywhere. Springsteen had disbanded the E Street
Band years earlier, in 1989, for a new creative direction. The Jukes
were largely absent from the Asbury scene. Promoters were not
interested in the bar bands of old. Grunge, jam, and punk were on
the rise. The Pony transitioned from a neighborhood bar with live
music seven nights a week to a more traditional venue, as a local
audience could not be counted on in the crumbling town. But the
Pony remained a draw, for music fans and new bands alike.

Eric Deggans: The industry was uncertain; it wasn't sure where the
lanes were. Rock could be a really stratified, codified, rigid kind of system. At that moment, all the boundaries were blurry and people weren't
quite sure what was popular and what was not, and what was making
money and what was not, what people would come out to see and what
they wouldn't. Bruce walking away from the E Street Band was a seismic
big indicator of just how unstable everything felt. There was a sense that
there was a chapter closing, and people who were attached to that chapter didn't necessarily want to see it close, and people who felt excluded
from that chapter, especially younger people, were eager to see it close.

Kyle Brendle: The people that are hot in the eighties, those people
were now in their forties and such. There wasn't a lot of classic Asbury
going around. Bruce was only in the club a couple of times. Southside
wasn't even playing the Pony anymore. It was just different musical

tastes. The current musical tastes were punk and hardcore, and the jam thing was just starting to brew out of there being the [Grateful] Dead and Phish to being a whole fucking genre.

Jorma Kaukonen: For jam, the rougher it is, the better they like it. There's no question that whoever was booking for the Pony realized what their demography was going to be like. And I'm sure those kind of bands gravitated to that venue because it was like that.

Kyle Brendle: Both punk and hardcore and jamming scenes, those people are fearless and don't care. They just want to see their bands, their music. That's it.

Al Schnier: There was something about it being almost abandoned and a bit out of the way or run-down, and maybe even less than blue-collar, and how it sort of suited our band and it fit our fans just fine. And it was a place we could go and have a good time and it was okay. It's not that it didn't matter, but nobody cared also, because everybody was there really just to commune and be together and have a great time. And we had a space where we could do it. And that's all mattered.

G. Love: As far as there being a music scene down here, honestly, I wasn't really aware of that except for the past. Again, with Bruce Springsteen, and Southside Johnny. And then I just remember coming here and we'd be coming and feeling it, but it wasn't popping off. It was pretty much like a ghost town, like a run-down ghost town. And you'd walk in these venues, and they'd somehow be packed out and we rock out.

Donavon Frankenreiter: In the beginning, I remember coming here and it was kind of like, "Where am I? I know the beach is right there, but are people going to show up to this? Where does everybody live?" And then all of a sudden you have a concert and you're like, "Where did everybody come from? Holy shit."

Christopher Thorn: When we got to the Stone Pony, because you're right there by the boardwalk and stuff, I remember it feeling really kind of dangerous and funky, and them saying, you got to be careful, blah, blah, blah. Don't walk around. Of course, that's immediately what I do, is walk around, and as soon as somebody says, "Don't go anywhere."

And I remember having a moment with Shannon [Hoon] on the beach where we saw hypodermic needles. So that was a tough first impression.

Dave Pirner: We were driving around and thinking it kind of looked like a ghost town. I remember an old amusement park that had been shut down. And a lot of really interesting places with characters that seemed like they were living in the past, in a weird dream or something. It was very ghostly. There wasn't much activity on the street. Again, it was at night, but everything seemed kind of boarded up. As we were driving around, "Born to Run" came on the radio and it was just too funny. I remember the guy who was driving was standing on the hood of the car with his fist raised. And we're all rocking out in Asbury Park to Bruce Springsteen. It was kismet or something, I don't know. They probably played it on the radio all the time, but it seemed like a bizarre coincidence.

Dave Wyndorf: I thought I was going to go in there, the kind of paranoia you get, and there's going to be a bunch of guys that remember me being an asshole and they're going to kill me. We went there and there was a bunch of happy fucking nineties kids rocking.

Al Schnier: We played at the Saint before we played at the Stone Pony. I mean, everything was like that then. It was like everything was a stepping-stone, and you had to play a Tuesday before you could play a Thursday, and you're never getting a weekend gig unless you knew somebody or you drew enough on that Tuesday or Thursday that they were going to stick you on as an opener.

Ryan Miller: I'm certain that that was the case for us and our fans coming to be like, "Oh my God, I've seen you guys play at the Saint four times. And now you're playing the Stone Pony," and like what that means for the show and the relationship of fan to band and band to fan. It wasn't the kind of place that you wanted to play because the amenities were great or the sound was perfect, or you got a really fucking awesome dressing room. I remember it being a little bit of like a slum.

John Popper: It was '85 that *Born in the U.S.A.* was just crammed down our throats. Bruce Springsteen's fucking ass, with the little hat hanging out of it, was just in everyone's face, was really the wrong way to be introduced to Bruce Springsteen, being some kids from Princeton, New Jersey. So I was pretty sure that Bruce Springsteen had nothing viable to offer us. I had made my mind up, and for years I would kick and scream as though he's selling this image of New Jersey that isn't real, because I'm in New Jersey and I don't see this blue-collar existence of working along the shore, and what that even meant. And it would take me years, decades before I would look back and realize that I'd been ripping off Bruce Springsteen a lot throughout all of my songwriting. There's a term for when you cram as many lyrics as you can onto a phrase, and Springsteen is great at that. And so in time, we came to appreciate what the shore meant.

By the way, "Run Around" was very much us doing our version of "Rosalita," without doing it. I was trying to allude to it without doing it.

Donavon Frankenreiter: One thing that we do ever since the very first time I've ever played here. I don't know if every band does that, but every time I play here, I always put Bruce on the guest list, but he never shows up.

Nick Hexum: I was familiar with the lore of New Jersey and the House That Bruce Built. It was a bit of a mythical place of blue-collar, super-rootsy rock-and-roll place. But for us, starting out a show at Convention Hall, and during the first song, I got hit with a flying Doc Marten. Chucked and hit me right in the face. I mean, who loses a Doc Marten? There's so many laces. It almost seems like it would have to be intentional, but maybe they were just being cool and not lacing up their boots, and then they fell off in the pit and somebody decided to throw it and he hit me right in the face. And I just remember, "I'm not going to react. I'm not going to stop the show and say, 'Who threw that?' or anything. Just take it in stride and just pretend it didn't happen and keep on rocking." I was like, "This is 'Welcome to Jersey!'" That's the way of someone saying, "Welcome to Jersey! Here's a Doc Marten upside your head!"

Dave Pirner: When we heard about playing the Pony, it was like, "Oh, cool." It definitely has some legendary status, and another place where you're kind of, "Let's not suck because this club has seen a lot of good music" kind of thing. And I was celebrating my birthday onstage that night, April 14. I do remember playing an extra-long set and going, "I feel like playing some more. Let's play any cover, every cover we can think of." And yeah, that was my way of celebrating my birthday, was to play a bunch of songs I really like that we don't usually play.

Dave Wyndorf: That first Pony show, back in those days, we're stage-diving a lot, as everybody was. The Pony had that great industrial exposed ceiling. You could climb on that shit. I climbed all over it. I was swinging.

> **Michele Amabile/Asbury Park Press:** At the Stone Pony Saturday, Dave Wyndorf and company played out every male Black Sabbath fantasy in front of a sweltering, sold-out, hometown crowd of headbangers, moshers, and crowd-surfers (who may have had a little bit of trouble holding on to the overhead ceiling pipes thanks to some strategically applied Vaseline).

Dave Wyndorf: Those guys came and tried to pull me off and said like, "What the fuck, you're hanging on the fucking toilet pipe." Good point. It didn't break, but kind of bent and stuff, and that stuff's not made for monkeying around. That's exactly what I was doing. I didn't see anybody mimicking it, but I'm sure other bands did it all the time. It was just too inviting. You had to jump up on them, you had to come do a running thing, leap off the monitor to give you good spring, and then go up, but still then you're, I don't know, twelve feet off the ground.

John Popper: When we would go to finally play in the Stone Pony, the first thing you notice when you come to Asbury Park, is where you're staying. And it was like 1972 in the hotel.

Nick Hexum: They put us up at a really spooky hotel that was kind of this really old, castle-looking place that had not been renovated since the sixties, it looked like. I mean, it was just so old and run-down. And we were like, "We're just going to shower here and sleep on the bus."

Tom Morello: I grew up on metal, and then punk, and then hip-hop, and really didn't immerse myself in the music of Bruce Springsteen till my thirties. It was then that I learned about Asbury Park, not realizing that I had played at the Stone Pony in my pre–Rage Against the Machine band, Lock Up. It was on a dreary tour when we've been sort of abandoned by our record company and we didn't have enough money to even have a tour manager or a guitar tech. The four of us were just bouncing around in a van and played a place called the Stone Pony, which I didn't have any reference for, so it was just one more gig. This one was along the ocean, which was kind of nice. You know what I mean? As we were on our way to our twenty-five-dollar hotel, Lord knows where. We were driving around in a van, those two years. It was just another stop on a dreary tour, can't afford hotels. One of those "Two of us have to sleep in the van tonight. I wonder, is it going to be me?"

Kyle Brendle: Almost weekly, there was a huge party at the Berkeley Hotel. We had the fourth floor. We had the two presidential suites. The presidential suite with two big wing rooms. It'd be a band playing and a DJ. Bathtubs full of beer, and it was part of the scene. It cost me two hundred dollars weekly. People knew they could come to the Pony and the party would continue to Berkeley till dawn. The rooms on the fourth floor were fifty dollars a room.

John Popper: We'd been going to play at the Stone Pony before we understood what that even meant. That's the result. And I think in that way, it allowed us to be more honest in our approach, because we didn't understand the shoes we were trying to fill, exactly.

Chris Barron: For us, trying to get into the Pony was like trying to play the Copacabana in the fifties, or something like that. Like really wanting to play there, because of Bruce Springsteen and the legend of it, and the kind of aura of it. We were not big enough, or I don't know if it was like we weren't the right kind of music or we didn't have a big enough draw, or something. But I do remember wanting to play there and not being able to until we got big.

John Popper: The thing is, all of our friends came to see us, and then a bunch of people we hadn't seen, and then the real Pony fans. And it was a fun place to drink. And I think you could find drugs around there. And then there was always some girl. I was working on somebody.

I wasn't doing that a lot in the early days. Everyone in my band was having sex with the same people, so I never wanted to get into that. My sales pitch was that I'm the shy fat guy, and that's how I got laid.

Nick Hexum: I definitely remember beautiful suburban girls there. I can't say I found love there, but I definitely found fun.

G. Love: I'm sure I did a lot of crazy shit in these dressing rooms. But that was in the nineties and I wasn't sober then.

John Popper: When I said I wasn't doing as many drugs back then, just compared to my band, I wasn't. But compared to a normal person, I was doing plenty of drugs and having lots of sex. I was just with the guys who were lapping me several times. I was with the most drug-doing guy, and then the other guy in the band was getting laid in three-ways with models and stuff. So it seemed to me that I was like the wholesome one. But no, actually, if you compared me to your average banker, I was doing pretty good.

Matt Pinfield: There were crazy stories there like Oasis playing there the first time. I had a deal with Tony Pallagrosi, and he calls me up and he goes, "Hey, Matt, I booked this band called Oasis." And they had one single import out at the time, "Supersonic." And that first single's amazing. So it sells out.

Lexi Quaas: Having Oasis come was one of those real moments. It was like a real, like, oh my God, they're playing here. Their songs were really big and it was like having the freaking Beatles come over. They wanted to play there. It's not like they had to play there, but they have a tumultuous relationship, the brothers. They walked onstage, they did maybe two songs. They got in a fight and then they walked offstage at the Pony. Then I had to go out and get them back onstage with various treats to get them to come back onstage, and then they came back onstage and they were amazing.

Tim Donnelly: There was a lot of drinking that was part of the culture. It was kind of like, you know, you could call that hooligan culture or whatever. But that was just a fucking normal night on the Jersey Shore back then. People fucking partied hard, right? So the crowd was full of . . . it's kind of the Irish Riviera. Lots of Irish on the Jersey

Shore. Lots of them. Loved their fucking Brit-rock. Loved that fucking music, right? So all the rowdy Irishmen were out that night. Everybody was out, partying hard. Oasis comes up, they fucking crush. It was fucking brilliant.

Except they only played for like forty-three minutes. You don't play the fucking Stone Pony for forty-three minutes. Not when it's the fucking house of Bruce Springsteen, Southside Johnny, and everybody plays as late as they can possibly play because the expectations are for the full fucking night, not for fucking forty-five minutes. So when they said, "That's it, good night," when fucking Liam [Gallagher] just threw the fucking mic up, people started booing, "Like, fuck you, what the fuck? Boo, boo, boo, boo." Started throwing shit. They came out the fucking back door, and it might have been Noel Gallagher took a full bottle of something, and back then they weren't fucking plastic bottles. They were glass bottles. Threw it from the stage into the crowd. Basically most of the crowd went pushing through the stage door and chased them onto their fucking bus. Where they get on the bus and they start opening up the window, start throwing bottles and shit out at the people on the fucking sidewalk. And they're trying to shake the fucking bus. And cops come from every fucking direction, man. I mean, every direction possible. And then they fucking came out with their billy clubs, people kind of fucking scattered or were standing on the sidewalk. "Fuck you, fuck you, fuck you." Next thing you know, the bus just fucking takes off. Fucking makes a left down Ocean Avenue, and just fucking takes off.

Tim Donnelly: Porno for Pyros, which was equally legendary because it was a complete underplay. And the Stone Pony in the nineties didn't really have air-conditioning, okay? It was really hot in there. I mean, people were dropping. They were dropping. And I remember dudes crowd-surfing to get up, and then they would try to reach up and grab one of the pipes. And the pipes would be scalding hot. And then they would fall down and they'd have fucking burns on their hands. It was so hot that I remember [the bass player] Mike Watt took a hit of his bottle of Jim Beam, and it was so warm, and he just looked at me. "Oh fuck." And he just went like that for me to move. And I opened up the fucking back door, and he tried to puke as much as he could out the back door, still fucking playing. And then some woman, when he was bending over after he puked, kissed him.

Kyle Brendle: By 1995, we had a night at the Pony called Jam Band Fridays. It carried the place in the winter. A band called Splintered Sunlight played every other Saturday. We also had Secret Sound, Juggling Suns. There's plenty of other ones, but those three were the staples in, so especially in the winter months, the Jam Band team was really carrying the place.

Christopher Thorn: We did two days there in a row, like a warm-up before Woodstock. It was a way to get comfortable, in a sense.

Chris Barron: We didn't have a lot of time to grow into the exponentially increasing-sized venues. I think when Eric left the band and things got a little hairy, I think there was an inclination on our part to fall back on a comfort zone, and to play places that were a little bit . . . not a little bit, a lot smaller. So, we were playing the Nightingale Bar and Stone Pony, and packing the living shit out of it, which was cool. And we could just leak that we were . . . "It's the Weeds, but it's really the Spin Doctors," and have a shit ton of people. It was like going back to . . . I don't know how to put it, but training wheels again. It was a way to fall back and feel comfortable after so much had changed.

Christopher Thorn: Moshing became a thing every night. And we had songs that there's no business moshing for. And every night. During the nineties, everybody did that at every show. It didn't matter what the song was, it's just how the crowd interacted with the band. It was moshing, and it was always jumping on the stage. My pedals would get all up fucked, my guitar pedals. People jump onstage, hit your pedal, and you're like, oh my God, suddenly I'm loud, or whatever. And it was part of the show. Shannon loved it. He'd bring people up onstage. He was always grabbing people and bringing them up, and it was just, and throwing them off. And it was very active. Those shows were very active. And even though we're not a punk rock band, it looked like a punk rock show. Shannon had an energy about him where he could wind people up. He had that in him where he could kind of create a little fire in the audience, and they'd kind of get wild. But they would mosh for "Change," some of our mellowest songs. They did it for "No Rain." I mean, it was just bizarre. And that was just that time. Then you saw it at every show. It didn't matter what it was.

Tony Pallagrosi: Well, it was slam dancing back then. And it was very ritualistic. And there weren't any jock meatheads in the crowd. Everybody who was there knew exactly what they were doing. And what they were getting into. And so yes, the people get banged up. But nobody went home and cried to mommy and daddy. Nobody called the police. Nobody sued us. They would just thank me for having it, as they were bleeding and blood was pouring down their face. But there weren't fights. It was insulated. It was a real subculture.

Chris Barron: It was like, everybody was looking out for each other. And if you fell down, people picked you up. People were making sure that you weren't going to get hurt. That was a big thing. It was like, somebody got hurt, it was not cool. Then you had preppy assholes moshing in the nineties. And then it became about hurting people, or being the toughest person who could take the most punishment, and shit like that. We'd been playing "How Could You Want Him (When You Know You Could Have Me?)," like a ballad. And these fuckers were just moshing their brains out. I forgot about that until a little while ago. I was thinking about the nineties, and I was like, "That fucking sucked." I hated that. I hated that.

Matt Pinfield: That was my joke. Whenever people would slam dance and mosh to a mellow song, I would go, "Are they listening to the same song I am? What are they hearing in their head right now? Because I don't think it's the song the band's playing onstage."

Nick Hexum: It was always a crazy crowd at the Pony. Super-wild, energetic . . . It was oversold. You really could not count on the promoters at that time to stick to true capacities. And the lack of oxygen was a problem because there was just so many bodies in there. And we're, I guess, fortunate that there was never any sort of trampling or anybody really getting hurt because those shows were so oversold. But there were plenty of minor injuries, stitches, people passing out from lack of oxygen or being too intoxicated. Fights. I mean, it was just complete mayhem.

John Popper: It always kind of bugged me that we didn't just start going to Asbury earlier. But again, Springsteen was presented to me as a pop artist in the eighties. *Born in the U.S.A.* was literally everywhere. So I didn't want to be that. And what I didn't realize is that I wanted to be a lot more like that scene than I had thought. It was really what kind of ruined it initially for me, was that Springsteen was presented to me on MTV, as the Top 40 thing. And so I didn't know about all of his earlier work, which it took me years to discover and go back. And it was kind of almost a redundant feeling to me that I worked so hard to look for a scene, and there was one right there. And that always kind of bugged me. It should have been on our radar more. We were so hell-bent on getting out of the burbs and going somewhere where we could have our band do something, and that was always New York City. But had we gone to Asbury Park, I think that we would've really thrived there a while, before even anyone outside there. We could have completely existed in that scene, and been completely happy, and we just didn't know enough about it.

20

Rock Roots Remain

Los Angeles, Springsteen's new home, was a long way from the Pony. And new music, with heavier guitars, thunderous drums, and simpler arrangements, was the new norm. But the spirit of Springsteen and the Jukes was inexorable from the walls of the bar. New albums by the Jukes and Joe Grushecky, a longtime friend and collaborator with Springsteen from Pittsburgh, brought the old days back to the Pony. Occasionally. And briefly.

Joe Grushecky: [Bruce] was not playing at that time. The E Street Band had disintegrated for whatever reason. And we were driving along the beach in California, listening to the mixes of *American Babylon*. He said, "I'm going to go out and play with you guys." It was totally his idea. At least that's the way I remember; he might remember it differently. So when we talked, he said, "I want this to . . . We'll start off in New Jersey." He had his agent book us about six dates. He wanted to start in New Jersey and he wanted to kick-start the Pony again. He said, "I want to kick-start Asbury Park in the music scene again, in Asbury," because it's really the pits, the city at that time. So he specifically wanted us to do it. And we went up, we rehearsed a night. I said, "We've got to play a couple of your songs if we're doing this, one or two anyway." And so we picked "Murder Incorporated," which I try to talk him into giving me, haha. But he wanted to do "Light of Day." So he taught us "Light of Day" at the Pony.

Bruce Springsteen: When it was on tough times, we played there, but it was just a good thing to do. People came out, old folks came out, and it just kept the place pumping a little bit.

Joe Grushecky: He definitely wanted to play New Jersey. I can remember specifically, he said he wanted to give it a kick start.

Eric Deggans: There was a sense that there was this transition going on. There were a lot of fans trying to figure out what that meant. They were hungry for scraps of that experience again because it was a really unifying force for people when it was big. They remember the glory days when Bruce could sit anywhere and people would run out to pay phones because pay phones still existed back then. . . . They would call their friends and they're like a tree, and then the next thing you knew, there'd be two hundred people waiting for Bruce to sit in with a band. Sometimes you'd do and sometimes you wouldn't, but it was always this kind of excitement. I think people were looking for that again.

Joe Grushecky: It was packed. I was having a meltdown because I didn't think we were going to get to the club. Bruce was driving. You couldn't get anywhere. It was the worst-kept secret in the world.

Stan Goldstein: I'll never forget, he came out the stage door there, and a girl said to him, "Bruce, will you sign some stuff for us?" He goes, "Yes, just don't hang on me."

Joe Grushecky: But it was great. Sweat pouring off you. It was the first time we played a lot of those songs that eventually became the *American Babylon* record. I mean, we had been rehearsing them, but we were keeping them under our belt until we went out and played it, until the record came on. So that was the week the record came out. And it was just great. And then people always said, "Well, what's it like playing with Bruce Springsteen?" I said, "A band is like a team." So you're like a football team and all of a sudden you have Joe Montana playing for you, or Bo Jackson on your team, or if you're a baseball team, all of a sudden you have Roberto Clemente or Mickey Mantle on your team. Of course it's going to be fucking better.

Bruce Springsteen: [Joe] had a good tight little band and he was a good songwriter, and we'd had scenes in common and we liked each other. And so if he came around and I felt like playing, I could see Joe and say,

"Hey, you want to sit in?" "Can I sit in?" "Yeah, sure." So we started to sit in with each other and it was just a nice place to go and sit in and play with a friend of yours.

Dave Davies: Venues hold on to a vibe. Audiences are like an energy that lingers I think, and for a long expression, because it brings out a height of emotion in people. So I believe that. I think gigs and venues hold on to a vibe, an ambiance, like a real energy. Like one of those energies that you feel that you've been where they are. Music is a great way to convey those kind of almost invisible forces that drive us emotionally. So it's a cool place to play.

Joe Grushecky: At the time, Asbury was trashed. You could drive a tank down the middle of the street and not hit anything on a Saturday night. It was empty, except for whatever band was playing, the people would be in that particular bar. But there was nothing going on in that section where the Pony is and all that. That was deserted. But the Pony was still rockin'.

Dave Davies: We did the warm-ups at the Pony because it's got a certain vibe about it that lends itself. And some places can leave you cold, where it's too loud or everything's off. So we felt the Pony was a good place for a warm-up, to do a rock show, and still have the subtleties to pull off acoustic stuff, harmony, that kind of shit. It was good for that. But compare it to someplace like the Royal Albert Hall in London. It's this really fancy and beautiful building, but it feels flat. And you've gotta really work the room to get it. And playing there can sometimes be very difficult. And I'm sure they've changed the PA there and acoustics and some things there. But the Stone Pony just had such an interesting vibe to it.

Dave Davies: In a small place like the Pony, you're much more alert to the band and the people around it. It was a great warm-up for that tour. . . . You get confidence from the crowd, the people. Because good rock-and-roll shows, making sure getting the songs right, making sure the fuckups work, just getting it all together.

Eric Deggans: And then later, Little Steven and Max played with Bruce. It was a big deal because those guys weren't working together. A shitload of people showed up for that just because it was a taste of the old Bruce magic. You had that going.

Rich Russo: There was a show where Southside played indoors, and it was so hot up there that they had no ventilation, no air. And everybody would always look at that door, because if anybody was coming, because it was a Southside show, it could have been Jon Bon Jovi, it could have been Steven, it could have been Bruce, could have been whoever; you'd always look. There was a point where that door opened, and it was Bruce, and it was so hot that all that heat just literally just shot at Bruce. You can literally see sweat beading off him. He just shut the door and he never came in. He was like, "Holy." It literally must have been like opening up a blast furnace because it was so compressive and he opened the door and that hot air just shot at him.

Eileen Chapman: In the Nasar era, Bruce was never really there to hang out and listen to music. It changed. He knew Butch and Jack. He was comfortable going in there, comfortable with the people that were in there, liked the bands that were performing, knew most of them. There was a reason to go and then it stopped. Now he's going to Cheers in Long Branch or other places where he knew people and felt comfortable.

Eric Deggans: I guess you could call it a tension. There was this type of fan that we used to call the Bruce Kooks, people who were super-fixated on Bruce Springsteen and all the artists that were associated with him. That would've been Southside Johnny, that would've been Glen Burtnik, that would've been even really Jon Bon Jovi. Those guys, they had a lot of commonality in their local audiences because people would claim them in similar ways. It was obvious that that era was in decline because Bruce had disbanded the E Street Band and some of the guys were flailing to figure out what they were going to do next. In particular, I wound up covering keyboard for Danny Federici, who had a lot of issues. He wound up auctioning a lot of his stuff off while I was there, which was really sad. Max Weinberg, I think he got a law degree or tried to get a law degree and then just founded a record company, and then, before he landed the job as musical director for Conan O'Brien's late show. It was obvious that that whole era of music was in transition. The standard-bearer was trying to do something different.

21

Punk Roots

In basements, VFW halls, and firehouses, a DIY punk scene was forming across New Jersey. Green Day's *Dookie* became Nirvana's *Nevermind* for a generation. Sparked in large part by the Bouncing Souls, punk in Jersey became a statewide movement, a lineage that would lead from a Lifetime show at a Legion hall to My Chemical Romance at Madison Square Garden. And like all Jersey music, it would be drawn to the siren call of the Pony, and Asbury.

Bryan Kienlen: So Timmy Chunks was one of our crew, one of our gang. He was the singer of Token Entry, which is the New York hardcore band that we looked up to. They were like a CBs matinee mainstay. I think Token Entry holds the record for playing the most CBs hardcore matinees. They were a big part of the New York hardcore thing, and we were big fans of all that, and showgoers there too.

Pete Steinkopf: He ended up migrating down to our punk house, came down for a show, and then he just never left.

Bryan Kienlen: He was a Green Day guitar tech as *Dookie* was blowing up, as they were at their peak, there he was onstage, changed the strings, handed Billy his guitars.

Pete Steinkopf: Last minute the opening band dropped off and Chunks was like, "Oh, my friends are in an awesome band and they live like half an hour from here."

Bryan Kienlen: "What are you guys doing next Saturday?" And we're like, "I don't know, nothing, Timmy." He's like, "Good, you're opening for Green Day at the Stone Pony." And so that was that. And that's when we met Green Day. So we go there. The show was in that big white tent.

Matt Pinfield: *Dookie* just exploded. At this point, you already had . . . All those singles were out. "Longview" was the first one, and then "Basket Case" came. "When I Come Around," "Welcome to Paradise," "She." All those singles were being released in pretty rapid succession with support from MTV. They just got so huge so fast. There was so much excitement for that Stone Pony show that people had come down from everywhere, from New York City for that show.

Kate Hiltz: Their tour blew up; their record and their lives blew up after they booked their tour. So that in multiple markets, the promoters moved them to bigger venues. And here in Asbury Park, this doesn't exist. Because at that point in time, Convention Hall is just condemned, or maybe only doing basketball. I don't know. So I think that basically was what got the Pony to tent out.

Bryan Kienlen: We gave them the shirt that we had, the Souls shirt that we were selling at that show. Just Bouncing Souls hand-drawn style and the back's a big "No MTV." We thought that was awesome because we were playing with Green Day and we were like the anti-MTV band and just spreading our message, and they loved it and they all got the shirt. . . . There was a Green Day postcard in the nineties too, I don't know where else, maybe a poster, wearing a Bouncing Souls shirt and it actually did a lot for us because they were the biggest band in the world and they were wearing Bouncing Souls shirts and stuff in these pictures and interviews.

Pete Steinkopf: It was such chaos. It was total fucking chaos and there were kids climbing over everything in and out of the tent and the merch guy from Green Day was so overrun with kids. I got in a fight with him. He tried to fight me. Because he was so overrun, he didn't know how to handle it; he was like manhandling all these little kids. And I ran over: "You can't do that." I think he hit me actually. Or tried to. And

Chunks had to come and chill it out. But in his defense, he's probably feeling attacked, thousands of kids coming for one guy selling shirts.

Matt Pinfield: That show got crazy. One of the security guys got his hands stomped by the crowd and almost lost his hand.

Pete Steinkopf: One thing about that show is I moved down to this area about maybe sixteen years ago or so and I think every person I know of a certain age, ten years younger than me, every person I've ever met was at that show. Every kid in this whole Asbury Park and then suburban area of Asbury Park, everyone was at that show. It was the biggest thing and they all say the same thing, like, "It was the biggest thing that ever happened in my childhood, was going to that Green Day show and then seeing the local band, and were like, 'Dude, this band's from New Jersey.'"

Kate Hiltz: And at that point in time we're just still total punks. So I think it gave them that sort of idea, like oh, now we could really do this. This isn't just about, all our friends came to our show at the Knights of Columbus. This is like, wait, there's people out here who want to . . . And I think they sold all their shirts for whatever, six dollars at the time. You know what I mean? But it was like, that's a big deal when you're making your shirts yourself in your basement and you're handing people seven-inches when you're trying to find somewhere to stay after a show, whatever. And Green Day were huge. Huge.

Bryan Kienlen: We weren't playing the Pony a ton before that Green Day show. We were in New Brunswick. There was just the Court Tavern and we were underage. We couldn't even play there. So we're like, we just have to have parties and play to people. We just wanted to play to people. And we also just wanted to party. So it was perfect. And that's what we did. And then that kind of gave birth to the whole DIY, New Brunswick basement show thing.

Pete Steinkopf: Basement shows.

Bryan Kienlen: Just out of necessity.

Pete Steinkopf: We would just invite people to our basement, come see us, because we had nowhere else.

Bryan Kienlen: We had a basement, which was our jam room. And we're like, everyone comes. We're going to steal some beer somewhere, and right? Drink some beer, play some music.

Brian Fallon: I don't know if the scene was starting to form down in Asbury Park yet in the mid-nineties. There was more going on in New Brunswick at the time for the music that I was listening to.

Brian Fallon: Rutgers used to have these crazy shows that were free sometimes. It would be all these punk bands and then like, the Beastie Boys would play or Tribe Called Quest would play and all these people that you wouldn't really get to see unless you bought a ticket to Madison Square Garden or somewhere that was big. And Rutgers used to have the shows on the campus. And then at the shows, there would be all these flyers getting handed out and they would just have a bunch of band names that you probably never heard of. And they would have an address or a phone number and you would call and go to the show on the day of the show. And that was usually in New Brunswick. So a lot of my upbringing started there and kind of coming around to the Melody Bar and the Court Tavern and those kinds of places, but also those houses on Handy Street. And like all these other houses that had basements and then kids would have shows on all the time.

Heath Saraceno: The shows at the firehouses, I mean, you could go see seven bands for six dollars, two or three nights a week. It was Friday, Saturday, Sunday, there's a show somewhere for six or seven bucks. You'll be there all day.

Brian Fallon: I went to PNC [Bank Arts Center in Holmdel] once when I was eleven. And I was like, "This is stupid, because the band's onstage fifty miles away from me, and there's nine million people around me and I don't feel anything." It was just a weird experience when the rest of my experiences were all at these small VFW halls or small venues where you're up in front of a band that you could see. You could see them sweating and you could see what . . . It felt electric.

Mike Doyle: You could go around Jersey and show up at a church or a Legion hall and you'd have an automatic crowd of kids. There was going to be a packed room or decently packed room or at least a hundred kids there.

Kenny Vasoli: Even in my Philly suburb town, it was still about Op[eration] Ivy or just super punk stuff, that if you didn't like that, no one knew who Lagwagon or any of these bands were. So once I got into the band that became the Starting Line, and those guys knew about the Jersey scene, and were showing me Lanemeyer and these bands from Jersey that were exactly what I wanted. Then I quickly learned that there was a place for the type of music I wanted to play, and it quickly became a home for us to play shows.

Benny Horowitz: When I really started falling in love with the scene and this idea that I'm just going to someone's basement in town whose parents were okay with it and these awesome bands are coming and playing in the basement. You could just charge at the door. You didn't need anything really. That's what started wetting my whistle in that way. Because of it, I started booking shows, and that ended up being really what was my main focus even more than playing for a few years there.

Jack Antonoff: The thing about that scene is it was special. I've done enough traveling and worked in music long enough to realize that what was happening in New Jersey at that time was incredibly important and influential and became sort of a lot of the stuff of mythology. I mean, you'd go to a firehouse, you'd do At the Drive-in, Get Up Kids, Midtown, and My Chemical Romance, and there'd be like 110 people there. That music has been extremely influential and there was really two huge hubs of it. There was the Jersey scene and then sort of this sprawling Midwest emo scene.

Kenny Vasoli: I do think that there's, I don't know, a bare essentials of punk music that to me is just three amps, a drum kit, a PA, and let's do this. It's when pageantry gets into it that I really start to become disinterested with music in any sort of capacity, especially something that is so rooted in like, "Let's just put on a show anywhere there's a basketball court."

Benny Horowitz: One of the things, and maybe it's because of the way I was brought up, was this unifying part of the scene where it was like we're all doing this together. I'm doing this show for all of us because we want to see it. We want to see it here. I would literally get onto the mic during my shows, like at one point during the show, and just be like, "Hey, guys, it's just me and my friends doing this shit. Try not to fuck it up or we'll never do it again. If you feel like it after the show, grab a broom, help us out." I really was completely sold on the positive, unifying part of the scene.

Jack Antonoff: We weren't listening to Avril Lavigne as a bit. We were dead fucking serious about our politics and our veganism, and Propagandhi was God and Lifetime were the GOATs. You couldn't go to a show without bringing a fucking can of beans that would get donated to Food Not Bombs because being a fucking human being was as important as the music. Whereas the hippies that were at Woodstock, their story gets told because the music was great and they were the hippies. This weird moment in New Jersey that I came up in so fucking quickly, the context of selling out changed so quickly and shifted that our entire story sort of gets erased and swept under the Hot Topic rug. There's zero connection, zero connection between what was happening in New Jersey at that time and fucking Machine Gun Kelly. Zero.

Brian Fallon: I would go see Lifetime in a basement, and every single kid around you is just singing and got their arm around you. And you're like, I'd never met this kid and he's got his arm around me and we're singing songs. Cool. That was what I was looking for. I was looking for a family, not like a scene report.

Jack Antonoff: What it felt like to fucking be at a Legion hall and hear Bigwig. But if I play you a Bigwig record, you're not really going to get it. If you're not from here, you might be like, "Eh, this sounds like fucking Blink-182 or some shit." It's like, "No, no, no. You don't get it." It was so subversive. It was so counterculture and there was so many fucking heavy rules. . . . Shows used to just get so fucking crazy. But there was also so much camaraderie. But yeah, it was a fucking crazy place. Everything was crazy then. There were these converging scenes, fucking hardcore scenes, straight-edge scenes, the punk scene, the pop-punk scene. They were all sort of coming together and there was an incredible amount of camaraderie.

Kevin Jonas: Those are the first times we got to see live music in that capacity. I remember me and Joe going to see as many shows as we could every weekend. We went to all the places. I think that taking that live performance aspect to what we did on our shows mattered, and I think it's still with us today.

Joe Jonas: I feel like there's certain venues where you felt like maybe I'm a little too young. For us, me and Kevin going to shows by ourselves, I think, looking back. But Stone Pony, those shows and places like that always had people our age, and all ages. And that felt comforting.

Bryan Kienlen: We were reminded, everywhere we went, that we were from New Jersey too. Early punk tours, like the van tours, where people, whatever city you were in, they'd be like, "Oh, Jersey? Huh." And everyone had some kind of attitude about New Jersey. They'd make the stupid exit joke. And then they'd say, "Bruce Springsteen." And we'd be like, "Yeah, Bruce Springsteen's fucking awesome." They'd think they were insulting us, in our punk world. And we'd just be like, fuck you, Boss rules. We were like pro-Boss punks before it was cool, dude. I mean decades before it was cool. And it felt good to be representing what was almost like an underdog, something that wasn't cool in the punk world. It felt good to be like, "Nah, fuck you."

Pete Steinkopf: At the time, there was nowhere to play in Asbury Park, besides Stone Pony. That was kind a pay-to-play kind of situation.

Bryan Kienlen: Yeah, you can play here, but you got to sell tickets to your friends. And we wouldn't do it. So we actually got blackballed from Asbury Park for while.

Jack Antonoff: We actually kind of grew up in this weird grace period where it was like . . . we kind of hated the legitimate venues because they saw all of us as . . . if they didn't have a national act, and they could sort of fuck around with us and get us to put eight bands on a bill and make sure everyone sells fifty tickets that you have to pay for, whether you sell or not, in a band.

Brian Fallon: My first time playing the Pony was probably one of those, sell a bunch of tickets to your friends and make your aunt come and see you play. And then you do this show on a Sunday afternoon at one o'clock . . . And then it's . . . And one way or the other, you just go, "Well, this isn't for me," or you go, "I'm never doing this again, so

I'd better write good songs." It's a definite threshing floor, I would say. Those matinee shows are brutal.

Tomas Kalnoky: Those horrible shows, those horrible show days where it's like, I don't know, Tuesdays or something, and it's like twelve local bands. Everyone sells tickets. There's no real headliner. You're playing at some random slot. I don't remember if the slot was determined by how many tickets you sold or just your general perceived popularity at the time. They were just awful. In the very beginning, it was playing for the other bands and their moms who drove them. You would sell your tickets. You're essentially playing for the handful of friends that you could convince to buy tickets and all of the equivalent of that from other bands. All of their poor sap friends that got duped into buying these tickets and getting a ride down there and also the suburban moms who would drive a good chunk of these kids down there. It just felt like a pay-to-play situation where you're just this sap kid who wants to play.

Brian Fallon: Punk moving to Asbury was one hundred percent the Souls. That was one hundred percent them. They made that call first. So, they sort of allowed the rest of us to do it. And they were big enough to make that call. So they had already developed the influence to do that. So, they did that and started it and then I think everyone else followed suit, like us and even the Loved Ones from Philly and all the bands that were in that scene. Hot Water Music would start to play there. And the Explosion would play there from Boston. And all those bands that were kinda in that scene at the time, I think, slowly started to gravitate towards playing in Asbury. So Asbury became more of a thing. And it influenced a bunch of bands. Even like the bands from Florida, Against Me! and Hot Water Music, those bands. They all started to play in Asbury too rather than going to some other city in New Jersey.

Kate Hiltz: The reason that any of us started moving here is our friend Matty O'Brien moved down here and his now-wife, Janna. Because of surfing. So everyone would come down here to surf. . . . And things started more happening here. I was like, now I have this giant house. You're giving up the practice space. Pete built the studio in the basement, and a practice space in the basement, and there's tons of room to store everything. I had the whole record label on the first floor. And it was just sort of a way to save money, honestly. . . . And then occasionally some of them would be homeless and stay here in between tours or breakups. Just in and out.

Pete Steinkopf: Before that, in the early nineties, we would come here at night, just with ropes and stuff and climbing the buildings. We're like, "Let's go to Asbury Park and just let's just go fuck around," weird break-ins, weird-ass shit and it's fine.

Bryan Kienlen: Because there were so many cool abandoned buildings and abandoned amusement rides and just shit that's just cool to go drink beer around when you're that age.

Pete Steinkopf: And I remember making homemade grappling hooks, you know what I mean? And throwing them.

Bryan Kienlen: We were idiots.

Kate Hiltz: Every building that was abandoned, which were very many back then, had all the copper taken out. When we would be climbing around in the Ocean Mile, which is now that glass cube, we would go climbing around in there and it would be like, "We got to get out of here because that wasn't a raccoon, that was definitely people over there." It was a weird ghost town filled with strange characters and many desperate people. But there was also—everyone still got that beach town chill vibe about them.

Benny Horowitz: Kate Hiltz and the Souls were some of the first punk explorers who bought a cheap house in Asbury and lived there, lived amongst the thing and started re-creating their scene. No one knew what the fuck Frank's Diner was, the Lanes, all that stuff until they started cementing a proper punk rock underground thing there again. I give them a lot of credit for turning—not turning the town around, but starting it where it felt cool.

Ben Jorgensen: When I found out the Bouncing Souls were playing at the Stone Pony, I had to go. And the Bouncing Souls were a big deal for me as a kid growing up in the New Jersey punk scene because at that time they were a band that came from New Jersey that was nationally recognized. So it felt like, "Oh wow, I go to punk shows in New Jersey all the time, but this one band is actually recognized and respected and on Epitaph," which was the coolest punk label at the time. They were respected nationally. So when I found out that they were playing in New Jersey at the Stone Pony, there was a feeling that this was their big homecoming show.

Brian Baker: My first time here in Bad Religion, which was '96, it was just this place in the middle of pretty much nothing. Now that I've lived here for six years, I know a little bit more about what would've been around there at the time. But my experience in there was that, where is everybody? Why is that rusted rebar foundation there? I can't believe that there's nobody here, because where I come from, every beach was already heavily populated and also kind of expensive. In DC you went to Rehoboth or you went to Ocean City. And I'm like, well, why? This is just amazing. It seemed dystopian and strange, which I guess to a degree it was.

J Mascis: I'd heard all about it already, so it's not a mystery or anything; it's like I have heard about the Stone Pony as far as I can remember. It definitely didn't seem out of the ordinary. It was just like, oh, we get to go there. That's cool.

CJ Ramone: To me, the Stone Pony is kind of like the CBGBs of New Jersey in a way, in that it gave birth to a musical scene and it lived through every up and down that a club or a bar possibly could make it through, you know what I mean? It made it through recessions and riots and strikes and everything. Not unlike CBGBs.

J Mascis: I didn't know if, you know, it was as many punk shows, or anything, were going on there. But eventually we were able to play the Stone Pony with Dino [Dinosaur Jr.]. It sort of reminded me of Coney Island or something at the time. I remember it was pretty trashed.

Jesse Malin: D Generation had hooked up with Daniel Rey, who had produced the Ramones and produced the first D Generation singles, and he was from Red Bank. We went from playing at, what's that, the Brighton Bar, and it was fun, to now we're at the Pony, and it's these packed-out shows.

Brian Baker: We were City Gardens people and we were Fast Lane people. So this was just like, okay, now we're at the Pony. . . . We were working an album that there was a lot of push behind it. And I think that somehow all of us, we had CAA booking us as opposed to calling Randy Ellis and borrowing his van and satelliting out of Trenton or whatever it was. So we've been coming in all my bands, Dag Nasty specifically, we came to New Jersey a lot. And so it was just a natural thing. This is where you go. And we just got in the Pony, I think, because we had the proper rock-and-roll connection now.

J Mascis: There were people there for sure who would go there. But I don't know where they would come from.

CJ Ramone: Stone Pony is as iconic as any other well-known club in the country or even in the world. So when you're doing your last tour, your final tour, that's the club you want to be playing if it's your last time in Jersey.

Brian Baker: I knew it was an important venue because I'm a 9:30 Club kid and I played CBGBs and I played Irving Plaza. And I was aware of music history. I was excited about it. So yeah. Wow. I'm in the Stone Pony. And another thing about it, even then, everyone knew it sounded good. It's just the way the room, just the way the room is made, the way it's built. I'm sure that the sound reinforcement equipment has changed fifty hundred times, but the room sounds good and it's where you want to play. So I was excited to do it.

Jesse Malin: By '96, the room was full of people that traveled from all parts of Jersey to come down there and see Social D [Distortion]. Maybe they came to see D Generation too. It felt like it was older people. The youth scene felt more as the later nineties came in that it was more of a younger energy and a young idea, as they say.

Ben Jorgensen: I was crowd-surfing during the Bouncing Souls at the Pony, and I smashed my face on the floor wedge, on the floor monitor. I crowd-surfed all the way to the front of the stage and my face hit the monitor. Then when I got to my feet again, I felt my mouth and my hand was wet, so I went to the bathroom, I looked at my face in the mirror and I was just gushing blood because I cut my lip open. And I actually passed out in the bathroom when I saw all the blood. My friends picked me up and of course I went straight back into the pit and had the best time of my life. It was the most Jersey thing ever.

Vinnie Fiorello: Less Than Jake never liked to go to Jersey first, and then New York City. We would always like to do New York City and then Jersey because the show in the city after the Jersey show would feel quieter. You'd know that you were going to party the night before in Jersey, if you were there. You'd know that the show in New York City was going to be a little bit more subdued. Doing New York City first, get all the suits at the show out of the way, and then go to Jersey and turn it up, party a little bit, and hang out and you know it was going to be rager.

Tomas Kalnoky: When Catch 22 got to headlining our own show there, that was actually my last show with Catch. I remember there was a tiny little part of me that was like—because I'd already decided to quit. I don't know if it was before or after that show was booked, but the guys in the band knew it was my last show. I'm not sure. I don't think we announced it or anything. I knew it was my last show. I remember there was a tiny sliver of me that was like, "What are you doing? You, quote-unquote, 'made it.' You're playing your own show. You're playing a headlining show at Stone Pony, and you're walking away." Literally, that's the last show. I remember being a little second-guessing my choices and being like, should I have stayed? It was too late already. I already was lining up college and real life and all that. I was already committed to leaving, but I just remember thinking to myself, "Fuck, was this a mistake?" because looking back, it's silly. It's like, what is it, eight hundred cap[acity], six hundred cap or something?

Geoff Rickly: I convinced my parents when I got my license that they should let me go to see the Deftones play in the Stone Pony. And it was weird too. I think opening for them, maybe even one of three, was Limp Bizkit. They weren't like a thing yet. And I just thought, this sucks. Yeah. I hate this band, this sucks. And I just, for some reason I thought they were the worst band ever. And then they were of course, huge. Leaving the show, there was a security guard who may have been either an off-duty cop or had been a cop at some point. And he was like, "Hey, kid, you old enough to drive?" I looked small. And I was like, yeah. He is like, "Don't stop at any lights."

J Mascis: Sometimes it seemed too desolate to be dangerous.

Benny Horowitz: We went to see 311 and the Urge at the Stone Pony. It was my first time, like I said, not only going to Asbury but also the Pony. We had a piece of shit like an old red Escort that almost broke down in a lot of bad places. We get out and I'm literally one foot in Asbury Park my first time, some dude just rushes to the car. He's holding that weird flapjack thing. It's like a piece of lead inside a leather. I think what you use to break windows if you have to. He's briefing us. He's like, "Guys, a lot of cars have been getting broken into around here," blah, blah, blah, where he's slapping his hand with this thing. He's like, "Give me ten dollars, I'll make sure your car is good." Essentially embezzling us, being like, "If you don't give us ten dollars, your car will be broken into." Of course, we gave it to him. The car was fine. Basically paid for security for the car.

Vinnie Fiorello: If you were in a punk band, anywhere that you could party in the parking lot and not fear being arrested, that was the spot that you would like to go to and hang out. . . . You're not going to worry about, "Oh, someone is drinking a forty out in the parking lot before they go in." No one is worried that the Asbury Park police are going to be there going, "You drank a forty." It's not like that.

Brian Fallon: In the seventies and eighties the Pony might have been more of like a rock club. And then it shifted to kinda of like, when I was younger, it felt like more of a punk club. So that after that Bouncing Souls show, that I saw when I was seventeen, then I would keep my eye on it more, to be like, "Oh, punk bands play here. I'm gonna go see punk bands here." And I think the Bouncing Souls had a lot to do with that. 'Cause they sort of bridged the gap first, between the Springsteen-era, rock-and-roll stuff and the punk stuff. And they sort of melded that together. So they actually did it before we did. And then we kinda followed suit and just took it in a different direction.

Bryan Kienlen: Fury of Five holds a pretty big chapter in the Stone Pony history, I would say. There was a whole hardcore world going on.

James Ramen: Fury of Five in late '94 became the Stone Pony go-to band. Like, if they needed a band, Fury of Five was that band. We were very, very aggressive in nature, violent. We'd come from that hardcore, tough guy, but [Steve] loved that we drew numbers.

Dave Wyndorf: Fury of Five. Their stories are fucking unbelievable. We ran into them a couple times. I couldn't believe it. It was like the Irish mob—it was like the Westies of 1952. Extremely violent on stage and off.

James Ramen: We're not the best band that ever did it, but the way we delivered from the stage and our stage presence just is so captivating. The people were drawn to that and the mosh was crazy, so people would always just want to come to see what kind of antics were going to happen. When Fury of Five played, is there going to be a big fight? It was always some element of surprise coming, so it just grew and grew.

Bob McLynn: There were huge fights. I remember playing, while we're playing there's like huge fights everywhere in the club. One of the fights spilled into the merch booth, and our merch guy was like throwing people out of the merch booth. And we had to stop the show. A lot of those hardcore shows back then devolved into a lot of fights back in the day, but that show I remember being extra, extra pugilistic.

James Ramen: I don't want to say we were a gang, but we had a crew, just like New York City got a crew. Boston got a crew. Like, everybody, even now, it's heavily run by crews. Music is run by crews. We used to bump heads with a crew. We had a couple of different names. There was a little rivalry there, and then it almost escalated at the Stone Pony. Then I got to talking to a guy who's deceased now. His name was John Egan. Sometimes, you're on the show, you didn't know what was going to happen. When you saw them and then everybody is rocking these letters on their hats or their clothes, you had to stay on point or you would get into altercations, for sure. After me and John had spoke it out or whatever, he simmered down. He was a hothead and he had "Fuck the Police" tattooed all over him. He just was a reckless dude. He didn't give a shit about anything, so once we squared up and got to talking, we squashed it and everything. The scene leveled out for a little while.

Brian Baker: In the early days, the first, the eighties and nineties, East Coast clubs, that was just the culture. It's like, shut up. Fuck you. There was a lot of . . . If not bikers, there was just a lot of tough guys around.

Jack Antonoff: My connection was all through hardcore at the time, ironic to my sound and kind of what I do. The more kind of Jersey sound, E Street, Southside Johnny version of Asbury I discovered a little later. There were a few places you could play in New Jersey that weren't fire halls. Most of the shows were fire halls or Legion halls. So the only place you could go play and do a real show was Asbury.

Geoff Rickly: Basically, nobody wants a kid to get hurt at a hardcore show. So often I'd catch a stray. I'd get hit by somebody hitting somebody else or whatever. From various crews, I definitely saw some violent stuff at hardcore shows, but I've also seen a lot of violent stuff, just like between metalheads and hardcore kids at shows back then. You know what I mean? The longhairs and the shorthairs when I was a kid, didn't really gel at hardcore shows. And I would see a Hessian dude get into a fight, and then I'd see seven hardcore guys beat up the Hessian dude. It was very like that for a while too, and I never really liked that. Asbury is definitely no stranger to that kind of stuff. There were some real problems there.

James Ramen: Violence was with everybody and anyone. It could be with the bouncers. It could have been with white-power dudes. It could have been with anybody that were just disrespectful. It was always some conflict that happened when Fury of Five played with bands, the way we would dance, or like fighting on the stage. Like I know I wasn't there, but there was a fight with Gwar right onstage. My drummer got his head split with a guitar. It was very crazy times. It was pretty violent, man. I'm not proud of it, but it built the legacy of the band, so the stories and people are drawn to that.

Stacie George: It felt scary to go see shows there.

Nicole Atkins: We went to the hardcore shows because they were all ages. When I was in high school, that was all you could get into. Then I went to them and I was like, "Oh, cool." Then I just got beat up and I was like, "This sucks." By dudes that were like twenty years older than me. I'm like, "What is this?"

Kyle Brendle: The hardcore scene of Jersey was brutal, and there was a lot of kids that were really roughing it up. It always had that element and that's where we had an in-house security force called the Peacekeepers. They were really good. It's a scene that needs to be managed properly. It can be tricky because there's a lot of angst, a lot of crazy people. That's what they do. They go there to release.

James Ramen: The craziest show we ever had was our record release at the Stone Pony. It was sold out. It was for our second record, which was *At War with the World*, and we had just come back from tour. It was us, DOD, and Candiria. The show was insane to a point that during the DOD set, the sprinkler system got broken from somebody hanging on it and the show almost got shut down because of it, because water was all over the stage and we had to get plastic over the equipment. They were going to shut it down and then I got super, super mad. I'm like, "There's no way that we're not playing." I told Steve, I said, "We're playing. I don't care. We're here." The stage is totally saturated with water and he let us play. The show was totally insane. One of the craziest shows ever, and people still talk about it.

Tony Pallagrosi: Well, hardcore and the whole Fury of Five thing got out of control. I always felt like every art form has a place. And initially, I thought it was honest. I thought the energy was amazing, and it just appealed to me on a certain level. And then it got progressively nastier; the tone of it, the purpose of it changed. And it was used and abused for other things, and by people, by groups of people, because of the fear of violence. They manipulated that, each for their own purposes.

James Ramen: There was so many fights, like it's hard to even explain. Our shows never got shut down for them, and people gravitated to it. They came to our shows looking for that. If we were at a show, then it was a different story. We just shut a show down. I personally made Pantera stop playing at Convention Hall because somebody sucker-punched my brother and split his eye. He had to get like fifty-something stitches in his face, and somebody told me they knew who it was. I went in the pit looking for this dude, and the whole place stopped moving. They had to turn the lights on. Pantera was up there, "Chill out, big dude," like I'm a monster. We just shut down the show. We had to.

Bob McLynn: Down here, there's something about down here that's a little more intense. We'd play the Pipeline in Newark, but it wasn't as intense. And the Pipeline had some serious hardcore shows. But down here, it seemed like another level of the intensity of it.

Bryan Kienlen: Before gang-y stuff, it was punks and skins. And skins of course being more prone to violence. There was always fights. It was a skinhead thing back then.

Benny Horowitz: Some of these hardcore gangs or whatever they were calling it were built around kicking skinheads out of the scene in a lot of ways. It was this sort of like "We're bodying up because they're bodying up" sort of thing, but then after a certain point, skinheads were pretty gone and they just started being fucking dicks themselves and just terrorizing shows, essentially. Asbury was a big, big place for that, for sure.

Tony Pallagrosi: It kind of became like that in terms of gangs. Initially, the gangs were formed. And then you'd have these pockets of three or four guys who you could call a gang because they operated as one, but they would operate as one within the context of the event. And they might come there with an agenda. So to me, it was all these groups of little gangs, individuals who had gang mentality, and actual organized gangs.

Geoff Rickly: That was an Asbury thing. Definitely.

Bob McLynn: Some of these bands rolled with gangs. And they're definitely some hardcore gangs throughout the whole Northeast. Certain bands had those crews around and would mix it up with whoever it was at the time.

Benny Horowitz: Fury of Five and their crew took over Asbury for a couple of years there, where it became an unsafe, shitty place to see shows because of what you almost certainly knew was going to happen there. I literally watched a kid, I think it was Biohazard at the Pony, and I watched some kid get chased out of there and jump into fucking Deal Lake to avoid this mob of people. They're just standing on the side laughing, and then a bunch of local dudes showed up and were like, "What's going on here?" They told them and they're like, "Yo, you mind if we run his pockets?" All the hardcore kids left, just this kid sitting in Deal Lake waiting to come out with these dudes waiting around him and stuff. It was dangerous. It was reflective of what was going on there at the time.

Tony Pallagrosi: The whole scene became a problem. We had one really bad day at the Pony where fights broke out everywhere. I mean, literally, it was like a movie. It was like a scene from a western movie in the saloon, when there are fights all over the fucking place. It was a Fury of Five show. Coal Chamber was there. And the guys from Fury of Five had been disrespected somehow—I hate that word—by Coal Chamber. And this fight broke out, and everybody was getting the shit beaten out of them. And I'll never forget this. I was walking from the back bar across the floor of the Pony, just looking around, looking at all of this fighting, and just going, "What the fuck?" And I'm figuring, at some point, somebody's going to come and hit me. And nobody did. Literally, nobody touched me. I think, on some level, they all knew that the only reason they had anything happening at all was because of me. Because I supported them. After that, I supported it differently. And this was interesting, I had also fired my original security force before that show. And again, I'm not naming names, but my feeling was that the security force that I fired had something to do with that day. I brought new guys in, and the new guys got the shit kicked out of them that day.

Tony Pallagrosi: I don't know why I wasn't put in the hospital that day.

22

Warped Tours

The Pony's reputation of bringing in bands like Green Day reached Southern California, where a fledgling national punk tour was forming. The lot behind the Pony and the nearby streets, all largely empty as Asbury reached rock bottom, proved the perfect festival "grounds" for the punk ethos. By 1997 and 1998, more than ten thousand descended on the city, proof that Asbury and the Pony, despite the plight of the town, could still attract music fans, laying the groundwork for festivals to come.

Tony Pallagrosi: We didn't go after the Warped Tour. The Warped Tour came to us. The Warped people knew of us. Their agent came to us because there weren't many markets that were embracing the music that we were embracing . . . and we were doing those bands at the Stone Pony. Again, much to the chagrin of the old-school Asbury people. They thought we had totally ruined the Stone Pony.

Kevin Lyman: Warped Tour was, when we started out, no one understood it. We were struggling, to be honest. We went out on the road, started in Salt Lake City. We didn't know if we were going to get past Denver, the show. We were making it work at that point, but it was more out of sheer will of a bunch of punks going down the road that we were going to make these shows work. We were downsizing into venues, smaller places and everything. However, we were booked into something called the Stone Pony Lot. We'd been downsizing into some of the smaller clubs, but this wasn't a downsize. This is where we were actually booked. So I just remember rolling into that day. It was a very interesting day for me because all of a sudden, it's like, oh, we got some barricades and we blocked off this street and blocked off this street. And someone told me, "Wow, Asbury is where Springsteen got his start. There's legacy here. Asbury Park." And I'd never been . . . And I'm looking around at all these buildings that were half-built, kind of start-ups that were kind of skeletons and just this really weird vibe. And then you got the vibe that this show was going to be just totally different. There were kids around in the morning and there was a lot of excitement. And we actually opened doors to people there and we were averaging in the hundreds, and all of a sudden, there might have been a thousand kids out front for the bands.

Heath Saraceno: The Warped Tour wasn't inside the Stone Pony, but it was around it, in the parking lots around it. And I remember when we were walking back to our car—well, first we got into a car accident on the way down there. Our car rear-ended the person in front of us. So we got into a car accident on the way there. And on the way back, we're walking back to the car and we just saw these, I think there had to be five or six guys just kicking the underside of a car, trying to get someone who was hiding out from underneath the car so they could beat the crap out of them.

Kevin Lyman: There was a good, good crowd, and it actually gave me inspiration that we were onto something here because everything was a little over-the-top. Everything was by the seat of our pants. They didn't really have a concession stand. They just had Domino's pizzas being delivered and they were selling by the slice through the fence.

Darius Koski: Sublime were all, especially Bradley, he was really fun hanging out with. He was a fun dude. They were all pretty wasted all the time, and I was just kind of like, "Oh, God, that's going to be a shit show." His dog was there and his dog ended up biting somebody and they ended up getting kicked off the tour later on.

Michelle Amabile: Louie dog, he was hanging in the Pony. They had a little doggie dish for him because it was so hot out. He liked me, maybe because I had a Dalmatian too.

Kevin Lyman: There was a rule for me on the road. No dog, no friends. Sublime was not allowed to have their dog or friends show up. And they showed up in Asbury Park. They flew in to see the band. They flew in to hang out. Now, the band I could handle, but some of their friends were just a bunch of drug addicts at that point and a psychotic dog.

Tim Donnelly: That fucking Sublime dog fucking got my leg. Me and Pat. My boy Pat Conlon.

Darius Koski: Bradley could barely walk, but they were kind of amazing live. I was like, "Whoa." Not making mistakes and just ripping on guitar and singing well, and I was like, "That's crazy," because I just saw this dude puking in the parking lot ten minutes ago.

Kevin Lyman: Behind the Stone Pony, there was kind of this gay cowboy bar. And after the show, we were all excited. People sold a little merchandise, there was people there, and we all went to the bar because Stone Pony wasn't open because it was still the production office and everything. We all went over there and it started the downfall of Sublime with me because their dog bit someone in the cowboy bar. So we had to get out of the cowboy bar, quickly. And then they caused problems and I ended up sending them home after the Nassau [Coliseum] show two days later. I sent them home for a week and they could meet us on the West Coast. I just had to get rid of their friends and the dog. I like animals, but that dog was not treated very well.

Lisa Brownlee: By the time I was there in '96, that was definitely established. It would be really exciting leading up to the shows coming up when it would be in Asbury, because I know Kevin felt that what he was doing was being accepted and appreciated by the people of Asbury.

I know he would be really excited about that show, looking forward to getting there because he felt the energy was what he was trying to create all along and it happened, it peaked that first year. I think it inspired him that we could actually do this, like people are really into this and we can make this work, and twenty-five years later, after '95, he was right.

Vinnie Fiorello: Warped Tour was a cool thing to see as it formed and got bigger, but I didn't know that punk rock could draw that many people. It felt like, "Wow, this is the biggest thing that will ever play. I can't believe it." It felt like a victory lap for a younger band.

Kevin Lyman: Going from the first year, we did 2,500 people the first year and everywhere else, we were doing 1,000 on the East Coast. So it was always our solid show. It was like pilgrimage to the beach. Everyone wanted to roll down there. Even from New York, a lot of people went down to the Jersey Shore. And then we'd go back up and we did better there than we did at Nassau or in the Park or Randall's Island. People were like, "I wanted to go down to the shore," because it was Warped. And if you're in New York City, there will be a lot of police around the show. That was a normal show. Down in Asbury Park, it was a free-for-all.

Tony Pallagrosi: I think the most amount of police we ever had was twelve or fourteen. Which was crazy. Which was crazy.

Nick Hexum: The Warped crew was particularly known as just very lax security. A girl could just come up and smile and be backstage. There was very little difference between being out in the crowd and being backstage. So, it was just a constant party. And our thing on the Warped Tour was that we had a fresh keg every night, so people would come over with their cups to fill up on our keg beer.

Tony Pallagrosi: We knew that people would come there because we were doing business there. And . . . we made money there. People were like, "How are you doing business in Asbury?" If I heard that once, I heard it a hundred times. They wouldn't believe that we had eighteen thousand kids there for a Warped Tour in 1997.

Vinnie Fiorello: By midafternoon, it was intermingling of local lunatics and just families that wandered down from ten blocks away that had no idea what was going on.

Pete Steinkopf: The Asbury shows, outside the Pony, those were the most crowded in Warped Tour of all the shows. They'd fence it off. But it seemed like the smallest area with the same amount of people as any of the big areas.

Bryan Kienlen: And people could just climb the fence. I remember everyone could just get in. It was loose. They ran it fast and loose back then in those early years.

Brian Baker: The next time I played was '98 and that was the Warped Tour. And that felt kind of crazy and unsafe. And I think because we were playing outdoors ad hoc, where there was just sort of a cyclone fence just thrown up into cinder blocks to mark where places were, and nothing really worked. Kevin took a big jump on trying to do it here.

Kevin Lyman: Each year, it just seemed like they just blocked another street off or just took a parking lot.

Darius Koski: A lot of times you play at festivals and you don't always get—if you're not the headlining band, if you're a band like us, you don't always get thousands of people watching you. There's a lot of times they're just milling around. You'll always get a good crowd because festivals are usually pretty big and stuff, but that Warped Tour, what I won't forget is everybody was watching it. If there were eight thousand people there, there were going to be eight thousand people watching us. That was supercool.

Ben Jorgensen: My old band in high school that I played drums for, called Random Task, we won an Ernie Ball Battle of the Band thing. . . . Seeing all those people squish together at that parking lot in Asbury was one of the things that helped me think about what I was doing artistically. And I think in the back of my head, maybe the gear started turning, like, "Hey, what I'm doing in music might not just be confined to basements forever."

Lisa Brownlee: Blink-182 were riding on our bus. It was me and Kevin in the production bus, and Blink was riding with us because they weren't anybody at that time and they rode with us. I used to have to give them my leftover pizza. They hadn't really developed yet and weren't getting a really big crowd yet, so we used to close the office down or wherever we were and put a big sign that we'd be closed during the Blink set. We'd always put, "Gone fishing," so we could create a bigger audience for them.

Eileen Chapman: We were doing all their merchandise. I don't know how we got involved with it, but we were doing merch for all the bands. And Blink kept trying to sneak in more merchandise because you count it all, and then you do the percentage on the count. They kept bringing in suitcases, and throwing more merch in there, thinking nobody saw it. So I'd be chasing one of the guys down with this suitcase.

Kenny Vasoli: The first time we saw Blink at Warped Tour, just as spectators. A fight broke out in the mosh pit, and they were just calling it, like ring announcers, instead of trying to break it up. It's a different time.

Benny Horowitz: I remember a Warped Tour where the singer from Fury of Five was just terrorizing the pit the second that guy started dancing. It was just like the sea parted because no one wanted to get touched by that dude.

Kevin Lyman: Fury of Five. Notorious. Notorious. They somehow one night didn't like something about Warped, so they decided to come fight the whole tour. And then the police came and they wanted to fight the police. We thought, "Okay, the police are here. It'll calm down." No, it almost escalated more. And I think the cops knew them or maybe we were related to them or just didn't want to mess. . . . They didn't want to mess with them or didn't want deal with them and it was pretty wild.

James Ramen: We just wanted to sell merch, but they wanted a percentage, and we're like, "You're not getting nothing." They called the cops, but that's our area. We know how to escape.

Kevin Lyman: Usually in West Coast, the bands are kind of neutral. The kids, if I worked the show, I would have the long hair and it kind of looked like the weird dude working. It was kind of like they kind of left you alone. In Asbury, they didn't give a fuck. They beat up the stage managers, beat up the crew, then the cops showed up and then were willing pretty much to fight the cops.

Jack Antonoff: In the late nineties and the years when NOFX was properly headlining the thing, it was really feral. It's amazing more of us didn't break our necks.

Mike Doyle: Pennywise set, that's when they did that giant circle pit. It ran around the sound guy.

Vinnie Fiorello: Everybody would call for circle pits from the stage.

Mike Doyle: Tom Petta got like arrested afterwards for almost inciting a riot when they're playing "Falling Down." Tom was just like, "This song is about the authority" or "Fuck the police" or something, and they break into "Falling Down" and that was literally it. And so Tom gets off the stage and the cops are there and like, yeah, we're gonna arrest you for inciting a riot basically.

Tom Petta: I got arrested, yeah. I had said a bunch of stuff to the cops that were behind me. The year before I got harassed by a bunch of cops at Warped Tour. . . . So that didn't turn out too well. That was a lot of court, a lot of money, a lot of fines. So they had to bring me back to Warped Tour to finish "work" because I was technically at work. I guess that's a law in New Jersey. So they brought me to the Asbury Park Police Department and booked me and brought me back to the Warped Tour.

Bill Stevenson: I don't know if it was the '97 one where Descendents played or the '98 one where All played, but Sick of It All was on one of those two. As far as the pit violence, I don't know. I did several years of touring as a Black Flag drummer, so I know that from a different angle. People would beat us up at our own show. I don't know.

Kevin Lyman: And I think some guy was losing his virginity behind the pizza or the taco stand by that point in a pile of pizza boxes, and you just stepped over and kind of went on with your day.

Miles Doughty: It's a punk rock tour, so I didn't even think anything was outside of the ordinary if you saw anything weird. To me, we're on a giant punk rock tour with fifty-seven bands, so I don't think there was anyone that could be more hardcore than a lot of the bands.

Pete Steinkopf: One thing we did realize when we did our last Warped Tour was we did the math and we spent over a year of our lives on Warped Tour.

Danny Clinch: I set up a backdrop at the Warped Tour once, and outside the Pony there was a chain-link fence that went around. I think we just clamped it to the fence. And it was the first time I met Kid Rock. He was with [publicist] Shelby Meade. "This is Bobby Ritchie. And he's going to be huge, I guarantee it," she said. And I got all these portraits of him in a cowboy hat.

Kevin Lyman: I'll never forget the show was over and all the trash. They had no trash or they're not picking it up as it goes and the trash is fenced in by the fences that they had set up around the streets. And the local fencing crew came and just started pulling the fences up and the trash was just blowing out to the ocean. And we run over and we're trying to stop the guy, but in true sometimes Jersey fashion, they're like, "The boss said the fence got to go. The fence got to go." And we're like, "You're putting all the trash in the ocean." "Boss said." So you kind of start to understand, wow, Asbury Park.

It was a free-for-all, which eventually led to me taking it away from there because everyone got greedy. Like we had to rent parking lots. And we would show up and we'd say our agreement was five hundred dollars for the parking lot and he goes, "It's a thousand dollars today." The Jersey shakedown really got pretty intense around there. So we eventually had to say that we were going to move that show.

Tony Pallagrosi: There were still plenty of people that didn't come to Asbury Park. They had their fears or their reasons, right. But things like the Warped Tour showed some business people that, yes, the Monmouth County suburban kids, given a reason, would come and their parents would drive them there and drop them off and pick them up later.

Kevin Lyman: It was a great place for us to cut our teeth as a tour and it was a perfect vibe for the Warped Tour. A little rough around the edges, a little dirty.

Jack Antonoff: I did Warped Tour in 2001 or 2002 with Steel Train. We were acoustic and it was still in the lot, and I remember my sister was really sick at that time and I left tour because she got so sick she ended up dying of cancer. But I remember my dad and I went to the Asbury Warped Tour show like two weeks after she died to pick up my amp and my guitar, and we kind of lost a little bit of it. And this is obviously an insane comparison, but for me at the time, I felt like my whole world had fallen apart because she had died. And I was obviously in a mountain of grief, but I also remember standing there being like, "Oh, also the scene's dead." And it was just a funny . . . In the context of my life, it was 9/11, the death of my sister, and then leaving that tour. And then I remember going back and seeing it and just being like, "Oh, every ship has sailed. It's a new time. My friends are gone. The scene is gone."

23

The End, Again

In the late eighties, the Pony proved resilient to the gravity of a dying town, brought down instead by new liquor and insurance laws. But by the late 1990s, the drag of a dying Asbury Park was inescapable. Marquee shows were more infrequent. Shows by previous-era legends like the Jukes were few. Drugs and violence plagued the town, and the Pony.

Rich Russo: In the late nineties, there was no reason to come here other than the Pony. When it wasn't here, it was bad.

Dan Jacobson: You have this failed redevelopment, which scatters everybody because of the rampant speculation. It fails, everyone's stuck with these properties.

Tom Marshall: There was a shell of a construction project. It was maybe an eight-, nine-story steel girder building. There were people living in it. You passed it and you heard them in there and it was scary as shit. . . . My friend got mugged during the day. During the day. Guy pulled a knife on him.

Kenny "Stringbean" Sorensen: One night I'm coming back from playing, I saw somebody running across the bridge in between Ocean Grove and Asbury, carrying a TV barefoot at two in the morning.

Bobby Jones: I am born and raised in Asbury. So I was aware of the Pony but I wasn't active to the Pony. My first time stepping into the

Pony is when I worked here. When I was growing up in Asbury, I wasn't even allowed to come down to the beach.

Governor Chris Christie: We went back a few times in the mid-nineties after we had had our first two kids. So '97, '98, somewhere in there, we started going back. That's when we went to see Southside. But you didn't want to park around there. It was not safe. It definitely, by the late nineties, started to deter us from going because it had gotten really seedy and you didn't feel safe doing it. Now I was a father, and I was like, "What am I doing? Grow up and stop coming here because it's not safe."

Adam Weiner: I grew up every summer in Atlantic City. And so I knew from grimy and Philly. Philadelphia is my city. So grimy is what I'm used to.

Jake Clemons: I was nineteen on tour with a band called Sturgeon General from Salt Lake City, Utah. We were playing at the Saint. It was 1999. Asbury wasn't in great shape. We spent a little bit of time just walking around. It was like ruins. Legitimately, like ruins. Like *Mad Max* a little bit. Meanwhile, we did a little photo shoot on a jetty. One of the guys slipped. It didn't seem like a big deal at the time, just a cut or something. Two days later, it was green. . . . The previous drummer of the band was from there, and he had some crazy story about, I guess when he was in high school or something. He was surfing and his board snagged a bag in the water, and he pulled it out and there were body parts. His nickname was Fish ever since that day.

Robert Randolph: Sammy [Steinlight] used to tell me, he was like, "Man, you need to get an investment place down here, and the Pony. It's coming back. It's going to come back." Him and Danny Clinch would always tell me, and I'm like, "Man, Pony ain't coming back, Asbury ain't coming back."

Jake Clemons: We were walking around reflecting on what we knew about the town and history there, but yes, almost standing on the ashes. Wow, there was so much here and it's just gone. It seemed like fiction.

Kenny "Stringbean" Sorensen: Every time you thought it couldn't get worse, it got worse. I'd see waves of well-meaning people come and try to start a music thing or a restaurant or whatever in the last six months, a year tops, year and a half, and just give up because of the combination of street crime and government. I'd say there was a lot of corruption.

Eileen Chapman: There were public officials that were going to jail for different reasons. The mayor was caught buying coke in a bar in front of City Hall in the lunch hour. There was another councilman who took a bribe and another one who got a free driveway. There was a lot of that going on. A lot of people lining their pocket.

Governor Chris Christie: I did some of those cases when I was U.S. attorney. We had Terry Weldon. He was the city manager at Asbury Park and the mayor of Ocean Township. . . . He was the guy who said he was taking the cash to take his kids to Disney World. We found the money when we did a search of his house. He had these old plaid sports coats in his attic, and we did the search. We went in the pockets of those jackets, and that's where he kept the cash.

Jean Mikle: Nancy Shields used to cover Asbury Park for many, many years and was covering at that time. She said to me, "There's certain people in the city who are profiting from keeping it beaten down." From keeping property values depressed so that they could buy buildings, rent them out to people, make a lot of money.

Eileen Chapman: People were getting hurt. They were doing heavy-duty drugs and getting hurt.

Tony Pallagrosi: Asbury can bring out the best and the worst in people, particularly when it comes to women, drugs, and music.

Eileen Chapman: Steve Nasar was married and had like a gazillion kids. And I think he was going to get away from his kids, quite frankly.

Tony Pallagrosi: He had five kids or six kids and he was living beyond his means. So it was draining the club. And I think the club was doing enough business to survive. But I don't think it was doing enough to support him and his family at the level that they were accustomed to.

Kyle Brendle: The writing was on the wall. He had personal issues. He was going through a divorce and I believe he was going to be losing a lot of assets, including the Pony.

Lexi Quaas: He was having a lot of issues. Greed is a big factor. You really can't push greed on alternative rock kids. They're not into greed.

Eileen Chapman: Then he made everything pink and turned it into a dance club. And that really didn't work.

Kyle Brendle: He tried to turn it into a dance club for about two or three months, didn't finish the renovations. He wanted to call it Club Vinyl and that never really happened.

Tony Pallagrosi: When they turned into Vinyl, Steve Nasar owed us money. So I tried to kill him. But I didn't have the chance. I missed him in Miami. I tracked him, went after him, but he was a slippery motherfucker. He still owes us fifteen grand.

Eileen Chapman: We did three days of music for the closing party. Friends of mine played. The Outcry played, Redhouse played. I wanted to make sure that the house bands that were popular at the time and had good audiences got to have your last stand at the Pony. We worked on themes, getting Smithereens in there, and Southside in there, and all of those people. We did one night with newer music. And then one night with traditional Butch and Jack–style music. I was in the box office the whole time. Because Steve told me he didn't trust anybody. "People know I'm leaving. They're going to want to steal from me."

Jim Babjak: At that final show, the Pony's last ride, it wasn't really people partying. The vibe I felt was sadness. It felt kind of almost anti-climactic in a way. It's weird, hard to describe. It was pretty dead. It was pretty dead.

Jean Mikle: It was just like, man, this is it. I never thought it would reopen. Rock clubs have a shelf life normally, right? I went with my boyfriend at the time and also a couple other people and I said, "What's funny about this is we're all sad, but we haven't really been hanging out here that much lately."

Governor Christine Todd Whitman: We had already made it as an urban enterprise zone in Asbury Park, and we were actively looking for people to develop. So when the Stone Pony closed, that was something that shook us up.

Graham Parker: I thought I'd love to live here in the winter. I love desolation. It was kind of Kerouacian. It was a beat town that Jack Kerouac would write a poem, tons of chapters on in one of his books or something. You could just imagine it. I'd walk along and the wind whipping in the winter, cold and not many people, hardly anybody there. All those amusement arcades that Bruce featured in *Greetings from Asbury Park*. And there they are, all closed up.

24

The Thunder Before the Storm

In the late 1990s, there was no immediate drive to reopen the Pony. Or anything in Asbury. The town felt dead, forgotten, inexplicably derelict along the precious finite stretch of the Jersey Shore. The boarded-up venue sat like a gravestone at the corner of Second Avenue and Ocean, now just a quick photo stop tourist attraction for Springsteen fans. But in 2000, a Cuban restaurant owner from Jersey City looked at the desolation and saw an opportunity: bring back the Pony, bring back the city.

David Cruz: I had just gotten fired from the paper. And the owner of the paper, Joe Barry, he was a big developer in Hoboken. So he owned the paper, but he wanted me to work for his development company, doing some projects in Monmouth County, and wanted me to do some advance work for him. So I was going down to a city council meeting at Asbury, and I was hanging out at Domenic's and he said, "Oh, I'll go down with you."

Domenic Santana: David Cruz. Joe Barry told David, "Hey, David, go and snoop out. Tell me what you think of Asbury Park. What do you think? Should I invest in there?" Then David didn't have a car. So I had my Suburban. I came down here with David, and I saw the for-sale sign outside of the Pony.

David Cruz: We went to this council and then we're driving around, and we hit Ocean Avenue. Make a turn at the Empress and it's like, "Oh shit, the Stone Pony." And then I see a for-sale sign up, and I was like, "Wow, I didn't even know that it closed." And he goes, "What's the Stone Pony?" I'm like, "The Stone Pony, you don't know?" So I told him the whole story about the joint, as much as I knew about it. So he goes, "Oh, interesting. You got a pen?" So I had a marker. And he wrote down the number.

Domenic Santana: I needed money. Nobody would believe in this place. I had to call mom, grandpa, let's take a drive. When they came in, I'll never forget it. It was like, "Domenic, what are you smoking?" I'm like, "What do you mean?" She says, "Look at this, look around. This is a ghost town." And I pulled up in front of the Stone Pony, and so help me God, there were two buses, full of Asians, all with their cameras taking pictures. And I turned around and said, "That's why." And my father looked at me, and he's like, "How much did you pay them?" And I'm like, "That's a good one, Dad. That's a good one. I didn't pay them!" And then he said, "Hmm. Maybe you have something here." Then all these Asians were in front of the Pony, taking pictures of that dilapidated sign.

Southside Johnny: One day I was walking on the boardwalk. I guess my mother was still alive. And I was just taking a walk in the boardwalk in the middle of the day and four of these guys come up from South Korea and go, "Oh, oh, oh, oh. Can you take our picture in front of the Stone Pony?" They didn't know who I was. And so I'm taking a picture of these people in front of the Stone Pony and I thought, "These are people from South Korea coming to Asbury Park, New Jersey." It just was astonishing.

Stevie Van Zandt: You would hear about tourists going down there when it was at its most vacant and just a wasteland. There were still tourists going down there to see where we started. In that sense, we kinda, it kept a little mystique, it kept the mystique alive. It kept the town alive in that sense. That little bit of, no matter how weird it looks now or how much of a dead town it may have become, it had this magical mystique of being where we came from, which especially for fine rock-and-roll fans, it was a big deal.

Domenic Santana: And that's when I think my family realized, maybe he has something here. If this is a ghost town, and you have a bunch of tourists coming to take pictures of an abandoned, dilapidated building, maybe he does have something here. So that was the saving grace, that got them convinced: "Okay, we'll finance you." But I'm dealing with my parents' retirement. If this fails, I can't have my parents come out of retirement to start working again. So that was a big pressure. I had to succeed.

David Cruz: Against all odds, he was able to make that deal. So I got brought in—I didn't have a job at the time—technically, as a partner. . . . My job was to work the locals. The mayor, the council people, activists, all those people.

Domenic Santana: The first time that I came to meet the mayor, Butch Saunders, may he rest in peace, people say that I killed him, but I'll tell you why. I came to him and I said, "I come here as a prospective investor. I would like to know what's going on in here." And he said, "If I were you, I wouldn't put my money over here. We don't know what's going on up in here." I'm like, "What?" I went to the next city council meeting, with a packed house, and I sat and I got up in front of the council and the mayor there, and I said, "I've come here before you as a prospective investor, and I came here in front of that man," and I pointed at him and I said, "That man told me . . ." and I repeated the sound bite, "If I were you I wouldn't put my money up in here. We don't know what's going on up in here." "Shouldn't we fire him today?" "Order! Order!" And the place went crazy.

David Cruz: So we're getting close to the opening weekend. And it was maybe a week or two before Memorial Day. . . . And I hear through the door. He goes, "Don't worry about him, fuck him, I'll take care of that. He thinks he's a partner, he only thinks." And so I'm like, is this motherfucker talking about me? Then the door opens and he looks at me, and I look at him, and it's clear that I heard what he was saying. Then later, we're at the Pony in the back offices. And he just starts screaming at me. "Fuck you!" Calling me a traitor or a schemer. And he pushes me. And then one of the people who worked there separated us. But everybody heard. And then he says, "You're done, get out of here." And he called the fucking cops, and they took me out of the place. And so that's how it ended.

Domenic Santana: David did get squeezed out. He did, because basically, he didn't bring no dough to the table, no money to the table, so he was sweat equity. As far as equity was, he was demanding more than what I thought the sweat equity was worth. He was demanding things in black and white with real estate and everything. I'm like, "Sorry, I can't give you that." . . . Unfortunately, because David Cruz is an awesome person, and I really looked at him as a big brother.

Lee Mrowicki: Then, all of a sudden, Eileen says, "There's this guy who wants to talk to you." I said, "What does he want to talk about?" Says, "He's going to buy the Pony. Wants to know if you'll work for him." So I sat and talked with Domenic for a while. He was from Jersey City and he had about four or five guys from Jersey City that were investors. I'm from Jersey City originally, so I said, "Oh, well, if it's going to bring it back to the way it used to be." He says, "Yeah, we want you to come back and just help me make it back to the way the glory days were." That's what happened, and it worked. It worked from day one.

Domenic Santana: I came out of nowhere telling them, "I need you. This place needs you. I can't do it without you." So I humbled myself to accept that it's not about me, and it's not about Bruce. That it's about the people. Tracey, the bartender in the back, we need her back there. And when Bruce came in, "Oh shit, you're still here." Like he'd never gone. Like oh my God. It was still the same, the brick treatment on the walls, I replaced that because I saw the photos of yesterday. I'm not inventing it. Give me the same paneling that was on the walls before. I wanted it to look the same. And we had 254 sprinkler leaks in there from frozen pipes bursting. Because in the winter, there was no heat in there. All the water inside the sprinkler systems burst.

Donavon Frankenreiter: Nothing's changed in here since I've first played. All the photos, and the guitars on the wall, and the history, the whole vibe. That's kind of fun too, to go to a spot that has really stayed the same over the years.

G. Love: It's a lot of same staff too. These guys been working here for a while. Which is a cool sign too. You don't want to go to a venue every year and be like, "Oh, who are these guys next year? What's going on?" These guys were family. And they hold it down and they're keeping it going.

Kyle Brendle: There was nobody being really energetic and out there really waving the flag, "Let's go Asbury Park." But Domenic really was doing that really well and it definitely helped.

Domenic Santana: One of the sound bites that I used was "We are the thunder before the storm." Domenic, you gotta hit it out of the park. And the only way you're gonna hit it out of the park is if you get the governor here. A conservative Republican governor. And everybody said, "She'll never come down for the ribbon cutting. Because you know what rock clubs are associated with, sex, drugs, and rock and roll. God forbid. She's never going to touch that."

Governor Christine Todd Whitman: The Stone Pony was an iconic rock-and-roll destination. I mean, a visit is a pilgrimage. It was a big attraction and it was something that really needed to be nurtured. We did the rededication of it after it had been taken over and revamped because we didn't want to lose it.

Domenic Santana: Once she showed up, it showed the state that Asbury Park, it brought attention to Asbury Park, and that's what I wanted. It wasn't about the Stone Pony, or Bruce. It was about, this is an endangered American treasure. This city. We believe that rock and roll will resurrect the city. So that was my emphasis: rock and roll resurrects the city. And that was the spin on that weekend.

Governor Christine Todd Whitman: To me . . . Asbury Park was an ideal place for development. It had everything, the shore, easy access to transportation, it really had it all, which is why we struggled so much trying to figure out how to bring it back.

Domenic Santana: After opening day, I had thirteen satellite trucks here from around the world. CBS, ABC, NBC there, everybody. *Behind the Music.*

Governor Christine Todd Whitman: We thought that the Stone Pony was so important to Asbury Park overall, this whole sort of aura, that we needed to bring it back if we were going to be successful at all at helping Asbury Park get back on its feet.

Bruce Springsteen: I don't think anybody expected it initially to come back. So it was kind of a surprise, I suppose, when it did.

Stevie Van Zandt: It was like the first time I went to Liverpool. I said, "Okay, what's the address of the Cavern?" And it's a parking lot. There was no sign that the Beatles had ever been to Liverpool when I got there. It was kind of a similar . . . but of course, a lot of people like me, who were coming to Liverpool because of the mystique of, that's where the Beatles started. Now eventually, the town figured it out. "Oh. Maybe there's something to this."

Domenic Santana: I went to the west side and I made some friends. I went to the churches and I made some friends with the fucking pastor, with the priests and shit because I told them there were going to be opportunities that we could do some shows to help finance whatever cause that they needed and we could do fundraisers. That's what the club was going to focus on, giving back to the community. We're going to do events, a lot of benefits. That way the community, when I get into trouble, they're going to come out and support me: "Leave Domenic alone. He's a good guy."

I also went to the west side, and I forget the name of the barbershop, but I went in, and I said, "Listen, what do you think about that Stone Pony and shit?" They started yelling, "That's home for the white rock and rollers and everything." I said, "Hey, you know what, I'm a disco kid. I don't even like rock and roll, but brother, I think this place could help spark and resurrect the city. I was thinking of opening up, but I can't open it up without security. I'm going to need some brothers to help me out. You guys could recommend to me a couple of good brothers that we could have and employ and keep the peace." "No problem. You got it, buddy. You got this." All of a sudden they became my friends. I went there every two weeks to get a shape-up from there on and we became best of friends.

Eileen Chapman: Domenic hired Concerts East to be the music promoters at the time. They were doing some shows, but not a whole lot. And then when we sat down with the numbers and realized that the shows that they were doing were not necessarily bringing in bar cut, they'd bring in a crowd at the door and that's where the promoters make money. But they weren't bringing in a bar crowd.

Domenic Santana: Tony Pallagrosi thought that he was the one that controlled the Jersey music scene. I tried to work out with him. He tried to blackball because, on Memorial Day before I opened, I didn't give him the exclusive that he wanted. He wanted to run the house and I wanted to be independent. I'm not going to let you run my business.

Tony Pallagrosi: Domenic Santana came in and took over the Pony and restored it back to its past and demonized us. . . . If you look at the writing, any kind of discussion about the nineties here at the Pony and in Asbury, except for Tim Donnelly and Danny Clinch, everybody else makes like the nineties didn't even exist. Almost to the to the man, to the last man standing in the world. It's like it didn't fucking exist. And what kind of bullshit crap is that.

25

The Domenic Era

Bombastic, eccentric, and affable, Domenic's stewardship of the Pony attempted to re-create the intoxicating draw from years past. But a direct return was impossible; the town was still in bad shape, and the Pony was no longer a neighborhood bar. Yet by sheer force of will, Domenic and a crew of Pony staffers new and old would drag the horse back to life. Soon big names were calling to play. Benefits were back in the Pony, including the "Light of Day" fundraisers that almost guaranteed a Springsteen appearance.

Lee Mrowicki: I saw Bruce one day at a place called Jersey Freeze in Freehold, New Jersey, having lunch, and we start talking. He says, "How's the new guy?" And I said, "Well, he's got a good heart," for one thing. And that, to Bruce, is probably more important than anything else. Eventually Bruce shows up, gives it the blessing.

Joe Grushecky: It seemed like it was going to make a resurgence with Domenic, the early days of Domenic. And we started Light of Day around then. Light of Day was always in November. November in Asbury Park in those days was like, what are you going to do? So Bob Benjamin, our manager, he found out he had Parkinson's. He asked me to come up to do a concert at the Pony. And I called Bruce, and Bruce and I were hanging out a lot in those days, at that particular time period. And I asked Bruce if he'd come down and play with us. And he gave the whole thing legitimacy, right off the bat, other than just the local guys playing. Even though I was from Pittsburgh, Willie Nile is from New York. But we all consider ourselves Jersey Shore musicians.

Jesse Malin: I played there at the Light of Day benefit that has moved to several venues now but it was there. Bruce was in the greenroom with Patti, and we just started talking. He said he liked some version I did of "Hungry Heart." I was wearing a Clash shirt. Bob Broom was there. The photographer took a picture of us, and he [Bruce] said that he'd heard about my first record. I was like, "Oh, well." He says, "I've read good things." I was like, "Okay." We talked about music and Joe Strummer's new album. Then I said to my roadie, "Go to the merch table, grab a copy, and bring it over here to Bruce. Give him a copy of the record." Then they left. That opened a lot because after that, about a month later, I got a phone call from him about wanting to play some of the songs on that record.

Willie Nile: When Bob Benjamin got diagnosed with Parkinson's, he called me up and said, "Hey, for my yearly birthday party, why don't we do it and everybody would raise money for Parkinson's research." And I said, "Absolutely. I'm in." Didn't think twice about it. And Bob had done the work for Bruce, and Bob invited him and he came. Bruce loves to play. He loves to play but he came to support his friend Bob, which I'll always respect him for. It's on his shoulders that Light of Day lives. He came year after year, and built up an international following.

Debbie DeLisa: This room in the Wonder Bar, this is the after party. And Bruce is the server. Me and him and Gary pour shots of tequila in the back for everybody. Bruce goes around with a little tray and serves it.

Nils Lofgren: Bruce has also sat in jamming with my bands at the Pony a number of times. One gig, outdoors with the ocean in front of us, was fabulous. With Timm Biery on drums, Wade Matthews on bass, and Buck Brown on guitar and keys, Bruce played and sang great with us. My fave memory of that night was a rock version duet of "Fall Behind," one of his all-time, great ballads.

Domenic Santana: First time that Bruce came, we're sitting backstage together, and I say, "Hey, Bruce. Why did it take a Juanito-come-lately to resurrect this dead horse? I don't even like rock and roll. I'm a disco kid." And he looked at me. He says, "You Cubans are crazy." And I turned around and I stopped. I thought there for a second. I said, "You know what? You're right."

Robert Randolph: What's funny is it kind of makes you kind of nervous, because of all the history. I remember they were like, "Hey, man, we told the Boss, we think the Boss is going to come down and watch you play." So you're playing nervously, performing thinking the Boss is somewhere in the back, the bar or something, which you can't really see because there's a lot of people there. . . . So it's that kind of energy happening the whole time. And I remember telling, I was like, "Man, it's kind of nerve-racking thinking . . . You tell us before the show that Springsteen may show up and watch you perform." I guess if I was probably from another state, I wouldn't really care. But being that it's Jersey and this is where I was born and raised, it's that whole, well, and I've had many people, legends that come to on our shows. Prince, Clapton, B. B. King, all these different guys. But it wasn't the same kind of nervous energy. It's like I'm in Jersey and Springsteen is back there.

Jeff Kazee: I thought the Jukes don't play the Pony anymore. I feel that sometimes people will say, "I'm done. I'm leaving. I'm not doing that anymore." I don't know if he said that. It felt that way. Guys want to do other things. It's so closely tied to the town every year and to that club every year. At one point, any artist wants to shake something off a little bit. I was like, "I guess we'll never do it." I didn't know if the Pony would be in business, to tell you the truth. But when I saw that crowd in that bar, made sense. It was what I thought it would be. Johnny was sweating his ass off. The air conditioner sucks. It was rock and roll. To that degree, I was like, "Yeah. I made it as a Juke. I finally get to check the Stone Pony box off." I was like any other slob walking around looking at the pictures. Now my picture with Johnny is above the men's room.

Domenic Santana: Bruce knew where the cooler was in the back. He knew where to get his beer. He knew my liquor room. He knew where I had his Patróns. One night, he was here all night, it's four o'clock in the morning and he's still carrying on and we're tired. He's just, "Shots for everybody! Yeah!" We're running out of tequila. We ran out of tequila. Then he comes in sweating into my office and grabs more.

Danny Clinch: Patti Smith started playing early on, and then she made it a tradition every New Year's. She would come up and play the Pony and her mother would be there and she'd be up there cursing, cussing, spitting, punk-rocking all over the place. And then she'd be like, "My mommy's here. And I just wanted to tell her how much I love her." And we were all like, oh my God, I love this lady.

Patti Smith: My mother really loved rock and roll and she loved our band. She would come and sit and really hold court. People would come and want to talk to her or sit with her. She was always trying to get me to play the Stone Pony.

Lenny Kaye: It was always a good place to go and warm up for our annual Bowery Ballroom shows. We'd go down there and usually before my birthday, which is December 27, and we'd have a good time. Patti's mom would come in from South Jersey, be up in the seats and just rooting us along. It felt very family.

Tony Shanahan: Her mother would be holding court in the back with a bunch of gay guys.

Patti Smith: She was treated like a queen. She had her little table. I think there's a little upstairs area where it's a little elevated. She had her own table and her own area. My mother had some sight problems. She would wear these huge big wraparound sunglasses at night and have her cane, and she liked to have a margarita. One time, we were doing the concert, and I was talking about something. Sometimes I start telling a story in between songs and my mother yelled, "Cut out the yap, and get to the rock and roll." I laughed, but of course we started playing. We do what Mama says.

Lenny Kaye: It's a strangely shaped room because it's a narrow throw from the stage to the back wall. Then it goes out, which can be somewhat disconcerting. The spirit in the room that you can communicate with everybody one-on-one. You can see the people. You can reach out and touch them. They can watch your inflections, your subtleties of what you're doing, and be on a rock bar. The inhibitions are flying away. You're there to have a good time.

Patti Smith: The Stone Pony always felt very current. It's an old club, but the energy there was great. For me, the Stone Pony wasn't so much about history. It was about the people. The people, they were electric. They were completely wild from beginning to end. They were with you. Whatever mistake you made or if the sound was bad or if my voice cracked or I had whatever, I forgot my lyrics or anything that happened, they were just right with you. They were right with you. I'd love to talk to the people there. That was the other thing, is that you could just almost do a stand-up at that place because the people just went along with—they were open to wherever you wanted to go. You could improvise the whole night.

I'm from South Jersey. I'm not hugely talented as a musician—I'm talking about technically or even singing—but I know I'm a performer, basically, and I respond to the people and every night is different. We don't play by rote and I don't perform by rote. Those concerts were always like—they were like an experience because there would be storytelling and poems and agitated moments and excitement and doing a song halfway and saying like, "Fuck that song. It's not going anywhere. Let's do a different song." It was like being on a roller coaster. You just go up and down and up. If you're on a roller coaster, there's no static moments. It's always going up, coming down, making a loop, and it's all exciting. That's what it was like. You could be drinking a glass of water and looking out at everybody and it was still an energy-filled moment.

Domenic Santana: I got a call. Russell Crowe always dreamed of playing in the Stone Pony. Because he had a band in Australia.

Russell Crowe: I started playing in bands in 1979. My first record came out in 1982.

Domenic Santana: Russell Crowe had already sold out at the theater at Madison Square Garden. Clear Channel said you can't play the Stone Pony. He says, "Why?" Because it's a fifty-mile radius or something. He said, "Well, cancel Madison Square Garden. I'm playing the Stone Pony."

Russell Crowe: I'm not sure of the details this far along, but yeah, we did have the choice of finishing the tour in NYC or at the Stone Pony and we took New Jersey. We ended up having to cut the dates short to make it work and sacrificed going to Boston to finish the tour there. However, it was a fortuitous change, because the original dates had us finishing in NYC on September 11, and we would have been staying at 60 Thompson in the shadows of the Twin Towers.

Domenic Santana: He brought a van full of Louis Vuittons to give out to all the girls in the front.

Kelly-Jane Cotter/Asbury Park Press: The New Zealand–born Crowe is notoriously attractive. His audience at the sold-out Pony gig was overwhelmingly female. Women in their twenties, thirties, forties, and fifties staked out their positions and, as one male fan described it, "paced like hungry wolves."

Russell Crowe: It was wild. After the bigger gigs where you're separated a little from the crowd, the proximity brought a surge of excitement and energy. They were very close and very vocal.

Kelly-Jane Cotter/Asbury Park Press: Crowe walked onstage smiling, sporting a long-sleeved black shirt and a scruffy beard that was, needless to say, rugged and handsome.

Russell Crowe: The main memory was just how many people they squeezed into the place that night. They ended up opening a door to the car park and you could see across the room to a big crowd outside.

Kelly-Jane Cotter/Asbury Park Press: I can tell you this was one of the most territorial crowds I've ever seen. These chicks would not budge. Given the option, I like to breathe during concerts, so I tried to squish my way back to the patio for some oxygen. It was a rough journey, and many dirty looks were launched in my direction. Relax, I said, I'm heading away from the stage. I have no intention of fighting any of you in order to get closer to Crowe's rugged handsomeness.

Russell Crowe: That night there certainly was a "leave it all on the field" mentality from the band. We definitely wanted the Stone Pony to know we had been there. It took us quite some time to leave the venue that night.

Domenic Santana: I realized that the old school was not going to keep me open. So John D. and Kyle booked a couple of hardcore things. Kyle and John D., it was both of them. Both of them helped. They realized that was a fresh market and a lot of people didn't want to open up the doors.

Domenic Santana: Oh my God, we had a couple of hardcore shows, and this big one, Holidays in the Sun. I didn't know that they were skinheads. Neo-Nazis and we had employees that were Black. They wanted to kick the fucking employees. It was raging. It was like rage against them. They came here and destroyed the city because they started squatting. Since all the buildings were abandoned and this place was Beirut by the shore, this was perfect for them. These squatters came from all over. There were no hotels. The Berkeley, there was only one or two floors working and all the rooms were sold out, so they camped out. They took over all these abandoned buildings. The police chasing them out. "Well, we don't have a place to stay." They started to graffiti the whole city. I got in a lot of trouble for that.

> **Nancy Shields/Asbury Park Press:** Some of the estimated fifteen hundred young people, many with bright red, green, and yellow Mohawks, leather outfits and body piercings, got into trouble breaking into empty buildings, including the Casino, to find a place to sleep. They also broke car windows and were cited for disorderly behavior at the Berkeley-Carteret Oceanfront Hotel, which was booked solid for the weekend with festivalgoers. Some spray-painted graffiti on Convention Hall, boardwalk pavilions, and city equipment, and littered the waterfront streets, officials said. The event, "Holidays in the Sun," featured the Exploited, the Business, and the UK Sums among sixty bands on two stages, according to the event's website. The music went on as scheduled all weekend after the trouble, which occurred primarily on Friday night.

Domenic Santana: I didn't realize what I was getting myself into, but hey, we're here. We've got to make this work now. We're not going to stop the show, because you will have riots. Then you could have a problem.

Kyle Brendle: We had a bomb scare during a Clarence Clemons show. Terry Magovern, who was Bruce's personal manager, also worked with the county and the dog team. Training the dogs, the bomb squad. He took the lead with the county. We cleared out the building and said, "We'll keep you posted. We're going to hope we can put the show back on." They did a sweep of the property with the dogs.

Eileen Chapman: Once they realized the bomb-sniffing dogs were coming, Clarence's now-whole entourage is running down the street with suitcases because they think they're going to smell the weed in their suitcases.

Domenic Santana: The Great White fire. Those fucking guys were clowns. "Oh, the club knew what we were doing." Bullshit. You did it to me the week before, and it wasn't on your rider. Nothing on your contract said fireworks. I would have made you come to Asbury Park Fire Department. The minute I see fireworks, "Fire department, go talk to them. I'm not dealing with that. That's not my department to deal with. Fireworks, that's fire department, talk to them."

Eileen Chapman: I wasn't working that night. Kyle was on as a manager. I went in to paint the side office because La Bamba's big band and a bunch of people were coming in. We needed an extra dressing room. So I was there painting. And the manager said to Kyle, "We have some sparklers onstage, is that going to be okay?" And I heard him say, "Yes, sparklers. Yeah, that's fine." So I'm back there painting, getting all the dresses finished. I go to walk out into the club and Big Bill, who was our head of security, was walking toward me and he said, "I need to know when pyrotechnics are going off." I said, "What the hell're you talking about?" He said they just shot these things off onstage that went up and hit the ceiling and came back down. And I said, "I had no idea." And now people were freaking out. I was freaking out. Everybody was freaking out. And then the band went on a plane. Like I said, I wasn't there in official capacity that night. But I was there when that happened, and saw the fear in all of our floor people that these things, whatever they were, hit the ceiling and then came back onto the stage. Just freaking out.

Domenic Santana: They never mentioned it to us. To them, it was like a big joke like, "Hey," because basically, they caught us off guard and we reacted. We were like, "Fire on the stage, fire on the stage." I was in my back office and I'm like, "Call security, all the fire extinguishers, and everything." Thank God we didn't have the foam. Thank God we also had a sprinkler system, which the club didn't, but it was the foam who ignited it.

Kyle Brendle: The Station fire [in Rhode Island in 2003] was a travesty in a place that shouldn't even been open at all. It was horrible, horrible. I sat and watched that with Pony staff that night. Just like crying and people really upset. Because they played the Pony three days before.

Domenic Santana: They did it the week before and they didn't tell us of their fireworks. That could have been us, but for the grace of God, there go I type of thing. It could have been us. Oh my God, that fucked with my head. That really did as a club owner, to see so many innocent people die and the families who you're going to have affected for a lot of people's lives. I was not the same after that, to tell you the truth.

Eileen Chapman: I actually bought the first Stone Pony summer stage. When I worked for Domenic, I had suggested we put a bar outside. So you open those garage doors, and you put a bar outside. So we did, and then I had a fight with the city about mercantile licenses. Then I had to fight, because it was Mrs. Jay's lot. It was grandfathered. There should be a bar there; there was always a bar there. So we fixed all that, and my husband had told me we needed a new car. He said, "Take fifteen thousand dollars. Go buy a new car." So later, I'm talking to Tinker, and Tinker says, "You know, I have my original stage in my trailer. I'm going to get rid of it." And I said, "How big is that?" And we started talking. I said, "I think I want to buy your stage." And I drove to Tinker's shop. He opened up the trailer. All I could see is decking. I couldn't really see anything, and I bought Tinker's stage.

Domenic Santana: We knew I couldn't afford a big professional mountain production, big rig out there. I didn't have the money to put that kind of stage together, so I knew we were going to have to depend on some local resources. Tinker had it abandoned somewhere, and I'm like, "All right, come put it together." It was all warped with all the playing. It was bad, but it did the job.

Eileen Chapman: And so Tinker has his friends bring the trailer, but I said to him, "I don't know how to put it together." He gets this piece of paper, and he makes these dots on it. I couldn't even tell you what this was, and he says, "This is how it goes together." I should've saved that piece of paper because it was priceless. "Tinker, I have no idea what this says." So he sends his guys down, and they built the stage, Tinker's friends. And then my husband came in from work. . . . So one of the bouncers said to him, "Hey. Have you seen your new car?" And he said, "No. Did we get a car?" Like: yeah, come on outside. Walking outside, he's like: what are you talking about? They're like: that stage is your car. After he got over his initial shock, he built us another bar, so he was okay with it.

Carl "Tinker" West: I built it. I designed it and built that stage. I always had a portable stage. The trailer out here is full of them.

Domenic Santana: We realized that we were not taking advantage of all that square footage in the beer garden. That was what to do. Then, all the noise complaints from that building across the street, the same citizen is this old lady, that fucking bitch was always dropping the dime on us for this and everything. We had to deal with that. We had to deal with that, with the sound and everything and the hours and everything. Yes, we got a lot of noise complaints, but that was part of the course. It wasn't like, "Yes, just turn it down." "Okay. Thank you, Officer. Goodbye." That type of thing. You just have to do your job and tell me to turn it down and I have to respond and tell you, "Thank you. We will," and the show goes on. That type of thing. Cat and mouse.

Joe Prinzo: The first time we had played out back, we took a flyer because Domenic, we believed in Domenic because he's a salesman. And they didn't have it together quite the way they do now. So the monitor rig was in the back of a box truck. And it was just Mrs. Jay's property, because the Golddigger was still standing at that point, I believe. And so, of course, Bruce shows up and we don't have a microphone for him. And we're just totally unprepared. But we just, we're winging it in typical Jukes fashion.

Southside Johnny: But Asbury Park was a wasteland. I mean it was just terrible.

Eileen Chapman: The first summer we reopened, Tim McLoone did this huge Holiday Express show and his car was stolen while he was on the stage.

Jorma Kaukonen: It was like the dark side of the moon or something like that. It was like a war zone in a lot of ways. And I remember the question always was, because again, I've worked there off and on since the sixties, "How can that possibly be?" I'm sure there's reasons for it, but I don't live there so I don't know, but "How can that possibly be?"

Patti Smith: I felt that it was struggling and down-and-out, but most of the places I'd lived in my life have been struggling and down-and-out. New York in 1967, I promise you, was a really struggling city. It was not the city it is now. Struggling in terms of financially and was pretty beaten down, and I never felt—I don't have a lot of fear of things like that. I think if you cloak yourself in here or if you let out a frightened vibe, that will attract people that you don't want to attract. If I can't go out into a situation with confidence, then I don't do it. The short answer is, I never felt any danger there. I knew that it was suffering in some ways or dilapidated here and there, but I sort of like a dilapidated beach town. I know it's not good for, I shouldn't say that in terms of the people's needs, but aesthetically and personally, I feel a great affinity with a failed beach town. I guess I'm just an old beach bum at heart.

Nicole Atkins: When I got to high school, I'd always see shows at the Pony, but I remember my friend's parents calling my parents to make sure that we would be safe going into Asbury. There's a lot of families that live there in communities. It wasn't all just gangs.

Patti Smith: A strange thing after my mother died, in September 2002, I don't know when it was that I was back there, but right in front of the Stone Pony, somebody had painted or printed a big sign out that said, "This too shall pass." I think it's from the Bible. It was my mother's favorite phrase. I actually saw it and burst into tears.

Governor Jim McGreevey: Asbury had been in steady decline for some period, and despite repeated efforts to attract private capital investment, the city was still very much struggling. There was repeated corruption. So you had the status quo, which was an almost unbroken lineage of venal corruption while waiting for a savior to transform the city. But the private sector had little confidence in the structure and the wherewithal of the municipal government.

Governor Richard J. Codey: Corruption, of course it damaged the city. You gotta clean up your own act first.

Dan Jacobson: In the early 2000s, when a lot of us were here working to bring the place back, to make it a place that was a little different and more broad-minded, a place that was anticonformist, a place that would appeal to creative people who were going to bring this place back. There was the Stone Pony, and what pissed me off about the Stone Pony, I think, I guess Domenic Santana reopened it, which was nice of him. It was great. But I used to trash it a lot. Although I gave him credit, because it would be like that would be the only thing that people talk about. It would always be like someone talking about how I saw Springsteen there near '82 and they live in Long Island now or Marlboro now and all these suburbanites talking about the Pony as if that's the only thing the city is about. They'd say the rest of the city is a shithole. "Oh, I was at the Pony so-and-so." It's not like they come back to spread out to the rest of the city. It's just really, I thought that it was almost getting in the way in terms of what it was and I really couldn't stand it. At that point, I started to really hate the Stone Pony for really, in a sense, in a strange way, representing all the ignorance about Asbury Park because that's all people could see about Asbury Park at that moment when there was so much else here. They brought their suburban biases and prejudices to it.

Governor Jim McGreevey: Asbury Park was perennially the glorious impossibility. Almost any person you could see a glorious promise that it had for those who had known the city and its experience was, you know, it was an impossibility that almost never had been achieved.

So when we saw Asbury at the crossroads, and first approached the idea of the state providing oversight over municipal processes, the first reaction on the local level was to kill the messenger. But our perspective was that if this dream is ever to become a reality and the potential for Asbury Park, then difficult governmental decisions would have had to been made which required confidence by the private sector and the objectivity and the competency of the municipal government. And we took over some municipal functions.

Governor Richard J. Codey: There were some efforts but not a full-court press, which is what it needed.

Danny Clinch: When we're going through the late nineties and the early two thousands, I was living in New York City. My photography career was cooking. I was doing tons of album covers and publicity shoots with all these different bands. And occasionally a band would come to me and they'd say like, "Yeah, we want to do something really rock and roll, and gritty," and like that, "but we don't really want to do New York City. Do you have any thoughts of where we could go?" I would bring people down here, and I would come down here. There would be absolutely nobody here, no one. I would have the whole boardwalk to myself. Inside of the Grand Arcade was the most incredible natural light portrait studio that you could have. All the texture, and all the patina, and all the half-painted walls, and rusty this, and art deco.

Robert Randolph: My manager was like, "Oh, it's still a little sketchy."

Russell Crowe: It certainly looked like the best times had passed. Having no reference though, we weren't focused on what wasn't there anymore.

Eileen Chapman: When Bruce did the whole *Rising* show here, you know, with Matt Lauer and the whole *Today* show, there was nothing going on in town, and one of the reasons that he did that was to show that there are now businesses trying to open in town and trying to garner some interest in having people come here.

Robert Randolph: I think to get the Black people going, they were kind of like, "You know, Sammy Davis Jr. performed here." So I don't even know if that was correct or not. But yeah, we wound up playing inside the Pony. It was a total shitty day during the winter. I think we might have had . . . It's probably like a hundred people there. Eventually I told my manager, "Don't book a show at the Pony in a wintertime."

26

A Changing of the Guard

The impossible seemed to be happening: investors were coming back to Asbury Park. Though the LGBT community had been slowly redeveloping the city block by block since the 1990s, the oceanfront remained largely desolate except for the Pony. Its reopening helped Asbury Partners, deeper-pocketed investors led by the Fishmans, to see the opportunities in the exceptionally undervalued beachfront town. But with that potential came yet another battle for the Pony's survival.

Domenic Santana: All of a sudden, development, developers came out of the woodwork. They wanted to develop, but I was conforming and I'm existing. I'm not going to let you build condos around me. And the people buying the condos complaining that my bongos are too loud for you. I'm like, "I don't want condos around there." I was going to throw rocks in progress's way.

Larry Fishman: There was no way we were going to destroy the Pony. The question was, in our opinion, it needed to be enhanced. It needed to be brought up to a level. My thought was to create something almost on the level of the Hard Rock Cafe using the Stone Pony. That's the anchor. I wanted to move the Stone Pony to where the Casino is, because it was a much bigger venue. You have the opportunity to create like an auditorium—a large stage, a large interior stage, and so forth.

Eileen Chapman: Domenic was having conversations with the developers. But he didn't tell us that. Don Stine, who worked with the *Asbury Park Press* at the time, came in and said, "I think we should do something to save the place. It's got historic value. It's got an international name."

Don Stine: Why would you tear down the only establishment at the beachfront that has been bringing people here for two decades during the dark, bad times in Asbury? I mean, why would you even consider that, that's insane.

Eileen Chapman: Don Stine, my friend Leanne, and I said, why don't we do this whole save the Stone Pony campaign? We can go international. There are bands that play here who want to make sure this place stays here. We don't want to be in a Cavern Club where it gets moved and then it's meaningless. Domenic kept saying, "No, no, no."

Larry Fishman: The building itself didn't have any additional value to me—the name Stone Pony had a value to me. . . . The Stone Pony name and the history that came with it, I think if you moved it down two blocks, wouldn't have destroyed anything. That was my position. You would have real restrooms, higher ceilings. There were a lot of things that, even to this day, the building lacks. You would never build a club that looks like the Stone Pony, that's for sure.

Eileen Chapman: Domenic walks in the office, and he looks angry, and he said, "Start your 'save the Stone Pony' campaign." So I got a bunch of people together. We called these bands. We got the word out, internationally. We did a parade on a horse again, down Ocean Avenue. Did this huge campaign to save the Stone Pony.

Kyle Brendle: There was this huge rally. We stayed up all night. We all got pickets, placards, and old posters. It was crazy. Motorcycles. People dressed up like Uncle Sam or Abe Lincoln. It was like a circus. It was exactly what Domenic created. It was a circus.

Domenic Santana: I rode in on a horse, all dressed up in white with a Che Guevara hat on. I thought I was leading a revolution here. Here's the little Cuban Juanito-come-lately to resurrect the dead horse, riding on a white horse. Leading a procession of over five hundred people on

Harley-Davidsons and everything. And the police department was like, "Domenic, we don't want problems."

Larry Fishman: That was a starting point where people started understanding that Asbury was about to change. It was a conflict between Domenic and our firm, and I represented the firm so that it was pretty public. Domenic was a promoter; he saw an opportunity to promote. Nobody ever threatened Domenic with "We're going to tear it down tomorrow." Domenic created the illusion that we were actively trying to demo the building. Then you had a lot of the Bruce fan clubs that joined the bandwagon. Domenic being the entertainer that he is, and the personality that he is, he hired horses to go up and down, and created events, and it worked well. It also brought a highlight onto the project; it became news. Written up in all the newspapers, and people say it doesn't matter if it's good news or bad news, it still focuses people's attention on the project, and that's what we needed. I was happy with it. I knew the truth going all the way through, and me and Domenic were never enemies. It's not like we wouldn't sit down and talk with each other.

Domenic Santana: The master planner hired by Asbury Partners was Andrés Duany, an outsider Cuban from Miami, an architect. I'm like, "Oh, I've got an in." That was La Familia. I'm going to meet with Andrés Duany. And Andrés Duany, I remember my first meeting with him. And I started on the wrong foot with him. I'll never forget. I went, "Mr. Duany, it's a great pleasure. And as a Cuban American, let me tell you there's no greater pride of knowing that I resurrected American rock-and-roll history." He says, "Domenic, cut the Cuban shit out. Let's get off that subject." You know? I'm like, "Uh-oh, back up." And he's the one that told me, "You're the Eiffel Tower of Asbury Park. And you're not going nowhere." That's all I wanted to hear. For the planner to say, "You're not going nowhere."

Larry Fishman: The Stone Pony was never envisioned to disappear. Relocated, yes, I said it publicly. That conflict, if you will, raised the blood pressure of a lot of people, and it put a lot of focus on Asbury, and we needed the focus on Asbury.

Domenic Santana: The hippie army was there in force. And they thought that, "Oh, these rockers won't get up. We'll have the meeting at six in the morning. These rock and rollers will never get up early." Were they wrong. We had a party. I gave them free booze. And they were ready. But I was like, "Hey, listen, guys. We don't want problems." Because I knew Andrés Duany, so I was safe. But people, when I came back after the meeting with Andrés Duany, I had a party waiting for me at the Stone Pony because everybody knew I was having lunch with Andrés Duany. And that I was going to come and tell them my meeting and what was the future of the Stone Pony. So I came on the stage across the street, and I said, "Guys, I'm sorry, the bulldozers are coming." I wanted to keep the army enraged. Andrés Duany told me, "Okay, you guys can go to sleep now. Rest assure, you guys are okay." No, I wanted to keep the army raging. The war is still on. I didn't want to get my guard down. So I came back like, "It doesn't look good." And they were not happy. Yeah, I'm a fucking scam artist.

Larry Fishman: Over the course of three or four months, I met with Domenic fifty times. Mostly after shows, or after hanging with stars or whoever did. Had fun, and came up with a number. Again, I have to emphasize that Domenic was not the sole owner. We had four owners, and three of the owners were all aligned. Domenic was separate. Even, when I actually acquired the Pony, the closing was in two separate rooms, because they weren't even talking to each other. I basically had to close with one group of people, and then another group of people. I owned the Stone Pony, not Asbury Partners, because they didn't want to get involved in any liquor-related businesses because of the liability. The fund was not set up to own bars. Because of my background, I used my funds to acquire the Pony.

Domenic Santana: So after that whole procession, the Fishmans realized I was going to fight. Larry was like, "Oh, this guy's going to cost me money. This guy's going to fight. He's going to give me hell." Once they realized that I could give them a fight, then it's like, "Okay, let's get rid of him. I'm not here to fight. I don't have the millions I need to keep it going." And they gave me a contract. They let me, the trademark, international trademark is mine. Abroad markets outside the U.S. So that's what I kept out of the deal.

Eileen Chapman: We were not aware of any of that going on behind the scenes. We were legitimately trying to save the Stone Pony, but what we did was we raised the value of the Stone Pony.

Don Stine: After we saved it, [Domenic] turned around and sold it right to Asbury Partners. And that created a lot of bad blood.

Eileen Chapman: I said, the day the developers come in here I'm leaving. The day that deal is signed I'm going. And when they signed the deal, I left that night. I've never worked for anybody I didn't know and felt comfortable. In that business and in that place, you would call a Bobby Bandiera and say, "Hey, can you come play on Thursday night? I'll give you eight hundred dollars." Whatever, and it was all words. We didn't have contracts. We had relationships.

Patti Smith: My mother died in September 2002, and she was in the hospital for a couple of days. Right around there, right before that, there was a lot of talk about the Stone Pony closing or going out of business or somebody buying it. . . . My mother read about it in the newspaper, and she was very upset and she wasn't doing well. We had a job there and she would call me and say, "Patricia, they haven't closed the Stone Pony, have they?" and I said, "No, Mommy, it's still going strong."

The last day of her life, in the morning, she would go in and out of consciousness, and I'm not telling this as a sad story. I'm telling it as something so typical and wonderful, my mother. My mother, I'm sitting at her side and we're all there. We know it's her last hours. She wakes up and she looks at me and she says, "Patricia." I said, "What?" She said, "Did we save the Stone Pony?" I said, "Oh, yes, Mommy, we saved the Stone Pony. The Stone Pony will be there forever." She said, "Oh, good," and she went back to sleep. She didn't die at that moment. She passed away some hours later, but it was one of the things that she was concerned about in her last hours, was that the Stone Pony would prevail. I've never seen her love a venue so much as she loved that place. She loved the people, the atmosphere, everything.

27

A Slow Climb

The dreamer developers arrived with grand plans and big initial investment into the Pony. But like the cliché of turning around a cruise ship, improving the fortunes of Asbury Park and the Pony required time, or a lot of money. Neither was in abundance.

Caroline O'Toole: A friend of my best friend was doing a lot of work at the time with Larry Fishman, who was the voice of Asbury Partners. And my best friend, Jeanie, her friend Mike suggested me to Larry. So we got in contact, and I think there was several other people he was speaking to at the same time, but it just kept coming around. . . . I was thirty-nine, and I was like, "Well, if I do this, I'm going to give up any idea of having a normal life."

Larry Fishman: We enhanced everything, put a real high-quality sound system in, put a new board in. It made the experience better. It was an experience not only for the people that attended the show but the people that played the show.

Caroline O'Toole: Probably the first benefit show Bruce ever played there, we started collecting guitars with signatures. So we had a couple blank guitars up on the wall. And he's playing onstage, and we didn't have air-conditioning then, so he was sweating. And he gets up on the middle bar, and we barely had electricity, I think too, because there's just wires everywhere. So now he's sweating, but he promised to sign a guitar, so we bought him a replica of what he plays normally, a real Fender, but he went for this blank ninety-nine-dollar guitar. He's holding on to the wire trying to sign it, and I'm like, "We're going to electrocute Bruce Springsteen." Then he has Bobby Bandiera get up on the bar, and Bobby signs it. He goes, "Sign this guitar." So Bobby signs it too. So to this day, that's the guitar we have is this ninety-nine-dollar guitar that Bruce and Bobby signed.

Larry Fishman: We cleaned some house, and we kept the best employees. We were able to invest money in systems so that everything could work effectively. I did my very best to bring in a much higher level of national entertainment, much higher than you got today, let's put it that way. I brought in maybe not a class act, but pretty high acts. I spent a lot of money on artists. You get one level of artists for five thousand dollars, you get another level for twenty-five thousand dollars. I was willing to take a chance and see if we could upgrade the entertainment level, and it worked amazingly. We brought in national acts. I made inroads with both AEG and Live Nation.

Caroline O'Toole: Then there was the whole upheaval with the staff. Once you go into a place, especially when you're going to try and implement new policies and things like that, you have resistance.

Larry Fishman: The idea was to keep you in Asbury. The idea was to get you to come down, hang out at the beach in the day. You know what I mean? We weren't just trying to create a club. If you're trying to do that you would be a New York City.

Caroline O'Toole: Booking was mainly John D. and Kyle Brendle. They were the two. Domenic didn't really do much of that. It was really those two. Kyle was more the classic guy. And then you had John, who brought in the newer bands and newer genres of music that hadn't really been tested yet.

Kyle Brendle: It was an overwhelmingly punk and hardcore scene. The jam band community was still coming.

Geoff Rickly: When we finally played the Stone Pony, we did a MySpace show, which is a thing back then MySpace would do. They would have an event and you would play it for maybe even for free, and they would promote your profile or whatever. And it was kind of like a time. The major labels were still trying to get their heads around whether social media was going to be a thing or not. But MySpace seemed to be something. So we played there and we had a great screen print poster, and I just would always laugh with the guys about the fact that it took a weird corporate social media tie-in to get us to the Stone Pony.

Mike Doyle: Eight years later Lifetime got back together. That show we showed up and everyone there was just there to see Lifetime but we're there and it's like fucking there's Geoff and the guitar player from Thursday and just hanging at the bar drinking Coronas and then there's Adam from Taking Back Sunday there with his girlfriend. And fuckin' Frank and Gerard from My Chemical Romance are in the fucking crowd. Like it was what the fuck is happening right now.

Andrew McMahon: The first time we really played the Pony was with Jack's Mannequin. And by that point it was much more ingrained for me. We covered "I'm on Fire" that night. And there was rumor that Bruce might come down to the show and we're just like, oh my God, what if Springsteen comes to the gig? But I was also in a pretty weird place in my life. I think at that moment I was maybe a year out of my cancer and pretty fucked-up in general. I was looking at the intro on that "I'm on Fire" video. I was like, "Oh my God, I'm hammered in this video." And just hearing my voice and hearing the way I was talking, it is a bit of a relic from a tricky moment in my life.

Ben Jorgensen: We decided to have our CD release show for *What to Do When You Are Dead*, both because the Stone Pony was the ultimate New Jersey club, and honestly, at that time, there were not many others left anymore.

Jack Antonoff: The history of that is also one of the completely undiscussed and unreferenced one. And the reason why it's undiscussed and unreferenced is because what became of emo became sort of a weird, smudged thing. When emo started, it was post-Fugazi music. It was, we were all saying, Texas Is the Reason and At the Drive-In. All this really important shit. And then it got commodified. It became Hot Topic really quickly. The thing that was happening in New Jersey shifted so much and became something that people didn't want to talk about that I actually think that we lived through something that wasn't terribly different than DC in the eighties, the Bay Area in the late sixties, one of these great musical moments that was just undiscussed because the context of what emo became became, I guess, unsavory or some bullshit for the mainstream.

Nick Jonas: The history that was created there by some of the greats from Jersey and specifically in the rock-and-roll world, really make it the kind of place that you look at as a benchmark of not only a dream and aspiration and goal, but also the benchmark of success and taking on that badge of honor that you wear after you've played there. It's just the history and the real feeling that the greats have played on that stage. For us, I think growing up in Jersey and being obviously hyperaware of Bruce and Bon Jovi and all of that really made it someplace that we looked at as, Okay, let's get there someday, let's be able to play there.

Kevin Jonas: That's how we grew up, listening to those local-scene bands and going to Stone Pony and Starland Ballroom, places like that, mattered a lot to us.

Nick Jonas: Two thousand five was our first show. And there was probably a handful of people that came to the concert. We were helping load in our gear out of probably a minivan. And it's memorable. I think it's one of those moments, a career moment for us, because growing up in New Jersey, playing the Stone Pony was always one of those things you hope for, you wish for. And it's a challenge because you're kind of on the hustle at that point. And you're literally inviting people on the boardwalk to come to your show.

Joe Jonas: We were nowhere close to the capacity of what that place could hold at that time. Passing out flyers along the boardwalk, inviting people in, whatever we could do to make it feel like a full room.

Kevin Jonas: But the boardwalk was pretty empty, just like the show.

Nick Jonas: It was just us. I think it was a headlining show. But it was the start of our career. And there's a lot of, you know, a lot of time ahead of us to kind of continue to hone our craft and build our fan base.

Kevin Jonas: None of us were twenty-one yet, so we had to play early, which was part of it. And some of the locals that were there just for the bar, not expecting to see a Jonas Brothers crowd or show, were hanging out. I remember feeling a little heckled from the back, to be honest. But they got into it after a certain amount of time.

Joe Jonas: Bruce. We definitely thought that back in the day, like there's a slim chance. That never happened, but we've been to plenty of his shows.

Larry Fishman: I didn't understand certain music. To this day I don't still understand certain music and why people like certain music or not, but John had a good feel for what would sell tickets and utilized that.

Caroline O'Toole: He was being sought after by management companies, big promoter companies. And John, every time he had an interview or spoke to someone, he would make it clear that Asbury Park was his priority. So he wasn't going to take a job with anybody who wasn't going to let him do that. So, Live Nation said yes to that, and that's how Live Nation came here.

Caroline O'Toole: I think it was New Year's, there was a killing in town, on the other side of Main Street, and everyone came down to the boardwalk, I think because they knew these two officers were inside. And they left, and now I have just this crowd of people who are just angry because now someone's been killed in town. And they're on the steps of the club. It wasn't called the Cabana Club yet. Actually, that was later on. It was called the Deep. And here I am, and I had to send my staff home. So here I am by myself on the porch of this club, facing this mob, and with no police inside. The crowd verbally attacked me. But after a lot of yelling, it just toned down.

Benny Horowitz: It ended up really coming to an awful head. They fucking killed some kid outside of Club Deep. A bunch of the local hardcore dudes. It was right when they were rebuilding the boardwalk and it was right on the boardwalk up there. It started with some small thing and some of the more notorious hardcore kids around at the time.

Caroline O'Toole: One night, somebody got hit outside the club and they fell on the sidewalk and they died, and I've never forgotten that. And that was the time I really questioned, "What's going on here and who are the people coming here?" I did a lot of soul-searching that night to see if I could go on that night and all the time that followed. But I had to because now I was here and I wanted to be part of this town going forward, and the Pony needed to be part of that. And if I left, I don't know what would have happened. So I had to just pull out everything that I could from within and just go on. And that was really hard to do after someone dies.

Caroline O'Toole: I used to go over to Domenic's house because he lived a couple of blocks away from the Pony because he was the only one who could understand what I was going through, because he had just been through it. And this was even after he didn't work there anymore. And we would both basically be crying because he was the only person who understood.

Domenic Santana: I always had the shoulder out for her. She's a strong woman, and I think I helped mold her into being a strong person. That's what it took, especially for a woman manager in a rock club, and with those hardcore punks and everything. You got to growl at these mother-fuckers and let them know that you are the law and that nobody is going to come and disrespect the house. I am the house and you're not going to disrespect me.

Larry Fishman: We had issues. The country had issues. There was an implosion. Subprime. The housing market in Asbury was predicated on, basically, summer homes. The gay population had a lot to do with it, with acquiring homes there. They were pioneers. It was a very inclusive community, but when the subprime hit, a lot of the developers, and you have to remember we were not building, we were running the redevelopment, but we weren't doing any building. We couldn't. Basically, the deal that we had signed with the city was that we would bring in outside developers. After 2006 it slowed up pretty bad, and that created the environment where iStar and Madison Marquette made overtures to the true backers of the Asbury Partners project, and made a deal.

Gary Mottola: After quite some time, we negotiated an arrangement where we came in to basically take control of everything on the boardwalk and the Pony and Wonder Bar.

Larry Fishman: I had taken it to a level, but he had resources far beyond what I had. It just morphed into what he could do. A deal was made that was fair, that we did, and I worked for iStar for a year, and then I moved on.

Governor Chris Christie: In the first of the economic incentive bills we did, we carved out some special stuff for Asbury Park, and when we did, the reaction was almost immediate because there was a real community down there, as you know, that wanted to develop the place. The gay community down there was incredibly intense on taking it to the next level. There were plenty of art galleries down there that were really interesting and unique and some restaurants, but not a lot. But once we provided incentives for them on the tax side, it got developers more interested and it freed up some of the others. It was really the approach. It wasn't a lot more complicated than that.

Gary Mottola: You look at one hundred miles of the Jersey shore. There's forty towns or something. They are all different. Beach Haven is different than Harvey Cedars, and Wildwood is different from Spring Lake, and Sea Girt is different from Sea Bright. They're all very different, but they're all the same. They're all part of the Jersey Shore. Same fabric. Largely the same people. I mean, people from New Jersey. People from elsewhere too, but it's just a rite of summer for many, many people in New Jersey to spend some time on the shore, whoever it is. Obviously, Asbury wasn't that place. In the early 2000s, if you went on the beach on July Fourth, if there were a hundred people, that would be a lot. The streets were potholed and parking meters were leaning over. It was pretty rough, but it was only one mile out of a hundred miles.

28

The Last Wild West

There is freedom in being forgotten. For the rockers, rogues, and renegades of Asbury Park, that meant autonomy in their city that was either ignored or avoided for roughly twenty years. And even as the Pony became more of an establishment organization with the arrival of Madison Marquette, the corporate overseer of the Pony and boardwalk that bought the rights from Asbury Partners, anarchic joy still spilled inside the walls.

Tim Donnelly: I look at up until about 2012 as the last years of the Wild Wild West of this place. Because it was just like fucking gnarly, dude. It was get-away-with-anything. It was like, most of the lights were still blinking, or traffic lights weren't even fucking working, cops weren't pulling you over for anything. It was pretty lawless.

Kate Hiltz: A lot of it, there was dog fights, cockfights, all this kind of stuff.

Graham Parker: There was just one place open where you got breakfast. I'd be staying in the Berkeley-Carteret. Nearly always the Berkeley-Carteret. Over the years, I'd stayed there and the things I saw there were extraordinary. At one point, I went in there and I was checking in and there was a clown convention. I'd go into the elevator and there'd be clowns. One of them would just have the big slippers on and a bow tie and nothing else. They'd be a bit sort of partially dressed clowns. Then I'd come down for a cup of tea at the bar or something before going to sound check, might have a bit of time, and they'd have a bit more clown clothing on. They seemed to be going up and down the elevators, getting bits of their costume or maybe borrowing costume. And all you wanted to do was look around and say, "Hey, clown." You really wanted to say, "Hey, clown." But I didn't do it for fear that they be . . . Clowns are quite sinister. Maybe they carry knives, I don't know.

Geoff Rickly: One thing that I always remember about playing Asbury and in Jersey in general is Vinny Magic. There's this guy that's either worked for one of the promoters, maybe he worked for John. Who knows who he worked for, but he was really good at close-up magic with cards. And he had that kind of a personality, like, "Hey, I'll show you. Oh, keep your eye on this card." And he also often, often also had cocaine, I'll be honest. But he was just like this character. And every band would be like, "Oh, you played Asbury? You see Vinny Magic?"

Kate Hiltz: One time someone stole a bike. We were sitting on the front porch. And the bike was parked on the sidewalk on the walkway up to the steps, and someone just kind of detoured off the sidewalk, hopped on it and rode away. And we were all like, hey. But also sort of "good for you, dude."

Robert Randolph: People snuck backstage easily, all the time. One time we played and literally a guy like that, I thought he was with somebody else, was just kind of back there the whole time and we thought he was with one of the other band members. Turns out he wasn't. He was back there jamming on our acoustic guitars and stuff. And finally I noticed that he was like . . . wasn't talking to anybody after the show. I was like, "Well, who is this guy?" They were like, "I don't know. We thought you knew him." Everybody was like, "I thought you knew him."

Bobby Jones: I walked Courtney Love from the greenroom to the front of stage and she walks in and everyone's calling her name. She looks around, come back outside, and she throws up on my leg. . . . And then she went back inside to perform.

Nicole Atkins: I was making my first record, and my manager was looking for tours to have me on. I was going out with Paul from the Parlor

Mob, and they were like, "Hey, can you go and watch this band, the Hold Steady? Because maybe you could go out with them." I was like, "Sure." So I went out, and Paul was like, "Yes, I'm not going to go backstage." Because he was a shy guy. He was like, "You just go back and do your thing." Then Kyle ended up getting him a bunch of shots at the bar. And I'm talking to Craig Finn, and Paul comes back with Kyle, and I think their guitar player at the time was a bad alcoholic. He's not anymore, but he was like, "Hey, rocker dude, what does your band sound like?" He's like, "Oh, kind of like the MC5 and Led Zeppelin." He goes, "Cool, so you sound like Jet?" And within two seconds, Paul flicked a cigarette at the guy. The guy bounded off and punched him in the face, the entire band on top of him, and I'm like, "Oh my God." And now Paul's fighting the whole band, and I'm just standing at the side like, "What the fuck is happening? How did this happen?" Then he gets up and he's like, "I'm done with this," and he leaves, and I can't find him. His phone's off, I can't find him anywhere. I run into Paradise. "Have you guys seen Paul?" "No." At the time, there was only a few bars there. I couldn't find him. I find him by the Big Beat Guitar, like the music lessons place in Neptune, Big Beat Music Studio, with cops, which is so far. It was just one of those ridiculous very Asbury Park nights that would've only flown then because it was still pretty desolate. It just was a bad moment. It was funny though. Paul started wearing the Hold Steady buttons on his jacket. Then the guy that punched him, his daughter was in a Parlor Mob video.

Kate Hiltz: For the first more than ten years I lived here, if you were a woman walking alone on Grand, you were a hooker. So it's not dangerous. It's just a different mentality of what people are doing outside during the day or at night or whatever. And I've been robbed many times, house broken into, everything taken. Luckily never stole stuff. I mean money, but not gear. And not for nothing. The cops are always like, "It's an inside job. It was some band dude that was staying here, whatever." . . . If it was a band dude, they would go for the Les Pauls. Trust me.

Donavon Frankenreiter: There's that one zone where you walk through that's really haunted. Near where Zeppelin played, Hendrix and shit. And where was the boat that caught on fire?

Tim Donnelly: That was in the mid-1930s, the *Morro Castle*, is what it was called. So it was a ship that went down. And they took the dead and stuff, at the back of the Convention Hall, and they took the dead bodies and they put them in the Convention Hall, and they had them all laid out. And someone decided to sneak people in and charge admissions to see the dead bodies. And there's a theory here that a lot of us subscribe to that started the bad negative energy. So there was always weird energy in and around that building. And this was a very happy place up until then. And then I swear to God, it took Hurricane Sandy to give this place a psychic cleansing to get that energy out. I have seen in the middle of the winter on a Tuesday afternoon in February, wet footprints in that back hallway.

Bobby Jones: One of the biggest injuries we've had was a Southside show. A lady broke her hip. She tried to go into the crowd and someone knocked her over and it just broke. At a Southside show. Out of all the punk shows and hard metal, it was a Southside Johnny show. The hard rock shows, you know what you're going to get. The Southside Johnny shows or any of the older people that come into the Pony or play, there's people who come and drink like they're twenty-one again, like back in their heyday. And it's not pretty.

Jeff Kazee: Johnny's crowd are beer drinkers. He sells a lot of beer. Club owners will tell you . . . Now, everybody has their audience a little older. They got more money and they'll just buy better beers. We sell a lot of beer for clubs. There's no question about it. They drink up. It's insane.

Tim Donnelly: The number one night for 911 calls related to alcohol, almost without fail, almost every year, is fucking Southside Johnny and the Asbury Jukes at the Summer Stage.

Al Schnier: We were playing the outdoor stage, and being Fourth of July 2008, there's fireworks on the beach and we needed a good Fourth of July song to play. And somebody suggests that we play the Team America song that the *South Park* had: "America, Fuck Yeah." It seemed a great idea at the time. It's short and sweet, nice sort of punk rock anthem, and pretty funny. And we got a good sense of humor. So we're like, okay, that's going to be our Fourth of July kickoff when they kick off the fireworks, we're going to play "America, Fuck Yeah." And it'll be great. Our fans will love it. They're all *South Park* fans, whatever. So we played "America, Fuck Yeah." Didn't think anything of it. Except for the fact that because we were outside and the stage is facing the beach, that all of that is being projected onto the beach where all of the families are. And that's exactly what they all heard too, which did not occur to us at the time. One of those families happened to be the mayor with his children. And that came back to haunt us; it backfired in a big way. And the folks at Stone Pony got a ton of shit for it, which in turn came to us. There was something that was in the paper, the following day, and we had to apologize. There was a whole thing. And we felt horrible about it after the fact. And it's not something we would've done intentionally, knowing that there were small children on the beach. But these things happen, the decisions you make in the spirit of a rock-and-roll show, not thinking about people outside of that event.

Al Schnier: We did come back, but I think it was a little bit tenuous at that point, just because of that thing. It really ruffled some feathers and it was literally because of the one song that one time. But you know, you piss off the mayor in a small town like that and it's not a good thing.

29

Home (for the Holidays)

Springsteen, E Streeters, and the Jukes built a lasting scene and an indelible mark on a fading town simply because it was their home. In the punk-strewn ashes of Asbury in the 1990s, the Bouncing Souls did the same, offering lifelines to the city and the Pony when times were tough well into the late 2000s, simply because it became their home. The Gaslight Anthem continued the lineage.

Bryan Kienlen: Home for the Holidays was inspired by the Bosstones. They're the originators of that. They had the Hometown Throwdown. And that was the "This is our hometown. We're doing a big show here."

Pete Steinkopf: We were at a time where we wanted to tour less and we were all like, "We want to do less long tours. How can we make people come to us and have a cool thing in our backyard?" That's where the conversation started. And then I remember being at Kate's house all together and talking about it and then came up with the idea. [A friend] came up with name. He's like, "How about 'Home for the Holidays,' homie?"

Kate Hiltz: Basically it's me and Caroline and the Pony staff are just going to put this thing together and not deal with any of this bullshit out in the bureaucracy. She really just gave me the longest rope you could possibly imagine.

Caroline O'Toole: It was great, just the whole atmosphere down there, because it was a holiday time of year.

Pete Steinkopf: The first year, I think we did three shows and they were all sold out. Because it was such a dead time here. At the time, in 2007, there was nothing.

Bryan Kienlen: At the time we wanted to uplift the Cookman Corridor or the Asbury Park scene. We wanted to bring people into Asbury Park, show off this cool place and energize all these businesses that are suffering the worst retail week for a lot of people. The bartenders of the Pony would thank us every year because they wouldn't otherwise make shit.

Frank Luna: Home for the Holidays, that was big for the whole city. They would do tattoo stuff, things like that. It became a festival. Every night there was something going on, at the Pony, at other places, Convention Hall.

Kate Hiltz: We tried to involve everybody. We would publish maps of here's where the restaurants that are open are, here's where the stores that are cool are, here's whatever. And go here, go there, do event. We would show movies at the showroom and just try to get people to go to stuff.

Eileen Chapman: Bouncing Souls were a lifeline at that point.

Bryan Kienlen: That's when we bonded with the Pony people too, like Caroline and everybody that worked there, the whole staff.

Kate Hiltz: Part of the Home for the Holidays was to have a charity aspect. And one year was this wolf rescue in Jackson. They were like, we can bring wolves to the Pony to meet people backstage. And I was like, cool. And later, there's a picture of me and Pete with a wolf, and Caroline was like, "What? We cannot have wolves. There's no wolves. Have you heard about insurance?" I was like, "Oh my God, I'm so sorry." I was like, "You are so right."

Bryan Kienlen: We would come up with weird, crazy things all the time to keep it new and fresh. Like one year we had a dunk tank, outside in the fucking freezing cold. All for charity. And then another year we got an old bingo machine with all the balls flying around. You pressed the thing and a ball comes up. And we had every song, every Bouncing Souls song written on all the different balls. And we had one guy up there and he would pull up a ball and tell us the song and we'd have to play it.

Brian Fallon: The celebrity set lists, I did one. I think mine might have been like the real sensitive, somber set list. Like "Late Bloomer" and "Anchors Aweigh." There wasn't a lot of funny songs in there. I tried to throw in "Neurotic" or something really weird from the first record. I don't know if I had the guts to put that "Inspection Station" on there.

Kate Hiltz: When they had that metal, really all-metal roof, there was a huge snowstorm and the roof of the Pony caved in.

Pete Steinkopf: One of the best ones was when the roof collapsed. May have been '08 or '09, don't remember. But they, like a week before the show, "What the fuck are we going to do?" And they turned the whole breezeway in Convention Hall into a venue.

Kate Hiltz: Sounded like dog shit.

Pete Steinkopf: One big venue. They decorated it. And we had Gaslight Anthem playing support that night. And H20.

Brian Fallon: I remember that show exactly. I played a black Telecaster custom with a gray hat and a white T-shirt on. And we knew the Bouncing Souls guys, but it was the first time that they were treating us like—I don't want to say equals but they were treating us like we're in now, we're peers now. And that blew our minds. At that time and how young we were to be playing for that many people. I mean, the Bouncing Souls were massive and they were a huge, huge part of our band being a band. As much as people give Bruce the credit for being our Godfather. I mean, if Bruce is our Godfather, they were our father. They were really pivotal in teaching us to be a band. And at that time, at that show, in the pavilion there in Convention Hall, outside in the hallway, we felt like this is our place on earth. I don't know if any other place will accept us but it doesn't matter because this is our piece of the earth.

Benny Horowitz: At first, I think the only way we could have played the Pony is if we got asked to open for someone there. All of our first shows in Asbury were the Lanes as a result, but it was also because of our connections. I already knew Kate. My good buddy Kyle, who we grew up with, was living at Kate's house and had a loose affiliation to the Souls. Our connection to Asbury was the punk rock thing. To be honest, I didn't really pay much attention to the Bruce Springsteen narrative until I met Brian.

Kate Hiltz: [The Pony] could string along a yearlong staff and bulk up in the summers, but they had the core bartenders and technicians and everything. They would just be, please, anything [in the winter]. So it's like, we can't cancel. Even when we got snowed out, that was two years after that, or three years after that. We just rescheduled it for February.

Kyle Brendle: The Souls really established that week in the winter for us, and since then, we've been booking all kinds of shows that week. That is a good week for us to this day. People like the live music that week. Of course, the college community is off. A lot of people take off. There is a holiday vibe for people willing to go out. Traditionally prior to that, there really wasn't much on that week.

Brian Fallon: The Souls kinda did the same southern migration that we did. Whereas, they were in New Brunswick and then kinda moved down to Asbury as the scene changed and the shift happened with the venues. And I was from that area of Monmouth County. I wasn't really from New Brunswick. So, I had moved when I was younger and then came back down. And kinda was like, "Well, this is my spot that I grew up in, so I would like to do what the Bouncing Souls are doing. Because they moved it down here, and this is where I'm from. So, I would rather play here than somewhere else." 'Cause it felt more local to me and more kinda like hometown. And watching them do those Home for the Holidays shows, kinda was like, "Whoa, this is awesome, this is working. And you know, we should play down here too."

Brian Fallon: The Lanes was our first entrance into the Asbury scene. We would start really going to shows there a lot. And for a while it was like the Lanes versus the Pony. And it was, there's definitely a thing like "the cool shows are at the Lanes and the corporate overlords are at the Pony." And I was like, I don't know about you, man, but I am definitely trying to go see that big cool show at the Pony. Like they'd have Steve

Earle or whatever, or the Pogues or Social Distortion would be down at the Pony. And I'd be like, dude, I'm going to both. Avail might be playing at the Lanes but I don't know, man, Social Distortion is playing at the Pony, I'm going to both.

Benny Horowitz: We took a little shit when we switched to the Pony. There was a little bit of pushback, in that way. I remember, not me specifically, but I do remember just a little harrumph thing about us making that jump to the Pony. But it became necessary. I mean, we were just drawing that amount.

Brian Fallon: No one ever made us make that choice, like are you with us or are you against us? Because they were like, well, you can't play here anymore. You got too big. Like, they would just say like, we can't have a Gaslight Anthem show at the Lanes anymore. There's just too many people. You got to go the Pony. And then they were like, at least you're keeping it local. . . . So, round the '59 *Sound* shows, everybody was buzzing and we knew, you can't know for sure, but you do feel like, "Okay, something's happening." And it felt like electric. And especially when we walk in those places, going and doing that hometown show and knowing this show is going to be packed. Everything starts lining up and you feel this electricity. And the Pony, that's like a professional place. When you reach the Stone Pony and you sell it out, you know you're doing something right. Because the Lanes are like two hundred people, three hundred people, whatever. And the basements are fifty people or less. But when you sell out eight hundred something people, you're like, "Okay, this is good. This is a real concert. This is a show." To me, that was a big marker for us.

Benny Horowitz: I'd been to a ton of shows at the Stone Pony by the time we played there for the first time. The coolest part about that to me was just being on the other side of the fence for once. It was like no lines, our own bathroom. Stuff like that was the coolest part about playing the Pony . . . like, "I'm here as a musician."

Brian Fallon: As time went on, we did a bunch of the outdoor shows and we went from filling up the inside to selling outside. We did our video for "45" at the Pony. I met my now wife there, which was crazy.

And when I met her it was just like a person that I saw and then didn't see again. Like we met at the Stone Pony at the video shoot for "45." And we didn't keep in touch. We didn't talk. I think we're both in relationships at the time. And then, I never saw this person again. And then a year or so later, two years later, or whatever it was, we ran into each other in another country. And I'm like, "Wait a second. I remember you from the video shoot," and we got to talking. And we ended up married. We have a kid. So it holds a special place. In my house, we have a picture hanging up of the first time we met. And it's not like we had any magic connection that day. We were both in relationships. I was married at the time; I didn't think anything of it. So I was just like, this is a cool person, nice to meet you, bye. But one of our friends took a photo, I was like, "All right, cool, good job on the video." And I gave her a hug. And then there's a photo of that moment, and years later when we got married, our friend was like, "Yo, I snapped a photo the first time you guys ever met and never knew each other." And here it is. And now it's framed in our house. And it's from the Pony.

Benny Horowitz: We felt like this is our place, you know what I mean? I think there was a feeling like you had to take all the steps in Asbury. Before we're going anywhere else, we're going to do all the cool shit in Asbury. We're going to do it here and play to our people. I think that was a big part of the motivation. Also, just options. There wasn't that many options. We'd also all gone to a lot of shows at the Starland and it's fine. We prefer shows at the Pony. Prefer shows down there with—It just felt like our spot for a little bit. I think we were always cognizant of trying to go back there because it's just where it felt like home I guess, at the time.

Brian Fallon: You could even see it in the Bouncing Souls' writing. Their writing changed when they moved down there. I think a lot of it became more about having to do with the beach and the boardwalk and the history. And they have that song "Ghosts on the Boardwalk" and all that. And I think it kind of, a lot of the scene shifted. And for us, it was after *Sink or Swim*, I think, is when we started to all gravitate towards Asbury Park. And then you can hear it in the EP that we did before '59 *Sound, Señor and the Queen*. That's where you can hear us start writing about the ocean and that kinda stuff. And it was really starting to come in more, that scene and that influence of all the Springsteen stuff and all the punk stuff that was coming from down there. So, it's sort of, our whole world came together down there. Where it was like the punk stuff meets the rock-and-roll stuff. And then, now we have this identity that we're creating. And that was really due, in part, to the work done by Bruce first, and then after by the Bouncing Souls.

30

Steady Ground

When Madison Marquette bought the Pony in 2008, it gave the historic venue the backing of a multibillion-dollar conglomerate. For the first time, the month-to-month budgetary fears dissipated. The venue could spend exceptionally large amounts of money on itself. Live Nation joined the fray. Up and down the boardwalk, pavilions were opening with new restaurants. Residential development by iStar, which was building a gleaming glass tower where the rotting C-8 structure was, was booming in town. The investment by the LGBT community in the northern stretches of town had rehabilitated entire neighborhoods. A far cry from the Jack and Butch era, but the Pony, and Asbury, were finally on steady ground.

Caroline O'Toole: When Madison Marquette came in 2008, that was a big sigh of relief because the years prior to that were some of the darkest of my life because the things that went on and the things . . . I mean, you basically had to sell your soul to keep going. So it was just a sense of "I don't have to do this anymore. I don't have to do the things that I'm not comfortable with that I didn't have a choice before. I have a choice now." Because I remember the first lunch I had with them, I was like, "Wow, I didn't know this existed."

Gary Mottola: The biggest question was, how do you overcome this incredible stigma about, don't go to Asbury? It was the combination of things. One was just doing some stuff. We did the Fifth Avenue Pavilion, and the Third Avenue Pavilion, and the First Avenue Pavilion. One of the things it did was build the water park. They figured, what can show safety other than kids playing right in the middle of the boardwalk. We also had a good police specialist. The police were very, both engaged and they weren't overbearing. They were very understanding and firm when they had to be, but also understanding when they felt it.

Caroline O'Toole: My favorite show wasn't a show at all. The day after Clarence died, we opened the venue because we knew people would want to maybe come and remember him, and we knew the Pony's significance for that. We didn't expect thousands of people, but that's what we got.

Kyle Brendle: The word was out that Clarence had passed away. Just people started coming in from all over the place. It's weird. I don't know, just streets were filled with people getting emotional with candles, and pictures, and stuff. It was pretty crazy. Very surreal that the fans had descended on the Pony as the place to commune with other fans and express their love and concern.

Caroline O'Toole: And there was one moment when I think Kyle might have been playing music and "Tenth Avenue Freeze-Out" came one, the one where Bruce introduces the band, and everybody was standing in a circle, and then when Bruce said Clarence's name, it was a feeling like I've never had in the building before or since. It was amazing. It was absolutely amazing. And out of all the music and, yes, beautiful, great artists that have come through there, that is a moment. It was one of those once-in-a-lifetime feelings that you want to feel again, but you probably won't. And that's what that was.

Kyle Brendle: It was surreal. The makeshift memorial stayed outside in the Pony sidewalk for weeks. No one would touch it.

Adam Weiner: My first show there was Clarence Clemons Day. It was maybe the year after he died. The city of Asbury proclaimed a certain day Clarence Clemons Day, and Rich Russo and Tony Paligrossi and some of these local people put together a night at the Pony for it. And Jake Clemons was playing. And there's a woman named Michelle Moore, who was in Bruce Springsteen's band at that time. She was a gospel singer. Her group sang, and then they booked us to open. And also my buddy Tony "Boccigalupe" [Amato]. And nobody knew who Low Cut Connie was, nobody. And then Rich came out onstage and was like, "I'm going to introduce you to this new band. Pay attention. This band is going places. Pay attention."

Jake Clemons: That was a heavy show. It was beautiful and I was super-excited to be celebrating Clarence Clemons Day. It was exciting. I don't know. It was a little bit weird because it was like my original music is not Clarence's music. I'm not going to do Bruce songs, so finding a way to honor him and celebrate him in a genuine way, I remember that being a little bit of a challenge just because I wanted to do it respectfully and beautifully. At the end of the day, it came down to the spirit of what Clarence was all about and that part wouldn't be hard or anything.

Caroline O'Toole: People still send mail for Bruce to the Pony. I do have currently a cooler full of tequila for him. I usually just throw the other things out. This, I was like, "He might want that."

Bobby Jones: I get a heads-up if Bruce is coming. And then a lot of times, I'm the guy that's next to him, overseeing things, with the people around. Sometimes he'll look at you and say "It's okay" and others he'll give you the nod like they're being a bit too much or extra. But sometimes he'd just come to relax and chill.

Caroline O'Toole: Usually, we know if Bruce is coming. Once our tech director, Jason Dermer, came on board . . . and he's just very good. He's just very good at what he does. And so he has credit in the industry. He has real cred. So, Bruce's Kevin would sometimes call Jason and say, "Hey, set me up the guitar and the amp and that sort of thing." So up until then, if you saw Kevin, then there was a possibility. Now we know a little bit.

Paul Janeway: I remember standing up on the bar during the show the first time we played because I just was reckless and still am. One of the bartenders said, "I haven't seen that since Bruce did that." I was like, "What?" I thought, "Holy shit."

Jake Clemons: At that early point in my career, I was really particular about making sure that I could stand on my own two feet and I was very,

very, very cautious about any kind of Bruce connections. So I may have even felt a little bit of reservation about playing Asbury Park for that reason. The pressure that I would imagine that I would've felt would've been to make sure I was able to somehow distinguish myself as a front-man and as a songwriter, and band leader, knowing that there was inevitably going to be a lot of E Street fans that were going to be there.

Dave Davies: I love the sound in the room, and the raw vibe. And you can't always feel that when you're in a building somewhere trying to play; it can't always work. It just natural because it's so close to the peo-ple. . . . It was interesting because at this particular time, I was playing as a four-piece because I had a stroke and I was little bit, not actually confident about playing. But a night before the gig, and my other guitar player became ill and had to go to a hospital. And I thought, "Oh shit, we still got to do the gig." So I thought, "Okay, we're going to have to do it as a three-piece."

Dennis Diken: I was on that gig with Dave. We were all on the phone that day: "Should we do the gig? Do you want to find a replacement?" Dave said, "Let's just try it as a trio."

Dave Davies: And it sounded punchy and louder and I felt my confi-dence, like I regained my confidence. There's something about three-piece to me that is heavier. And it kind of made up my mind to go back to a three-piece. Because you don't have to play all the time. Anyway, you learn to breathe. At the Stone Pony it persuaded me to go back to a three-piece. That gig helped me get my confidence back after the stroke. I could always make jokes and shit, but it doesn't always work. It had a really good crowd. The place lends itself to a vibe. It's got that intangible rock-vibe thing.

Kenny Chesney: I had come to Asbury Park a few times to shoot with Danny Clinch. It's a soulful place, beach and boardwalk. You can feel the history, all those characters and stories that just linger in the air. The people from SiriusXM wanted to do something special to launch No Shoes Radio. They said, "Whatever I wanted." I wanted to play somewhere iconic, somewhere legendary. So, I threw that out. Especially because it was close to their headquarters too, it was a place that would be special to them. And when I said it, they said, "Done."

Bobby Jones: We had people lined up all the way opposite Ocean Avenue for Kenny Chesney. We had security all around the Pony. We really had to block everything off. Normally, people sit there for normal artists. Like we had to lock down because of Kenny Chesney. So we really had to make sure we locked that down to make sure no one snuck inside.

Kenny Chesney: The night we played there, the people were feeling good. They live for the music; we could tell from the very first song. They were so with us, and they never let go. And when you hear people singing along in a place like that—thinking about all the people on that stage, all the bands and musicians they've seen—you get a little wowed.

Bobby Jones: But that one was particularly insane because Kenny Chesney sells out arenas. And now he's here at the Pony?

Kenny Chesney: We'd been playing stadiums for a long time, since 2005, and the thing a really great club does, it puts the fans right in your heart. BOOM! They're just there, and they're hanging on every song, every note, and we see every smile. There's an intimacy that gives you a rush that's so different from stadiums, but it's powerful too. But it's also that thing of, it takes you back to your own roots, those days when you're playing for tips, playing bars, and trying to make the party last as long as you can. There aren't a lot of lights, video, those things. . . . It's just you, the songs, and the people.

Bobby Jones: Kenny Chesney, no shoes on. The guy walks around with no shoes. And I was like, "Dude, you're in Asbury Park still."

Kenny Chesney: It was hot! It was steamy, and you could feel the humidity in the air. But you could also feel the passion of every single person who was crammed into that space. At a point, the passion is bigger than the heat. Those people light you up, and you just wanna burn it down for them. Once we got on that stage, we didn't want to get off.

Tom Morello: Getting to play a show on that stage, actually to be on that stage and to feel the good ghosts in the room of all the shows past, I hadn't really connected the dots before. There's a whole, I don't know, sort of seaside aspect to it and like, "Oh, what does it mean to have a bunch of bar bands playing along the ocean here?" That was new. I didn't recognize that as some of the lyrics in those songs, and then the mythology too of Clarence walking through the door on a blustery night and whatnot, and the kids huddled on the beach. Kids huddled on the beach. That's a very California thing to me. I didn't know that there was a Jersey analog to that. I didn't put two and two together till I actually saw the beach. I've huddled on that beach now too. Yeah, and so that was pretty cool to feel the boardwalk under my boots, and the Madame . . . What's her name? Madame Marie. That sign is still there. I don't know if it's actually the same place, but some of the stuff that was mentioned in those songs is front and center on that boardwalk.

Paul Janeway: A lot of venues we play don't have a personality. You show up, it's a black box, it's all the same. It's the House of Blues conundrum. You get the same fried mozzarella or whatever. There, there's a distinct personality and it's very Jersey. I love that. That's not where I come from. I love the idea of a venue having a personality. Even the people that work there, even the vibe, even the T-shirts. It's a distinct personality of Jersey.

Jake Clemons: That's an interesting thing about the Pony is those characters are still there in different ways. It's more than just the walls. It actually is some of the people there.

Tom Morello: The show, it was on my *Atlas Underground* tour, which was part . . . It was part kind of underground, art installation, part illegal rave, part mosh pit, shredding guitar festival. At the end, we do some, it's a combination of "Tom Joad," "Killing in the Name," "This Land Is Your Land," an electric version of "This Land Is Your Land," and a really rocking version of John Lennon's "Power to the People." It just sort of like, it kept ascending, and ascending, and ascending. It really made me feel like I had not dishonored the stage at the Stone Pony.

Brian Fallon: Sitting in with different artists at the Pony, I think that I always wanted to do that, because I felt like I always wanted to be part of a scene. I always felt like Bruce and the E Street guys, they were always sitting in with people. And it just felt like that's what bands should be doing. . . . I'm like, "Hey, you want to come sing with us? Want to come sing with us?" That's what I do. I want the party to have everybody in it, not just me.

Tom Morello: I had the whole crowd up onstage as we're doing "This Land Is Your Land," and there's some great pictures of these young New Jerseyans screaming this Woody Guthrie song with all the passion that anyone's ever mustered for Bon Jovi, or My Chem or Bruce or whatever.

Brian Fallon: I played with Jakob Dylan and the Wallflowers. And I got to play Jake's white Telecaster, which is, he knows that it's one of my favorite guitars in the world. And that was a real cool moment for me, to get to sit in with the Wallflowers at the Pony. I was like, this is great. And that was just spur-of-the-moment, total spur-of-the-moment. I was just down there to watch him play, and he's like, "You want to hop up with us?" I was like, "All right."

Jake Clemons: If you're capable and willing to take some risks and to go to stretch yourself a little bit to have an audience that's willing to meet you there, that's powerful, man. I don't know if that's every night at the Pony. I want to feel connected and I want to feel that participation. I'm right there with them. That's the cool thing about the Pony. It's almost a weird space because it's a club. It's just a club. You walk in there and it's just a club. The stage isn't very high, and it's—man, when it turns on, when that place is full, and the sound is what it is, it's amazing sound. It's electric, man.

Bruce Springsteen: It's amazing to go down there and see everything thriving. Like I say in my book, I'm kind of the Ghost of Christmas Past. I can invisibly walk down the boardwalk and everybody is busy going about their own current business. So it's nice. Bit of a surprise it didn't happen sooner. I mean, it was a beautiful town only an hour out of the city. But things happen in their own time. And so it's nice to see its resurgence.

Governor Philip D. Murphy: One of the coolest stories I think over the past number of years and certainly as we sit here is the rise again of Asbury Park. It's not perfect. The journey's not done. There's still challenges, but the place is finally back on its feet. And it's iconic. Just say the words Asbury Park, no matter where you are, who you're with, anywhere, you don't have to explain it. And the Pony is synonymous with Asbury Park. And you also don't have to explain what those two words mean to anybody. They're inextricably linked to each other. It's notable that we spent both election nights for the first time and on our reelection in Asbury Park. Because this is the place that is on the ascent.

Governor Chris Christie: It's really gratifying to look at it now and see, and there's still some glitches here and there, for sure. But when you look at Asbury Park in general and you see the Pony now with the outdoor venue and the fact that it's really become not this surviving seedy bar in a seedy town, but almost like a historic site inside the city of Asbury Park.

31

Summer Stage Saves

The land under the Pony is priceless to musicians, locals, and music fans. In the suddenly booming Asbury Park real estate market, it had a price, and a high one. What keeps the club alive now, ironically, is the empty lot next door. What was once the Pony Big Top in the 1990s was now triple the size and called the Stone Pony Summer Stage, the main source of revenue for the Stone Pony every year. Artists who could sell out theaters now came to the lot, to pay homage to the Pony history, and ink a gig on the ocean.

Caroline O'Toole: The outside was always there on some level since I started but it didn't mean a lot until we were able to take over the property next to us where the Golddigger was. And then we became like a city block. And then that enabled us to start having shows that had a higher capacity.

Gary Mottola: There was an outside thing but it was a kind of small stage and fairly limited capacity. So one of the things we did early on was buy a new stage. And I said, if we're gonna do it, make it big. Lights, sound. Have it be dominating. It was more to make a statement, from an entertainment standpoint.

Caroline O'Toole: And we were like, "Wow, we can actually make okay money doing this." Because without the outside, the inside doesn't exist, because the expenses are just too much. And that was another part of the years of being there early on, was just the constant struggle for staying in business, making payroll.

Stacie George: You basically break even in small clubs like a Wonder Bar or a Stone Pony, and you keep the lights on, and you keep people working, but it's like a river of nickels in a club. The higher the capacity of a venue, the more money a venue should make. Therefore, the Stone Pony Summer Stage basically pays for Wonder Bar and Stone Pony to exist because those thirty-five shows in a season bring enough fans.

Bruce Springsteen: They put on some pretty big shows, and they have their Summer Stage. It's turned into a very nice thing.

Tom Morello: The Summer Stage is a place where you could have a big-ass rock show. It's no longer just the place where the E Street Band played in the sixties. It's now like a place which is a significant venue.

Caroline O'Toole: We started hiring police officers for the shows, and that gives you a whole 'nother level of comfort because you know right outside your door you have officers that are there and they're on your side and they're there for the crowd. It takes a lot of that worry out. So you're able to do more things because they're there.

Miles Doughty: They know our crowd is a little chaotic, so they gear up for it now, because back in the day, they didn't gear up for it enough. That's when there's always little problems with security and whatnot. There's nothing you can do. Now they staff it well and have it corralled well. Just when it was out of control and it was understaffed, just not realizing how crazy the shows kept getting. Now they've figured out what it's like at a Slightly Stoopid show.

Michael "Buck" Crowell: Slightly Stoopid was always so down with having as many people backstage as humanly possible. Madison Marquette was always pissed. No one gave a shit. It was always just family. So this group was very close to that. But of course they're not from Jersey, so it wasn't all familiar faces. It was always known that their after parties were always so sick.

Miles Doughty: If you know the history of Stoopid, it gets a little crazy sometimes at the after shows and parties and just the venues. You still can get away with quite a bit. We still have some good parties there. There is definitely some legendary years of that little backstage area, the Summer Stage, and just turned into raging parties.

Michael "Buck" Crowell: They would do it on the artist side. They would have their own DJ that would come in and be the only DJ of the after parties; they had him on tour.

Miles Doughty: A lot of times when we do that, we'll just have them spin in between bands too.

Michael "Buck" Crowell: So everyone always wanted to go the Slightly Stoopid after party. It was like, oh my God. People were crawling through fences to get there.

Paul Janeway: It's a parking lot. It's weird because it feels like a festival. It feels like you're playing a street festival or something. You're still connected to the Pony, you're backstage and all that stuff, but then you're just in this massive lot.

Gary Mottola: The reality is it's a parking lot with porta-johns. But we wanted to make it the best parking lot with porta-johns. And again, bands love it there. They can see the ocean.

Wesley Schultz: I was a North Jersey kid. The first time I went was in 2016 and we played the parking lot of the Stone Pony. And was very excited to play it because what happens a lot with its relationship to New York is that a lot of New Jersey can get overlooked. It's an underdog state. We moved out to Colorado in '09, and then whenever we'd come back, we'd often hit New York because there's just all these venues there. To play there was a very special thing for us because of that fact.

Jeff Kazee: The last time Bruce sat in with us all night, forty-five minutes. And so, Bruce comes around. I don't remember him sound-checking with us but he was around after sound check. I saw Kevin, his guitar tech, setting up. I knew he was coming. My road manager told me, "Be ready for Bruce." I got to figure out with Johnny what we want to do to Bruce. We talked. "There's something Bruce wants to do. Let me give the guys a heads-up." If there's something we haven't done in a while, we're not going to change the world. There's enough stuff we know to do that. Sometimes it's like, in this particular song, "Kitty's Back," we have a good arrangement of it because we did it before. We learned it for some reason. Bruce didn't know we knew it. Johnny says, "After sound check, come back to the room. You and I will go over the set list." I go in there and by the time I get back there, it's just Johnny and Bruce. There's not much talking going on. Johnny's going through set lists. "All right. We got 'I Don't Want to Go Home.'" "All right. Yeah." Bruce is like, "Yeah." "Love on the Wrong Side . . ." just throwing songs that he knows Bruce knows or wrote. Bruce is like, "Yeah. Okay. All right. Yeah. No." Johnny goes . . . He said, "'Sherry Darling.'" "All right. Okay. Yeah." And then Johnny goes, "Hey, Bruce, we do 'Kitty's Back.' It sounds incredible. The horns. We got an arrangement." He's like, "Yeah. You got a teleprompter?" He said, "We don't have a fucking teleprompter. It's the Jukes, man." Bruce is like, "I don't really feel comfortable doing it. The words, you know?" And he's got a million songs. Johnny's like, "Come on." He's trying to shame him. Bruce wasn't having it. He's like, "No. I'm going to pass on that. We got enough." "All right. All right." Wrap it up, get seven, eight songs. "All right. We'll see you" at whatever o'clock. "Come up. I'll bring you on about thirty, forty minutes in." He's like, "All right. I'll see you later." He walks out. I hear the door shut and Johnny goes, "Fuck 'im. We're going to do it. Put it on the list."

Jeff Kazee: So we do it. Bruce is playing and we sing the first verse. "Great. Got it." The second verse comes around, and Bruce goes up to the mic, looks over at Johnny. Johnny goes up to the mic, looks over at Bruce. They both forget it. It goes around and they just kind of look at each other, like a standoff. All of a sudden you can see, Johnny looks at me. I used to sub for [Paul] Shaffer on the *Letterman Show*. They would play songs and the organ would play the melody. I start going and I start playing the melody. We play that and then we get to the pre-chorus and they jump back in. I play the melody in the verse and it pops back in, they come back on the pre-chorus or the chorus. Of course, the crowd's going crazy. They love it.

Wesley Schultz: I remember playing, I think I played "My City of Ruins" that night onstage. I was superexcited. I have a few memories of the night. Well, one was that I knew I was back home in Jersey because there were these workers that just were constantly taking breaks and had the worst attitude. I was like, oh, I'm back home.

Donavon Frankenreiter: The East Coast in the summer, every night's a Friday night. Because if you're an agent booking a band, you're like, "Dude, I know where the fuck I'm going to put you on a Sunday, Monday, Tuesday." And they're like, "Oh, Pony on a Sunday. Somewhere, whatever . . ." The East Coast is always every night's Friday night.

Wesley Schultz: There's something to that. I don't know, like where it's an interesting state to be from where like if you, wherever you end up going, you wear it as a badge of honor. The people who, even if you move, they're like, "You're still one of us," and it's true. It's like this weird kinship you have because everybody kind of shits on you for being from New Jersey. I remember my wife, I remember taking her when we started dating. She's like, "You are taking me to New Jersey?" Then she's like, "This is really beautiful." I think people fly to Newark and smell and they just judge it. Whenever I meet a musician who's from there, it was like, "Fuck you, you're from New Jersey?" It's really funny. Jack is like the same way where I've met him a couple of times and that's like definitely one of the things we talked about. It's like you've been through some fire together. That same idea of it doesn't really leave. You're tattooed with that, I think for better.

Jack Antonoff: I just was writing so much music about . . . I had written the lyric "Shadow of the city," about a song that I was trying to write, which eventually turned into "Chinatown." Not literally, just I don't want to write ten songs about the journey to and from over the George Washington Bridge one way or the other. I finally found it, which was through the lens of wanting to take someone home. But at the time, I'd written a song called "Shadow of the City," which wasn't a good song, but it was a really good line. And it was a line I had been kicking around about New Jersey, shadow of the city. And that's the culture in all of its glory, which I think is better than being in the city. I think it's more interesting and more thrilling and more grows from that. And also just writing about where I'm recording from. So then I thought, "Well, it'd be nice to have a meetup." And I didn't want to have a festival. I actually think that I'm not really into the whole idea of everyone having their own festival. I see it more as like a block party.

Stacie George: Jack Antonoff loves Asbury Park, considers it basically his hometown and where he grew up going to shows, and wanted to start his own festival, and Stone Pony was the only place he wanted to do it. . . . He does this and does not make money off it. Actually, he spends money doing it to pay all these artists.

Jack Antonoff: Jersey's also its own weird little community. Not necessarily mob, just its own backdoor shit. Trying to get that festival off the ground, I was like, "That's how much catering is? Whose cousin is doing catering? What the fuck?"

Andrew McMahon: I've known Jack for a long time and he reached out and was like, "Would you come and do this show?" And I remember Khalid was there. I had no idea who he was. Kids in Jersey knew who he was, but I was clearly not up on the new shit.

Jack Antonoff: The vibing sound of New Jersey is an emotional one, it's not a literal one, you know what I mean? It's not like, "We use these instruments." The line I can draw from Pine Grove to Lifetime to myself to Southside Johnny to Bruce to fucking SZA or whatever, it's this emotional outsideness. But not outsideness in this "I'm in a cabin," Bon Iver way, sort of this outside but community. It's communal because there's a tent there and everyone's invited, but it's not the center of the universe. It's reporting to the left of the center of the universe. And that's a real perspective that I feel in all the music that comes out of New Jersey. And I don't think it's possible to not embody that if you're being honest.

Bobby Jones: The Jonas Brothers, talk about something that was huge. That was big. That was an all-day thing. And it takes a lot.

Nick Jonas: We had discussed doing something in Jersey in a significant location to our kind of ascension. And it just made sense that it was the Stone Pony for a number of reasons. So, performing there yet again, kind of a nod to the history of that place, playing indoors and then walking outside to perform to a larger crowd. And that's kind of a story of our career and where we started, and how we remember our roots as well.

Joe Jonas: Inside, there's something that just, it feels right. Feels like it's something that every artist, I think sometimes need to be reminded of what that feeling is like. In a safe way, getting back onstage like that. There's a reason why some of the greats like Bruce love that place and still try to play shows occasionally there, because I feel like there's not a lot of places out there that have that same energy and history. You know, the floor is sticky.

Kevin Jonas: It was just a representation of who we are. Like we're Jersey guys that left and continued our career. But then coming back to our, let's call it hometown shows, at a place where we played when we were younger. And seeing a New Jersey crowd, a hometown crowd is always what's important. Anytime we can represent New Jersey, it feels right to us.

Nick Jonas: Seeing the size of crowds, and kind of the overflow of the crowd on the beach. I think we just felt it was right to show some more love and play some more songs. And they were an incredible crowd that night and such a memorable performance for us.

Stacie George: A venue has to evolve with the time. My job, I look at it, is like, "I got to get the younger generation coming to Stone Pony Summer Stage." They feel like it's a rite of passage that they grew up going to. Therefore, I have to book artists that aren't just Social Distortion and Bouncing Souls, and the jam bands. I have to book artists that the younger generation wants. That's why you see, whether it's Rainbow Kitten Surprise or like Louis Tomlinson from One Direction, which blew right out, or Fletcher or Backseat Lovers are a really young crowd. That's really important because the next generation that's going to be supporting the artists in Asbury, also supporting the restaurants. It's like an ecosystem that you have to feed.

Jack Antonoff: The fact that it's become bougie in many ways is perfectly strange. That this place that we played basement shows and then blew out of town pretty quickly because it felt sketchy is now a place where people go to brunch. And I think the throughline with all this is New Jersey is really weird. It's a really weird place because the true identity of New Jersey can be a little bit depressing, which is kind of like what I said. It's this "Get me out of here," slash, "Keep me here forever."

Sea.Hear.Now (and Then)

Thirty-five thousand people, packed on the north beach of Asbury Park, listening to Pearl Jam. An impossible scene for anyone who rode the lows of Asbury through the 1990s and 2000s. But the stubborn dreaming of two locals brought it to reality. Everywhere in Asbury now, there are signs of progress, and of change. Same with the Pony. Butch passed away in 2018. Jack retired, though he still drives a cab. Steve Nasar disappeared. Domenic retired to Miami. Yet the fifty years of spirits remain alive in the walls of the Pony. And on Saturday night of the Sea.Hear.Now festival, the good ghosts of the Pony awaken in a Super Jam, re-creating that spontaneity and collaboration that came so naturally to Springsteen, Stevie, Southside and the crew years ago. And who knows, maybe next time, Bruce will show up.

Danny Clinch: Tim Donnelly and I had been thinking about a festival and we'd one-sheeted it a bunch in our minds. And then the Gentlemen of the Road came through Seaside Heights and they put on that show there. We saw people show up out there and the lineup was kind of right up our alley. This was like, "Oh, this is kind of what we want to do in Asbury." And we looked at it and we went to the show and it was incredible. It was well run. We had a great time. Tangiers did a late-night show. And the guys in the band came over.

Tim Donnelly: Mumford & Sons dudes came over, Taylor from Dawes. At the Bamboo Bar.

Danny Clinch: That's when we really thought we could get it off the ground. And then we hit up a lot of people, because we had a lot of friends who had done festivals. We had spent, at that point, fifteen years, ten to fifteen years going to Bonnaroo from the inside, from setup to teardown to backstage, to onstage to everything.

Danny Clinch: I remember being at Bonnaroo and meeting Tim Sweetwood. He came to me and he said, "Danny, you and I could do a festival together because you know the people, and I've got the skills to do it." And I was like, "Sure." And he went his way, I went my way, and nothing ever happened. And then when we started to hit a wall, I was like, "Remember what Sweetwood said to us? Let's hit him up," and we did. And he was the only one to actually say, "Let me come to Asbury and have a look." And there were some people who were in New York City who didn't even say, "Let me come to Asbury and have a look."

Tim Donnelly: He came up from Georgia. He sees it. He sees exactly what we see. Then, we don't hear from him. All of a sudden, we were dead. It was not going to happen. Then he calls us back, says he just got hired by C3 festivals. And then he comes up and he sees Bruce Springsteen perform; his first time coming to Asbury Park and he gets to see Bruce Springsteen. And he was just like, "Wow, this is kind of crazy." And then Charles Attal from C3 came down, and I took a walk on the boardwalk with him. All he did was walk out that door, turned around. He goes, "Yep, I see it."

Tim Sweetwood: I was friends with Danny Clinch and he had been for a little while, he's like, "Oh, you got to come up and check out Asbury Park." Then, after probably not years, but months and months and months of bugging, he's like, "You got to get up here and just check it out." So I took it and I drank the Kool-Aid right away, as soon as you step in the town and walk the boardwalk.

Tim Donnelly: And then Danny, H.M., and I flew down to Texas, met with the team, and they asked us how much money we thought we were going to make in the first year. And we all laughed and said, "We're not going to make any money." And he goes, "That's the right answer." Because he was trying to test us to see if we were in it for the right reasons. And we were. And then it happened.

Jack Johnson: When I got there, they had all kinds of options for me, the whole thing. It was a bunch of surfers from the community to go hang with, surf with. It was fun. The waves were actually pretty good. Me and Garrett—G. Love—we got to go down for a surf. I remember actually surfing during Blondie's set. I love music with surfing. As a kid growing up and getting to watch surf films all the time, you always would get songs stuck in your head from the surf parts. Then you'd get to go surf and think about that or have it in your mind. To actually, just to hear Blondie play live while I was out surfing on the side was really fun, kind of surreal moment.

Tim Sweetwood: But the natural side of festivals is they can only go so late. In theory, we'd be out on the beach till one a.m. or in the park till one a.m., but that doesn't exist. And in Asbury Park, we had the Stone Pony and the Wonder Bar and all that kind of stuff.

Tim Donnelly: So the Super Jams, we had done these parties in the past with Tangiers Blues Band. The party for Danny's *Still Moving* book was at the McKittrick [Hotel in New York City], and it was an epic one. So, it was Tangiers Blues Band with Foo Fighters, Perry Farrell, Zac Brown, and that was a ripping party.

Danny Clinch: And Luther [Dickinson] from North Mississippi Allstars. And Luther hands Dave Grohl his guitar, and Dave doesn't know that he is like an open-tuning G or something and just starts strumming this thing. And he's like, "What the fuck?"

Tim Donnelly: And in my time working at Tipitina's, I got to see how Ivan Neville would operate that kind of shit. So, it's like Dumpstaphunk's show, but everybody would show up and play with Dumpstaphunk at the end of JazzFest at Tips that fucking Sunday night. And we knew that Danny's band, Tangiers Blues Band, can play anything. So we drafted a song list, and then we sent it out to all the bands. All right, what do you want to play? Off of this list, what do you know?

Tim Sweetwood: The concept of a Super Jam has always existed, whether it's Jazz Fest or Bonnaroo or whatever, but not how we were doing it here.

Danny Clinch: But we got G. Love there, and Jack, and Brandi Carlile.

Tim Donnelly: Jack played, they did "Iko Iko" with Pres Hall Horns. And Brandi came in and just crushed.

Jack Johnson: I was a little nervous. Those are real musicians. I mess around the acoustic guitar and stuff, and they're all just real players. They were so welcoming. They made me feel just like I should be there, right off the bat as soon as we were playing and helping me out. We did "Iko Iko," which is a song that everybody's heard. It's got a lot of history and meaning and depth to it. To get some insight from them and to be guided a little bit on ways to sing it, that was a lot of fun. Again, it was like a little history lesson.

Clint Maedgen: Rehearsing with Brandi Carlile backstage at the Stone Pony just as ten giant pizzas get delivered for the band and the crew, I mean, that feels like family to me. That's just like, we're learning what we're going to do on "Old Rugged Cross." We're choosing a key. All right, yeah, two verses, two verses. Yeah, Ronnell, you solo. Okay, Brandi, you'll take it out.

Jack Johnson: There's certain times where you just feel looseness is what everybody in the room wants. It's not a performance, it's a party. It was one of those moments where I just realized that it had a real similar feel to a song I have called "Mudfootball." I started turning around and showing people where the chords might go, and then we went into one of my tunes as well. I forget if we went back and forth a few times, but it was that natural playing with those guys, that we shift around. It's nice when you can just turn around, tell one person in the band what chord you're about to go to, and they communicate so well. You know that we're about to play the game of Telephone and that's going to get passed around real quick. You don't have to necessarily look at everybody, because there's usually, there's a language and a way a band communicates when they're that tight. You know that if you get eye contact with one person, they're going to spread the word pretty quick. You can do things like that. It's one of those things.

Clint Maedgen: So Nicole [Atkins] is singing a Blind Melon song with us, with Christopher Thorn on guitar. And we're learning to form the song with Nicole on the sidewalk outside of the Pony, about to walk

onstage. There has been no rehearsal. That's a sidewalk rehearsal, literally two minutes before we walk onstage, and we do it.

Jack Johnson: Right outside the back door. That was fun. Just making
sure we knew what key we were doing and that stuff. It's exciting. I've
seen those moments too. I remember Fugazi coming to play in my
hometown and getting to see them before the show, just off the side,
working things out and stuff. It's nice when you get to peek into that
world. Thinking back, yes, it's funny you start seeing a crowd building
up and you realize like, "Oh, we can't do this too much longer. This is
starting to get pretty packed around us here."

Christopher Thorn: The first one year, Preservation Hall was there
with Tangiers. I played quite a bit that night, actually. I had never
really played with a horn section like that onstage. So the fact that
the Preservation Hall guys were onstage with us, and I remember just
jamming and going, this is the best jamming with these guys. I was so
turned on. I like kind of playing without a net.

Tim Donnelly: So it's in that spirit and that spirit, I think, is what
we are able to tap into and operate off of that great spirit of what this
fucking city is. Which is, you never know. You never know what's going
to happen, you never know what's going to roll out. And that's part of
the excitement of it. And New Orleans is the only other place that it's
really like that.

Danny Clinch: Every bit of that first year became everything that we
ever wanted to do. From having Jack Johnson on the beach, and G.
Love and Brandi and just all those bands, and then having the art in
the gallery, Timmy [Donnelly] doing the art on the beach, us doing
the art in the gallery, and the surf contest. And then we end up in the
Stone Pony with the Blues Band and Preservation Hall Jazz Band as
our horn section jamming with Jack Johnson and Brandi and G. Love
and everybody. It was really, to me, it's hard to beat that initial moment
where something is so spectacular that you can't even believe it.

Mike McCready: When Danny asked me to play, I was like, "Fuck. Hell
yeah, I want to play. Please. I'll pay you to play there." That was one
of those things that's like, "Oh, yeah, I can say I jammed at the Stone

Pony." So it's a thing of, not an ego thing, but it's an accomplishment I think, if that's the right word. Bigger than that. I've played a million places. But it's one of the highlights in my career.

Tim Donnelly: Getting Mike McCready into Stone Pony, because they'd never been to Asbury Park. Pearl Jam's never been to Asbury Park, Mike's never been to Asbury Park.

Mike McCready: Danny invited myself and this woman named Kate Neckel. We had an art thing called Infinite Color and Sound that we were doing, which was painting and music, and it was a collective of those types of things. And Danny offered for us to play at the tent there where he has the pictures for sale and we we're into it. So that was my first experience going out there. And right when I got there, I went right out to the beach and I put on "Thunder Road" and I just listened to it with my headphones. And just to get into the significance of it and to Bruce's land and where he came up. I like to do those things and I like to feel that kind of music and his music and where he came up and whatever the legend of all that is, buy into that. So part of that is me sitting listening to "Thunder Road" and then "Badlands" and a couple other of his tunes.

Danny Clinch: People come here and they don't do their regular spiel. People get here and they go, "Oh, this is a soulful, incredible place, and we are here and we're feeling that, and we're therefore going to respond accordingly."

Mike McCready: It's exhilarating to play a small place like that because that's even more terrifying to play the club than it is to play the thirty thousand people for me, because that is a wash, the thirty thousand whatever it is, or fifteen thousand. That has its own sets of anxieties and fears. But I almost feel more intimidated when I'm at a small club like that because there's a dude right there in front of me just looking at me. And I feel like I have to really bring it and engage, but I'm right there, so I've got to be on, I got to be playing great. Maybe I can hide that when we're playing in front of bigger things, but I always feel a little bit more intimidated when we play small clubs like that, honestly. And that's good because then I'm alive and I'm feeling energy from the crowd that's different and it's right fucking there. The huge energy that we get I love and is amazing, but the intimacy of that is very special and it's nerve-racking. It really is a little bit because I'm more aware of what I'm doing, I think, when people are right in front of me. I don't play any differently, but I think I'm more conscious of, there's a dude right there having a beer and then there's this woman over. I can see people.

Tim Sweetwood: Those Super Jams never go as they're planned and it's always chaotic behind the scenes. It's not two p.m. and somebody's had their lunch and their coffee. It's one a.m., they haven't had enough coffee, they've maybe had a few drinks already and stuff like that. They're trying to wind down for the night, all that kind of stuff. Then you're saying like, "Hey, go kick it into high gear." It's chaotic, and that is the best way to describe it.

Mike McCready: And then out of that experience, I pitched it to our guys. I was like, "Man, we got to play Sea.Hear.Now because a), it's in Asbury Park and that's killer and rad." And I got to go there and Ed [Vedder] may have been there at one time, I'm not sure. But it was very significant and almost subtly life-changing in a way because I now have this feeling of love for Asbury Park because I was there two times and I got to be part of it, even in a festival sense.

Danny Clinch: Then we decided, "Oh, let's have a band do the house-band role for the Super Jam." And it was a good one: St. Paul and the Broken Bones.

Paul Janeway: Danny Clinch or somebody with the festival had reached out and just asked. They thought it was a good fit. There was a point in this band where I don't think that would have been possible just because of the homework and things like that. We had gotten a lot better, and improv was something we all were striving to do, just to think on your feet. We've been playing so long. We were like, "Yes, let's give it a shot."

Paul Janeway: We learned a lot about ourselves as a band because it wasn't as hard as I thought it was going to be. I remember playing in Wichita, Kansas, and we were playing like "Hungry Heart" and Dr. John. And I'm like, "No, no, no. We do other stuff like. It's an original show." But we were just so focused on learning. And then you're having to coordinate who's going to do it and who's not going to do it and who's in town and who's not in town. And truth be told, I like to be very prepared for stuff. We'll have improvisational parts in the show. But I like it so that if things do go off the rails, I want to make sure that I can put it back on.

Wesley Schultz: Danny Clinch approached me and just said, "Hey, I know you guys are in the middle of a crazy tour and everything, would you consider doing this?" We found out what time it was, and I remember just saying yes. Then my writing partner, Jere [Jeremiah Fraites], was like, "Hell, yes." Then I was like, "Wait, Jere's going to do this?" Because it's past midnight. I think it's like one a.m. and Jere goes to bed much earlier when he's allowed to. That's not his scene. Then on that night, he's like, "I'm definitely not doing it." He had to bail. So it was me and Byron Isaacs. Byron's got a really cool story unto himself, but we ended up playing "Ophelia" that night. Byron used to play with Levon Helm and he was a part of that band.

Paul Janeway: Wes, what's funny is, we did the Band. We did the Band on that night. And so apparently the Lumineers' bass player was the bass player for Levon Helm for a long time. He played bass with Levon Helm and so he was going to come play bass and Wes is going to do the song, the Band song. Our bass player is sitting there telling the guy, "So the movement here. Are you sure you got it?" He didn't know that he had played with Levon Helm. He's like, "Okay, you go. It goes to the four here," and the guy's like, "I think I got it."

Wesley Schultz: So I meet Jake Clemons and I meet the guys from the Struts and I see Danny and I see all these people, and I'm like, wow. You're just hanging on. You're like, "I guess this is happening now." You go with it. We did two songs. I forget the two songs we did. I just know one of them was "Ophelia" by the Band. We have a song about the same name, so we were joking, we were playing two different versions of "Ophelia" in the same night.

Jake Clemons: I love that stuff. To me . . . that takes me back to when I first started touring. At a lot of festivals back in the nineties, you would have moments like that. They're super low-key, underplayed and just a lot of really powerful moments can come out of that. At the jam, it was jumping up. I don't remember anything specific being thrown out, and that's what I love. Just that moment of you're feeling connected to it or inspired and at the moment leave.

Tim Donnelly: The Lumineers, so they had played the outside of the Stone Pony, the summer stage, a couple years before that, but he never played the inside of Stone Pony because he moved to Colorado and he was never in a band that played the Pony. So, he closed the Pony with us on the Super Jam night, and he's on the sidewalk with Jake Clemons drinking Budweisers on the sidewalk. And I pop my head out the door and I'm like, "Oh God, they're drinking on the sidewalk." That's like one of two things in Asbury Park you can't do. Drink on the sidewalk and piss in public. And here comes a cop rolling up. I'm like, "Oh my God. Oh, this is going to suck." And the cop rolls down. Thank God he recognizes Jake. "Hey, bring that beer inside and we're good."

Wesley Schultz: There was a community there that I think the elder statesman, like a Bruce, it brings out the best in everyone as far as not being so isolationist about everything. There can be a territorialness or a coldness or iciness around. If you ever go to a festival, you'd think all the bands are just all hanging out, but it's few and far between. Everybody's just on these long tours and just like it's not what people think it is often, but at that, I met so many people at both events. I have to believe it has something to do with—It's almost like the top-down thing. The people who are setting the culture are people like Bruce.

Jake Clemons: To this day, it's one of my favorite moments in my career because I was asked to be the resident surfer musician. It was the best gig that someone like me could ask for.

Wesley Schultz: My tour manager, who's the only one that stuck around with me, was like, "We should probably go because we got a flight tomorrow." I remember getting back to the hotel maybe three thirty or four. I was staying in Manhattan and then we were flying out or something the next day, so I was just like, "I'll take this on the chin. This is worth it."

Tim Sweetwood: One of the unique ones would be last year with the Jacket, who are very close friends with all of us. I think one of the cool, unique parts of that is most of the time at, and many of the times, again, whether it's Bonnaroo, Jazz, all these things with a Super Jam concept, it's more individual artists or one or two people from a band. That one last year was like, "Hey, everybody, Tangiers, get off the stage. The whole band's going to come on and do a couple songs." It's like, Jim will still join the band for other things, but that was a pretty unique moment where it was like, "Hey, we're taking over."

Patrick Hallahan: Tim [Donnelly] and Danny had reached out to us saying, "Hey, I know it's going to be late. I know you guys are probably going to want to pull out of town, but part of the spirit of this thing is getting up and having some fun at the Pony," and we're like, "Done." It wasn't just one of us. It was all of us. We took over the damn stage. Then when we do it and we feel it . . . In true Asbury Park and Stone Pony fashion, there was a chance that the Boss might sit in with us. He ended up not being able to do it but we had worked up a couple of Springsteen tunes. Then we always have "Purple Rain" in the back pocket because there are a few artists bigger in our lives than Prince. So, the legacy of the place knocks the stuffing out of the air and everybody just gels together. Well, something like "Purple Rain"—it doesn't matter who you are or what walk of life you're in, you hear that, it's over. You and the person next to you, you're singing along.

Wesley Schultz: You're reminded of the spirit of those artists, I would say from let's say the late seventies or something like that that I've been exposed to. I guess these artists go beyond that, but they had this idea that there was cross-pollination and you were going to hang with each other and you were going to sing songs together, and maybe we record something off the cuff. I feel like everything now, I would say, as a rule of thumb, doesn't happen that way. You really have to get people out of their comfort zones to do things like that. For me, it was a beautiful experience because of the energy of that, and it didn't have to be perfect.

Nicole Atkins: I remember my grandfather always saying he came over from Sicily and grew up in Asbury Park, and then lived in Neptune

City his whole life. He was like, "Asbury's never coming back. Never coming back." Then when I showed him a picture of the Sea.Hear.Now festival, that's when he was like, "Oh my God." He cried.

Brian Fallon: There was the first foolish person that said, "I think I'm gonna open a business in Asbury Park, and right now it's a train wreck." But they did it, and that's the thing, it worked.

Kevin Jonas: The town, it's seen everything. Being here still in New Jersey and I've seen it kind of change over the years. It's just a cool culture there now. It's like somewhere you want to go. You have amazing dinner, see live music, that beach experience but also have a culinary experience. It's one of my favorite places to visit now.

Jack Antonoff: It's a funny place because it's not like this undiscovered place like, "Oh, you got to go to Asbury Park and catch the scene. It's so undiscovered." It's like, "No, it's weird." It's weird when I was growing up. It's weird now. It's sort of like this is very New Jersey and we're sort of moving with it in its own weirdness.

Bruce Springsteen: I feel at home [at the Pony], sure. I've been going there too long. Everybody treats you great and, "Hi, how you doing?" And if we go down, yeah, it's a home away from home. It is still, at this point. So it's nice. They've amazingly kept it going. I'm surprised it's still there, to be honest with you. They managed to keep it going and it's been nice and relaxing in the summertime and sometimes in the winter, and local acts still play inside. It's a place. Hopefully it'll remain.

Southside Johnny: Rock 'n' roll acts have been a huge part of the renaissance of Asbury Park, even though it took twenty years. Because once Bruce put out *Greetings from Asbury Park* and all of us went out on the road with Asbury in the name and all that, people came here.

Mike McCready: It's got a life of its own, The Stone Pony. It's got the legend of it. It's in the fabric of Bruce's songs. It's part of the history of New Jersey. And it could be luck and timing that it's still open. Since its first roof implosion, it got fixed and people put money back into it. And Bruce and those guys in the early days cut their teeth there so they spent their ten thousand hours probably playing there, in that area at least. And so that's a significant thing. And it should always be there. It's a monument. I mean, I think I have to look at it that way too. It's a thing that people will go to travel to see because it's a tangible, exciting, historical place that people have been going to for forty, fifty years, even though it's had its ups and downs. . . . All the other clubs in New York are gone and there's many clubs around the world that are gone. Who really knows?

Patti Smith: We need these clubs. We need a sense of history. It's not like any of these clubs were the greatest club of all, or that they had the best sound, because some of them, like CBGB, had horrible sound, really. Sometimes it smelled of piss and beer, but it was ours. It was the one that we had, and these people need this sense of connection, and places to play, and also history. . . . If we're going to work so hard to preserve a cathedral or the birthplace of a great artist, why not the birthplace of a wondrous scene that inspired so many people?

Bruce Springsteen: I mean people look back and go, oh wow, Southside was playing there, Steve was there, I was there. But the regularness of it all was really what it was about. Three nights a week. Every week. There was nothing surprising going on. It was a very steady, comfortable environment. I'm sure it was like bar life in a thousand other towns going on simultaneously. There was that one club where your local musicians gathered and would get up onstage and play. I think the only thing that was exceptional about it was that it was unexceptional. Looking back on it, it was just a very down-home place where that group of musicians who inhabited Asbury Park at that moment could gather and be together and create, and very important in that sense, that there was a place. Because without the Pony, I don't know, would there have been someplace else?

Acknowledgments

First and foremost, I'd like to thank my parents.

My dad raised me on music. When I was born, he blasted "Overture/ It's a Boy" by the Who with the windows open, loud enough so that the neighbors could hear I had arrived. He filled my childhood with music by the Who, the Stones, the Dead, and Bruce. He braved mosh pits at Blink-182 and Bad Religion shows while politely declining offers to crowd-surf. He not only took me to my first concert in the lot behind the Stone Pony, he also truly gave me the gift of music.

And my mom encouraged it. From her generous refrains of "Wow, was that you?" during twangy and probably cringey attempts at guitar practice in middle school to never-ending rides from record stores, my mom was always adding fuel to my musical fire. In high school, she attended my punk band's gigs at shows in church basements (and once had to rescue my five-year-old sister from a quickly forming mosh pit). And that whole suggestion of maybe trying this journalism thing out as a career turned out to be some good motherly advice too.

My beautiful, patient, kind, caring, thoughtful, wonderful fiancée Moll has been my biggest supporter throughout this entire process. She endured a long-distance, "bicoastal" (Asbury Park and Greenpoint, of course) relationship while I dived headfirst into the book. She braved rocky ferries and parkway traffic to visit on weekends. She was always my first gut check after interviews and my first read on many chapters. She is my perfect teammate.

This book would not be possible without Tim Donnelly and Danny Clinch, two of the most important people in protecting and advancing Asbury Park. Every city would be better off if they had a Tim and Danny.

I've often referred to Tim as both the sherpa and shaman of this book. He helped me make countless connections with musicians, managers, Pony people and Asbury-ites—almost all of whom immediately said yes based on Tim's reputation alone. Vouches from Tim Donnelly can carry more weight than a presidential endorsement around this town—and the music industry in general. He had vision and ideas where I had blind spots, and he was indispensable in helping me get the full picture of the Pony presented. He was my near-daily call, sometimes multiple times a day (to be fair, some of those calls were just about the swell forecast), but he never grew tired of helping make this book a reality. Tim is always thinking of Asbury Park first, and I'm grateful to call him a friend.

Mr. Clinch needs no introduction from me. He is one of the most prolific, sought-after, and respected photographers alive right now, and I was honored to be able to work with him on this book. Probably 80 percent of the artists I interviewed asked me "Wait, do you know Danny Clinch?" There are few more vocal champions for Asbury Park, New Jersey, and live music in general, than Danny Clinch, and his relentlessly upbeat energy is infectious. Go see his gallery in Asbury Park—the Transparent Clinch Gallery—which in addition to being a breathtaking display of his work has morphed into an amazing live music venue with that spirit of spontaneity so unique to Asbury. It's really the modern Asbury's cultural living room.

Merissa Fleischhauer is my Asbury guardian angel. From providing me with a spare set of sheets when I first moved down with a mislabeled storage box (somehow I had a blender and other kitchen gadgets in a box labeled "bedding"), she has made it physically possible to write this book in Asbury Park. I conducted about fifty interviews in the front lounge of the St. Laurent over my favorite lunch deal in town (get the burger!). She generously offered me the hotel's in-demand rooms upstairs whenever I needed to interview artists who required privacy. She helped me find a place to live when my first lease in Asbury ended. Her enthusiasm for this project, her big heart, and her friendship have been invaluable.

My agent, Daniel Greenberg, was a believer in this project from the beginning, even when "a bar in Asbury Park" as a book subject may not have seemed the most compelling. He has been my patient guide throughout this publishing process, which, it turns out, is quite different from newspapers. I'm forever grateful for the many phone calls he fielded from me at any point in the day or weekend.

Noah Eaker, my editor through to the finish line, has been a fantastic partner in shaping this story—helping tailor a fifty-year history into a tangible narrative and believing it was one worth sharing. Noah also wore about a dozen different hats during the process, from editor to coach, photo wrangler, scheduler, and event planner, and did them all with the steadiest hand, and Edie Astley made it all come together.

Jennifer Barth, my first editor at HarperCollins, was an equal believer in this story.

I would never have had this opportunity if Carolyn Ryan had not given me a chance at this whole reporting path years ago, letting me loose on the campaign trail as we envisioned the role of a "digital correspondent." Carolyn has been my editor on many of my favorite stories and videos I've done at the *Times*. She saw a book in my original *Times* story on the Pony before even I did and became one of my most important confidantes in parsing interviews for the best nuggets and details.

David Halbfinger, my editor now for two presidential campaigns, was a consistent champion, cheerleader, and guide. Now, to get his violin chops on the stage of the Pony . . . Diego Ribadeneira was the first editor at the *New York Times* to hear my pitch that there might be a story inside the Pony walls, and was in from the start. Meghan Louttit made that first *NYT* article sing.

Every day that I show up to work, I am reminded of how lucky I am to know many of the greatest reporters and editors in the world, and to call them friends. So many have passed along tips, contacts, advice, and have shared general excitement for the book. Sopan Deb and Jim Rutenberg guided me through the book process as much as anyone, and Maggie Haberman always made time to talk Springsteen songs and lore. So many others were a lifeline, either on the book or on the campaign trail while it hung over my head, including Reid Epstein, Ali Watkins, Matt Flegenheimer, Joe Coscarelli, Lisa Lerer, Kevin Draper, Katie Glueck,

Adam Nagourney, Michael Bender, Jon Lemire, Ashley Parker, Eli Stokols, Ali Berzon, Astead Herndon, Jenny Medina, Jonathan Martin, as well as my current editors Zach Johnk and Kathleen Hennessey, and Patrick Healy, who told me that being the "Jersey guy" at the paper might be a good thing.

And a special thank-you to Lizzie Goodman, who wrote my absolute favorite oral history of all time (*Meet Me in the Bathroom*, which, if you haven't read it, donate this book and go buy that one now). Lizzie gave me guidance and encouragement when I was a total stranger.

Bob Santelli and Eileen Chapman need no introduction at this point, but they were both instrumental in helping me make sense of all the history and connect with so many essential characters in the Pony's wild history. Joe Prinzo was one of my favorite sounding boards, helping some reluctant artists feel comfortable in talking to me. Tina Kerekes and Zack Sandler made the Clinch gallery a second home and helped uncover some beautiful memories and stories.

Marilyn Laverty and Max Lefkowitz were critical in helping organize some of the most important characters in the book.

Sammy Steinlight was a great friend and a musical shepherd throughout the process, including lending me some rare recordings that I promise to return someday.

I also owe a debt of gratitude to the many reps, managers, and agents who helped connect me with artists, who patiently managed my many manic emails asking for updates, including Ken Weinstein, Vanessa Burt, Rich Russo, Brittany L'Heureux, Jim Merlis, Noah Goldman, Chris Scott, Jamie Oborne, Whitney Williams, Ken Sunshine, Robin Baum, Jeff Raymond, Emilia Kyriazis, and many more. And ditto to friends who played the role of agent and connector, including Allie Briskin, Noah Malale, and Francesca Smith.

Thank you to the current Pony staff, who let me wander around during sound checks and off-hours, chasing artists, especially to Caroline O'Toole, Bobby Jones, and Kyle Brendle.

I leaned on an assortment of family, friends, and colleagues to read random chapters to help guide me through the weeds, and they were key to helping shape the final cut: Aaron Levine, Andrew Moorehead,

Reid Prebenda, Michele Murphy, Julie Cohn, Brian Killea, Mike Sechehay, Caroline Corasaniti, Joan Corasaniti, Sopan, and Moll.

And a shout-out to my original punk crew, who braved church basements, VFW halls, and Elks lodges for shows, and are probably all suffering similar hearing loss at this point.

I overcame most of my writing roadblocks with "volume therapy." Many thanks to Nick Greer, Greer Amps, and Benson Amps for the creativity-sparking decibels.

To everyone who sat for an interview for this book, thank you for trusting me with your voice and stories. I hope I did you justice.

To anyone I missed, I owe you a beer. Come find me at the back bar.

Source Notes

Michele Amabile, article in the *Asbury Park Press*, May 23, 1995 (p. 180).

Kelly-Jane Cotter, article in the *Asbury Park Press*, September 1, 2001 (p. 234).

Danny Federici, interview with the *Asbury Park Press*, 1998 (p. 11).

Dave Marsh, interview for Epic Records release party, 1976 (p. 51).

Lee Mrowicki, interview with the *Asbury Park Press*, January 20, 1986 (p. 137).

Tom Petta, interview with *This Was the Scene* podcast, May 25, 2018 (p. 215).

Butch Pielka, interview with the *Asbury Park Press*, January 9, 1977 (p. 22).

Butch Pielka, interview with the *Asbury Park Press*, February 5, 1984 (pp. 20, 21, 46, 84, 102).

Butch Pielka, interview with the *Asbury Park Press*, January 5, 1986 (p. 136).

Butch Pielka, interview with the *Asbury Park Press*, March 4, 1989 (p. 145).

Butch Pielka, interview with the *Philadelphia Inquirer*, July 8, 1979 (pp. 22, 23, 35).

Butch Pielka, interview with the *Record*, February 11, 1986 (p. 151).

Butch Pielka, interview with the *Record*, February 11, 1986 (p. 106).

Carrie Potter, interview with NJ.com, March 28, 2011 (p. 16).

Margaret Potter, interview with *Rolling Stone*, October 10, 1985 (p. 10).

Howard Saunders, interview with Joan Greenbaum, Pacific Radio, December 24, 1985 (pp. 147, 148).

Ed Sciaky, interview for Epic Records release party, 1976 (p. 51).

Nancy Shields, article in the *Asbury Park Press*, September 10, 2002 (p. 235).

Ronnie Spector, interview for Epic Records release party, 1976 (p. 48–49).

Bruce Springsteen, E Street Band induction ceremony, Rock and Roll Hall of Fame, December 28, 2014 (pp. 10, 11, 15).

Bruce Springsteen, interview with the *New York Times*, March 28, 1976 (p. 42).

J. T. Sullivan, interview with the *Philadelphia Inquirer*, February 5, 1984 (p. 22).

Garry Tallent, interview with Salon.com, January 3, 2006 (p. 14).

Garry Tallent, interview with the *Asbury Park Press*, January 21, 1986 (p. 150).

Max Weinberg, interview with the *New York Times*, November 8, 1992 (p. 164).

About the Author

NICK CORASANITI is a domestic correspondent covering national politics for the *New York Times*. He has covered four presidential cycles, along with countless congressional, gubernatorial, and mayoral races in more than fifteen years at the *Times*. He was once the *Times*' New Jersey correspondent, tracking the politics, policy, people, trains, beaches, and eccentricities that give the Garden State its charm. He is a born-and-raised, and exceptionally proud, New Jerseyan who splits his time between Asbury Park and Brooklyn.